NCAD LIBRARY
WITHDRAWN

Communicating with pattern

Squares, checks, and grids

RotoVision

Published and distributed by RotoVision SA
Route Suisse 9, CH-1295, Mies, Switzerland
RotoVision SA Sales and Editorial Office
Sheridan House, 114 Western Road, Hove
BN3 1DD, UK
Tel: + 44 (0) 1273 72 72 68
Fax: + 44 (0) 1273 72 72 69
E-mail: sales@rotovision.com
Web: www.rotovision.com

10 9 8 7 6 5 4 3 2 1
ISBN 978-2-940361-82-3

Original book concept: Keith Stephenson and Luke Herriott
Art direction: Tony Seddon
Design and artwork: Keith and Spike at Absolute Zero Degrees
Additional illustrations: Keith Stephenson

Reprographics in Singapore by Provision PTE
Printed in Singapore by Star Standard Industries PTE

Communicating with pattern

Squares, checks, and grids

Mark Hampshire & Keith Stephenson

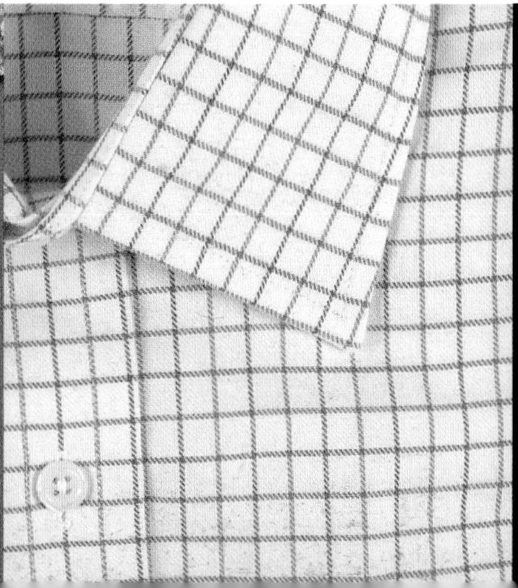

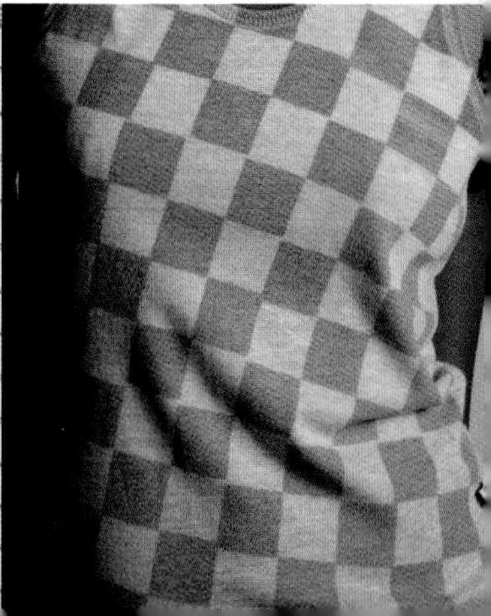

45
R.P.M.
CHS
TT17
MARKETED BY
CHRYSALIS
RECORDS LTD

Contents

Introduction 006

Classic Checks 008

Membership and Identity 032

Themes and Moods 064

Signals and Information 126

Form and Function 188

Appendix
Index 250
Contributors 252
Photography Credits 254
Acknowledgments 256

Introduction

For a period of 25 years starting in the 1950s, artist Josef Albers created over 1,000 paintings, drawings, prints and tapestries in his "Homage to the Square" series. A student and subsequent teacher at the Bauhaus, Albers was deeply interested in form, texture, and, most importantly, color. The "Homage to the Square" series is based on a mathematically precise configuration of concentric squares overlaid in diminishing scale. Each work in the series acts as a vehicle to examine the subjective experience of color, its meditative potential, and the effects that adjacent colors have on one another. Albers explored an illusion he termed the "interaction of color" whereby the square sandwiched between the inner and outer squares would subtly acquire the hue of its neighbors. By juxtaposing carefully chosen tones, Albers achieves the illusion of flat planes advancing or receding in space—effects that would later become central to the Op Art movement.

If color was Albers' chief concern, why choose the square as his means of expression? It is our assertion that the square is uniquely apt for enabling Albers to focus attention on the effect of color on the human condition. Paint in stripes, circles, dots, triangles, or any other tessellated configuration, and the pattern itself would become the focus of the work. When Albers pays homage to the square, he is revering its neutrality.

The square is a tool of abstraction, employed by Braque and Picasso during the Cubist period to emphasize the form and volume of their subjects. From Mackintosh to Mondrian, the Modernists rejected the romanticism and ornament of the 19th century in favor of the "form follows function" logic of the square, the grid, and the cube. For them, squares and right angles came to represent a rejection of applied pattern and adornment in preference for rational mindedness, functionality, and human achievement.

So rational is the square that its metaphoric use tends to be at best prosaic, at worst derisory: the description of a design as "boxy" is rarely invoked as a compliment; being branded "a bit of a square" is the classic insult levelled at the shy and unadventurous. But if the square lacks the life affirming emotion of the circle or the graphic pizzazz of the stripe, it boasts a more essential mantle. The square is useful. We rely on squares and grids as instruments to measure areas and order information, to generate structure and organize disparate constituents. The square is technical, uniform, a symbol of methodical thought.

It is a civilizing force, too. The grid represents the human quest to impose order on a chaotic world: evidenced by ancient Eastern settlements set out on strict axes running north/south and east/west. The forum provided the administrative and commercial focus of Roman cities. We still gravitate toward the town square as a recreational and social hub that evokes civic pride and a sense of community.

Communicating with Pattern: Squares, Checks, and Grids is our homage to the square. It examines the pattern's visual vocabulary in everyday applications and across a range of creative disciplines, organized in five key sections. Firstly, we consider the classic checks and their cultural associations—from fashionable houndstooth to Western plaid. Next, we look at how squares and checks have been appropriated as part of the identity of individuals, organizations, and countries: police uniforms, clan tartans, and heraldic shields all feature. The neutrality of the square enables the pattern to express a diverse range of themes and moods, including puzzles and games, retro, automotive, and learning. In the form of tiny pixels, squares are fundamental to digital communication and offer a means of expressing signals and information from warning signs to the Periodic Table. Finally, we turn our attention to the squares, checks, and grids that are intrinsic to the form and function of objects, materials and the environment, taking in mesh, weaves, tiles, and mosaics. The result is a comprehensive overview of the surprisingly diverse range of design solutions offered by the utilitarian square.

001 *"Homage to Square: Terra Caliente" by Josef Albers*

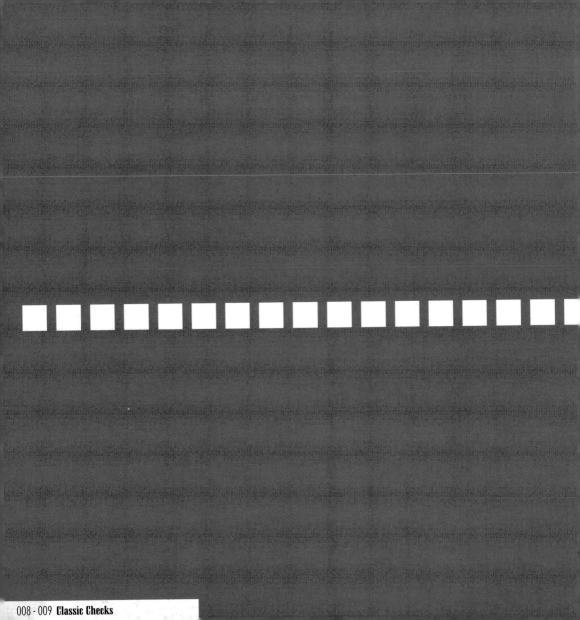

Classic Checks

The Burberry Check
Tattersall Check
Argyle
Houndstooth Check
Gingham
Western Plaid

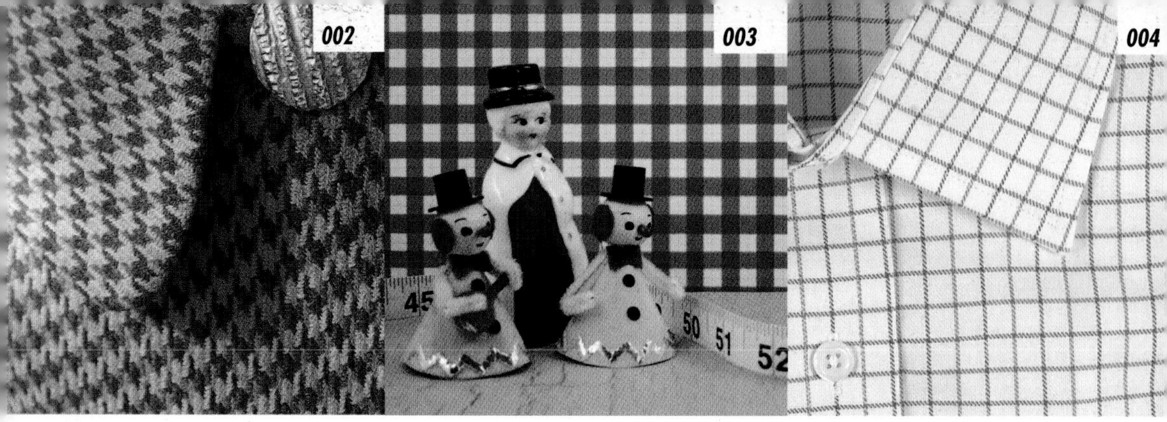

Classic Checks

The function of weaving lends itself to the creation of checked designs. Simply varying the colors on the warp and weft results in a checked pattern. No surprise, then, that we surround ourselves with checks on clothing, products, and home furnishings—smart, practical, and even elegant, but not necessarily remarkable. The checks that feature in this chapter, however, have adopted greater cultural significance.

Classic checks are known by name: the Burberry Check, signature of the celebrated British fashion house; Tattersall, named after the founder of the famous horse auctioneers; and Argyle, adopted by the Campbell clan of the Scottish county of Argyll. They have the power to evoke particular associations: cheerful gingham has a domestic appeal; chic houndstooth screams haute couture; and western plaid transports you to the Wild West. These checks represent best of breed.

002 *Vintage houndstooth.*
003 *Homely red and white gingham.*
004 *The Tattersall check from Cordings.*
005 *Zooty houndstooth floor tile from FLOR.*
006 *Worn with fashionable irony, the classic Argyle sock celebrates the retro golf look.*
007 *Unmistakable: Burberry Check is probably the most internationally recognized of all checks.*
008 *Western plaid.*
009 *Vintage Miss Dior perfume is dressed up for glamor in black-and-white houndstooth.*
010 *Monochromatic knitted Argyle.*
011 *Vintage American country dolls in gingham farm clothes.*
012 *More gingham in this Maine seafood restaurant.*
013 *Vintage gingham covered cookery book.*

005
006
007
011
012
013
Better Homes and Gardens.
Junior
Cook Book
FOR BEGINNING COOKS OF ALL AGES

The Burberry Check

The Burberry Check was first used in the 1920s to line Burberry trenchcoats. In the 1960s it was extended to accessories and since the 1980s it has been used in different colors. The distinctive Check has been synonymous with Burberry for decades, but it was first registered as a trademark during the 1990s. It is now registered throughout the world in all the major trademark classes.

To reflect the fact that the Check remains distinctive of Burberry, even when used in colors other than the classic colors of camel, red, white, and black, the Burberry Check is also registered as a trademark without any color limitations. Burberry is an international symbol of luxury.

014 *The Burberry Check in the classic colors, red, white, camel, and black.*
015 *A typical Burberry advertising campaign image captures the mix of classic and luxury featuring a Burberry Beaton bag in check. © Copyright Burberry/Testino*

Tattersall

Just the thing for a day at the races, the Tattersall check is named for Richard Tattersall, founder of the world's first bloodstock auction house in 1766 in London's Hyde Park. Various sources attribute the checked pattern to the blankets his horses wore when they were taken to market. The pattern became synonymous with the auction house and all the rage in gentlemen's fashion, worn as waistcoats, and, later, shirts. Now based in Newmarket, England, Tattersalls remains Europe's largest bloodstock auctioneers, offering more than 5,000 thoroughbred racehorses each year—still priced in shillings, not pounds.

The check lives on as a popular shirting. Usually made up of dark lines forming squares on a light background, Tattersall check is a symbol of English country life, combined with tweed jackets and moleskin pants. Nowhere can a better selection of these shirts be found than at Cordings, gentlemen's outfitters since 1839. Having passed through the hands of various owners, the company persuaded one of its best customers, rock star Eric Clapton, to become a co-owner and design director in 2003. Clapton said he did so because he liked its classic shirts and tweed shooting jackets and wanted to be able to continue buying them.

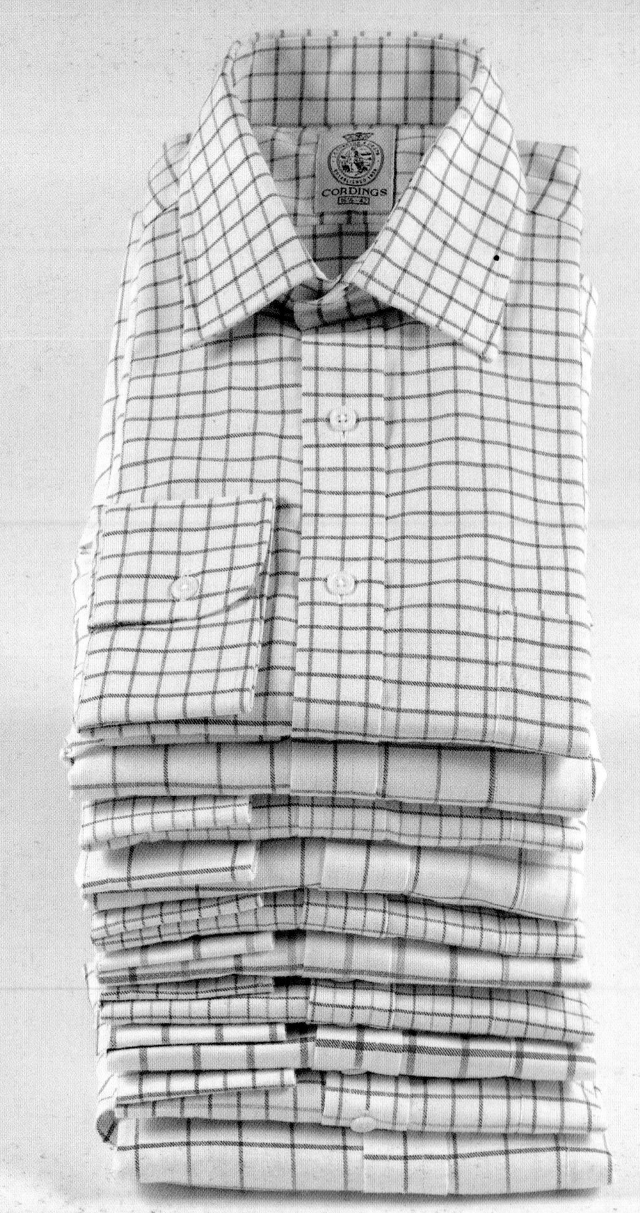

016 and 017 *Tattersall shirt collection from Cordings.*

Argyle

Considered part of the plaid family, the distinctive diamond-shaped Argyle pattern has been traced back to the 16th century, when the Campbell clan of the Scottish county of Argyll adopted the pattern for footwear in the same green and white colors as its kilts. The pattern reached England in the 1700s when it started to be produced commercially in a range of different colors. Its enduring appeal is surely largely due to the many possible variations on a theme. Women knitting socks for WWII troops challenged each other to create intricate Argyle designs; not an easy task, as it involves the intarsia knitting technique, in which various colors of yarn are twisted over each other and knitted simultaneously. Argyle socks have remained popular ever since, being the ideal preppy accompaniment to penny loafers in the 1950s and again in the 1980s.

It is the sock that secured the pattern's association with golf. Jazzy knee-high Argyle socks were popular with US golfers during the 1920s and Argyle continued to be affiliated with the sport throughout the second half of the 20th century. The golfing sweater became a staple of Scottish knitwear houses like Pringle and Lyle and Scott. Incongruity being valuable fashion currency, Argyle's countryside associations have found new favor with a young urban audience, putting Argyle back on the fashion agenda as these brands reinvent themselves through a combination of new designs and archive reissues.

019

020

018 Traditional golfing Argyle socks.
019 Urban Argyle.
020 and 023 Knitted Argyle jumpers.
021 Lyle and Scott has recently found new favor with a fashionable crowd.
022 The heritage of Argyle is apparent when worn with a kilt.

021

022

023

024 025 026

Houndstooth Check

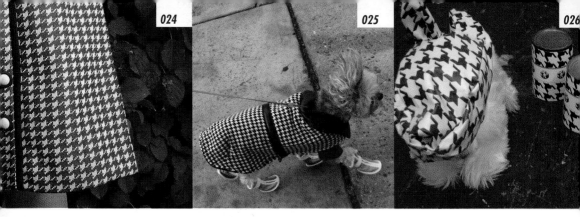

The houndstooth check arises from two colors of yarn woven in a 2:2 twill to create an abstract shape with four points. While it is used at a small scale for sober applications such as men's tailoring, it is the large-scale, black-and-white houndstooth that has become a fashion icon. Its popularity grew in the mid-20th century in the hands of fashion houses like Dior, adopted as the signature check for its first fragrance, Miss Dior, launched in 1947 to coincide with the introduction of the New Look.

Visual shorthand for all things couture, houndstooth instantly communicates Parisian elegance. The design was particularly popular in the 1960s and Pop Art influences have meant that artists and designers continue to play with the scale and context of houndstooth. No longer restricted to woven wool, it is applied as a print to a range of fabrics including cottons and silks.

Its appeal has gone beyond fashion and textiles and into the 3D world of product design. The regularity of the interlocking pattern offers opportunities to play with positive and negative space. Blown up into individual pixels, houndstooth's exaggerated form has a curiously technical quality that works particularly well laser-cut out of a variety of solid materials.

028 029 030

024 and 030 A vintage A-line houndstooth dress.
025 A hound in houndstooth.
026 Artist Emily Clay created this piece using the graphic of houndstooth as shorthand for luxury branding.
027 Photographer Ninon Tschaen perfectly captures the spirit of retro glamor with her houndstooth shoes and matching shoeboxes.
028 A fresh look at a classic—by enlarging the check the design of this coat feels simultaneously classic and modern.
029 Vintage Miss Dior perfume packaging.

031

034

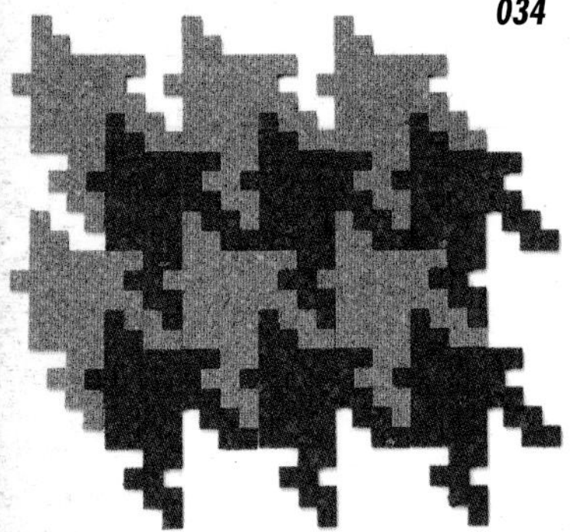

031 and 034 *Jaime Salm from Mio designed this Haute Surface houndstooth collection of coasters with the dual advantage of being both decorative and protective.*
032 *FLOR created these Zooty fashion inspired modular floor tiles in houndstooth.*
033 *The enlarged scale of the houndstooth pattern in this plywood screen by Courtney Skott exploits houndstooth's negative and positive space, literally taking the pattern into a new dimension.*

Gingham

Today, gingham is instantly recognizable by its regular checked repeat of same-size squares, but, like many textiles, the name originally referred to the weave rather than the pattern. Having made its way via Holland from the East as a plain or striped fabric, the first checked versions were produced by the mills of Manchester, England, in the 18th century—generally the blue and white variety. Arriving in the US, its manufacture in the factories of Virginia, Carolina, Georgia, and Alabama contributed greatly to the economies of those states up until the mid-20th century.

In the early 20th century, French boys and girls wore smocks of "vichy," as the check is known in France, named after the city responsible for its manufacture. The tradition is kept alive in the premium denim products of Provence-based fashion brand, Atelier LaDurance. Blue vichy check fabric lines the pockets of men's products, red the women's. Its combination of nostalgia and simple, honest style gives the pattern particular resonance for the French, adopted as the icon for French budget department store Tati. The store's bold pink-and-white vichy awnings and carrier bags announce Tati's promise of "always the lowest price" to stylish, yet thrifty consumers.

035 and 036 *Gingham makes hygienic and homely café tablecloths.*

037 and 039 *Red gingham (or vichy) pocket bags in these women's denim jeans by Atelier LaDurance differentiates them from the men's range which use blue.*

038 *The family-owned Farmer's Daughter hotel, Los Angeles, uses its icon farm girl on an enlarged gingham wall surface to evoke warm, friendly service and old-fashioned hospitality. Photographed here by Raphael Mazor.*

040 *Polo packaging for luxury denim company Atelier LaDurance with branding by Boy Bastiaens at StormHand.*

040

Atelier LaDurance®

LES BAUX DE PROVENCE

041 *Cheery red gingham on this breakfast table.*
042 *Gingham helps to communicate the "homemade" concept used on these two vintage Better Homes cookery books.*
043 *French budget store Tati uses vichy (or gingham) to give a friendly feel to its branding.*
044 *This vintage washing powder ad suggests that wash-day blues are a thing of the past when you do your chores in gingham.*

042

Better Homes and Gardens JUNIOR Cook Book for the Hostess & Host of tomorrow

043

Gingham is a particularly versatile textile—one of the peculiarities of its manufacturing technique is that the even spacing of colored yarns in the warp and weft produce a fabric with no right or wrong side in terms of color. The pattern shares qualities with the "hygienic" stripe, in that it both shows and hides dirt in equal measures. With cheerfulness and cleanliness in balance, it's the firm favorite for tablecloths the world over and is used as graphic shorthand for café dining. Being washable, the fabric became a favorite for children's summer clothing and it endures as a popular choice for babies' and children's clothing and accessories—especially in pastel pinks, yellows, and greens.

Americans have long held folk associations with gingham; along with dungarees and petticoats, it's a must at any square dance. Patriotic quilters use gingham as a staple pattern—its cheery checks serving as a neutral foil for florals and geometrics. Its domestic appeal is undeniably enduring. Used as curtains, aprons, pajamas, and bedspreads, gingham has a homemaker quality evocative of western settlers and 1950s housewives alike.

045 *Picnics, barbecues, and fresh outdoor summer food is celebrated with gingham in the large-format, 30-sheet billboard advertising for Coca-Cola by Nicholas Felton and Creative Director Chris Shipman for Berlin Cameron Partners.*

Coca-Cola®
make it real™

Western Plaid

Western style evolved from humble beginnings. Settlers arrived in Texas during the 1820s bringing with them simple work wear for their new jobs on the land. Influenced by the clothes of Spanish and Mexican ranchers, cowboy clothing incorporated elaborate embroidery and tassels. But the classic plaid shirt is most commonly associated with the Wild West and Denver-based Rockmount Ranch Wear is one of the last remaining purveyors of the real thing.

At the age of 106, its proprietor, Jack A. Weil can point to a lifetime of practical innovations, including less cumbersome slim-fitting shirts and practical snap fasteners to let loose if the shirt got caught.

Hollywood has helped create and perpetuate the cowboy myth—not least to westerners themselves. Seeing these heroes on screen in the 1930s, cowboys started to emulate the screen version of their own selves, blurring fiction and reality.

The influence continues: the popularity of 2005 movie, *Brokeback Mountain*, led to a marked increase in sales of western clothing (the two stars' shirts, one of them plaid, selling on Ebay for over $100,000), while the zeitgeist has carried western style onto the catwalks of fashion designers like DSquared.

046, 048, and 049 *USA-based photographer Abra Carroll Nardo took these pictures at the Raleigh rodeo in North Carolina.*
047 *Self-portrait by Christy Bindas.*
050–053 *Western plaid at work on the ranch.*
054 *Western plaid appears on the catwalks in this collection from Spring/Summer 2006 by DSquared.*

030 - 031 **Classic Checks**

Membership and Identity

Tartan
Heraldry
Date Plaques
Police Uniform
Harlequin
National Identity

Membership and Identity

Examples of squares and checks used for identification are many and varied. Firstly, tartan and its appeal as a signifier of identity is easy to understand. Being less regimented than the stripe (used for military and team membership), tartan carries an air of romance and has the advantage of offering an infinite number of color and pattern configurations. Sillitoe's Tartan, the nickname for the black-and-white checkered pattern adopted by police forces around the world, offers a badge of identification that creates instant standout. Ease of recognition was also key to identifying the archetypes portrayed in the Commedia dell'arte; a suit of multicolored diamonds that has become the enduring symbol of the figure of Harlequin.

The prevalence of squares and checks in the system of heraldry has influenced national flags, many of which are emblazoned with heraldic crosses in a variety of geometric configurations. Finally, the practical square offers the perfect framing device for a date plaque—a defining aspect of any building's identity.

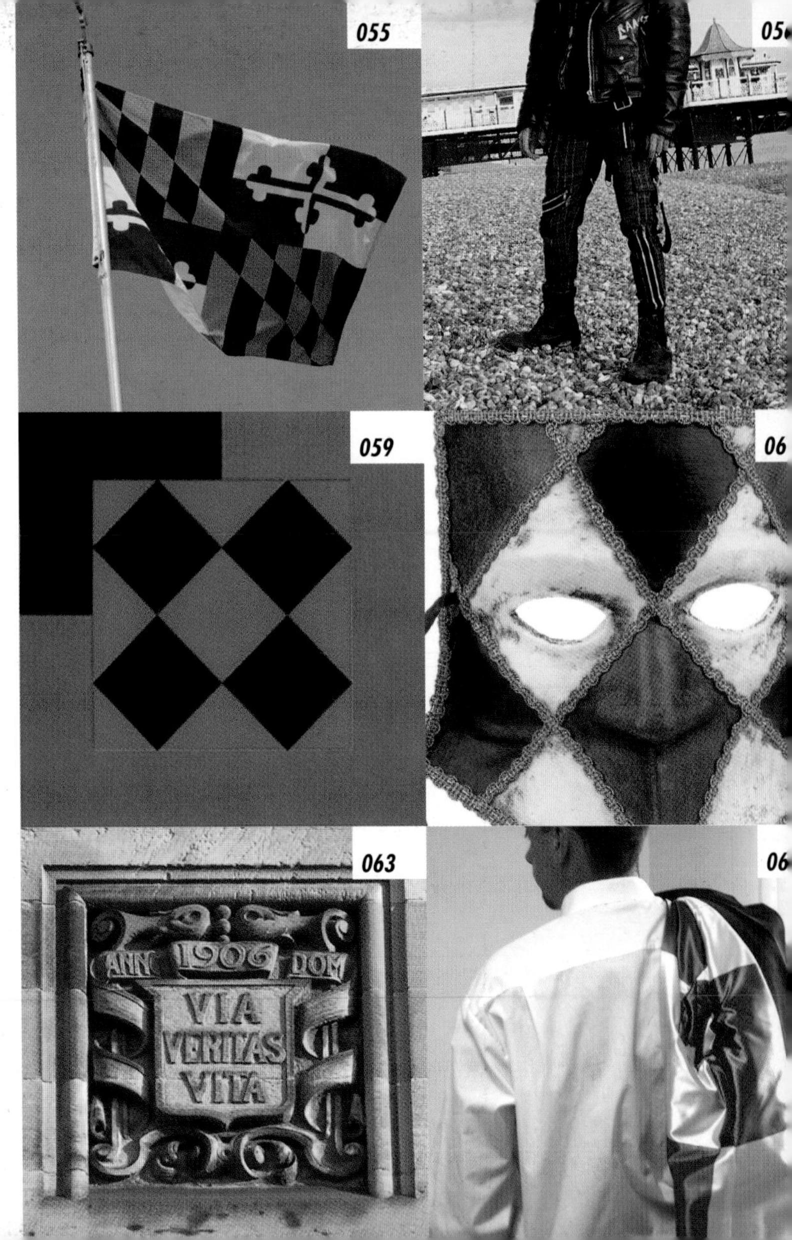

055 *Maryland flag.* ***056*** *Punk tartan bondage pants.*
057 *Panama flag.* ***058*** *Munro tartan.*
059 *An example of the Railfreight brand identity system by Roundel.* ***060*** *A Harlequin mask.*
061 *Two uniformed policewomen enjoy artwork by Milk, Two Sugars.* ***062*** *Opening illustration of Francis Bickley's 1923 book "The Adventures of Harlequin" by John Austen.* ***063*** *Commemorative date plaque.*
064 *Croatian flag jacket lining for the the project Croatian Silence by Boris Ljubicic.*
065 *The Scottish kilt in clan tartans.*

057
058
061
062
065
POLICE

Tartan

Of all patterned fabrics, tartan is surely the most emotive. We revere it as a symbol of ancient family lineage, a bond that unites people of Scottish descent all around the world. Yet much of what we take for granted about tartan is myth and legend. In his book *Tartans*, Brian Wilton, Director of the Scottish Tartans Authority in Scotland, traces tartan back to its roots, reveals a wealth of information, and quashes a few misconceptions.

But first let's deal with the basics. The word "tartan" probably comes from the French "tiretaine" and originally referred to the way the thread is woven: the weft two over, two under the warp, advancing one thread each pass to form visible diagonal lines where different colors cross. The resulting blocks of color repeat vertically and horizontally in a pattern of squares and lines known as a sett. Most tartans are the same viewed from any direction. →

066 *Caledonia tartan.*
067 *A tartan traditionally worn as a kilt with a sporran.*

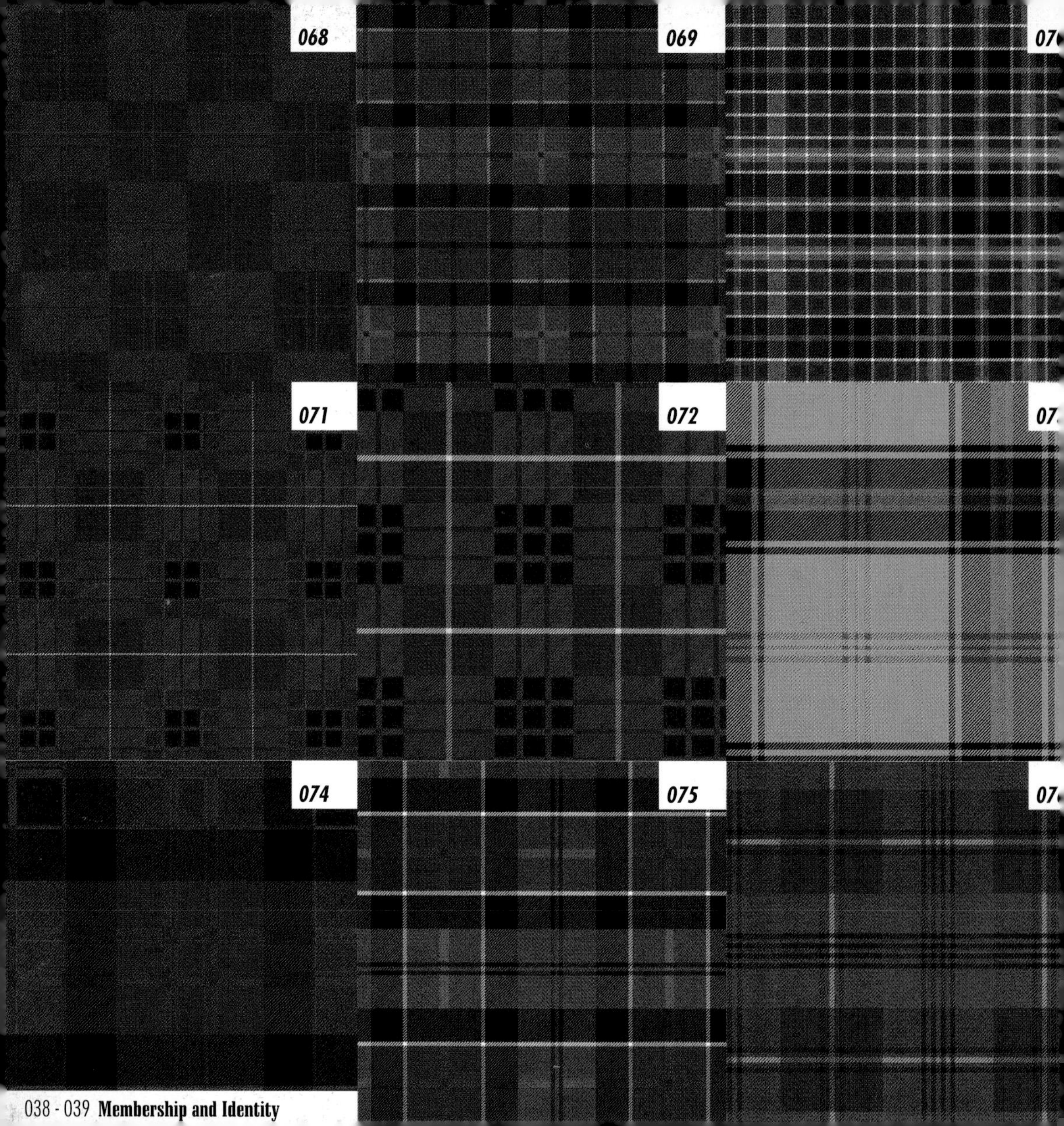
068
069
07
071
072
07
074
075
07

077

078

079

080

→ While there is evidence that tartan existed in ancient history, Brian Wilton explains that concrete documentation of tartan is much more recent: a German woodcut from around 1631 seems to show Highland soldiers wearing the tartan philamhor—the great kilt. After Bonnie Prince Charlie's army, organized into tartan-clad Clan regiments, was defeated at Culloden in 1746, the wearing of the kilt was outlawed along with use of the Gaelic language. Culloden was the start of what Wilton calls the "great Clan Tartan myth." We have romanticized the idea of different tartans woven as a means of identifying and unifying members of a clan. The variety of colors is actually due to simple geography. Each community weaver would use local natural resources for dying the wool: the west coast offered gipsywort and welks for greens and purples; inland moors offered heathers for oranges and browns. Wilton explains: "By its very nature, that community would be one huge extended family that soon became identified by its tartan which it wore, not to differentiate it from its neighbors in the next glen, but because that's what its community weaver produced!" →

068 *Erskine.* ***069*** *Forsyth.* ***070*** *Aberdeen.*
071 *Fraser.* ***072*** *Hamilton.* ***073*** *Bell of the Borders.*
074 *Clan MacDonald.* ***075*** *Colquhoun.*
076 *Baird.* ***077*** *Barclay Dress.*
078 *Chattan.* ***079*** *Erskine Black & White.*
080 *Buchanan.*

→ By the early 19th century the historical novels of Sir Walter Scott were helping to popularize and reinvent myths of Highland culture. When Scott orchestrated George IV's state visit to Scotland in 1822, Highland Chieftains were encouraged to attend dressed in all their tartan finery and the king himself appeared in highland dress. This royal interest in all things Scottish reached its peak when Queen Victoria and Prince Albert fell in love with Balmoral Castle and filled its rooms with tartan furnishings.

The clan tartan had become an industry and the border weavers were only too happy to supply Highland Chiefs with their individual clan tartan—after all, it created new business. If nobody in the clan could recall a particular pattern, the chief might simply request that the tartan manufacturer assign one to him. This was the start of the demand for bespoke tartan that today sees major corporations, around 40 American states, soccer teams, and even bands like the White Stripes creating their own tartans. →

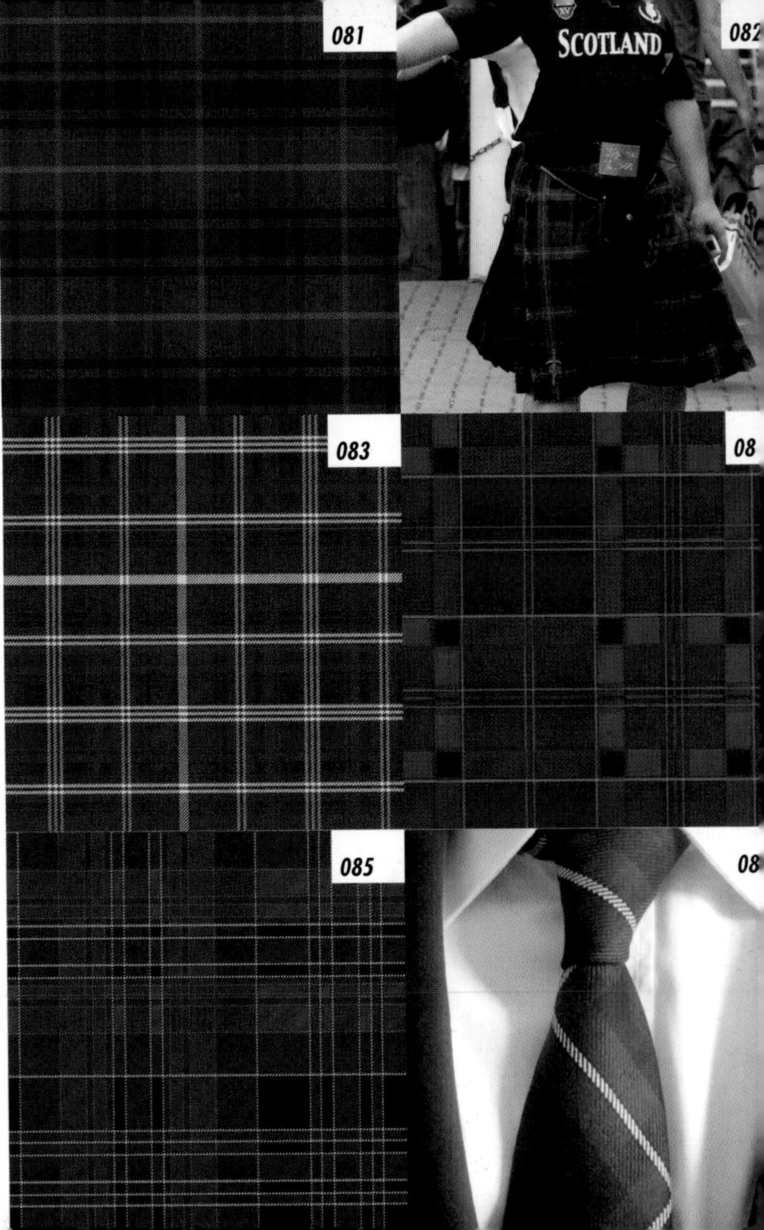

081 *MacArthur.*
082 *A patriotic Scot.*
083 *MacDougall.*
084 *MacGillivray.*
085 *MacDonald of Boisdale.*
086 *Mackenzie tartan tie.*
087 *A Scottish bull.*
088 *MacBeth.*

088
087

→ Families and individuals researching their family trees will often reaffirm their celtic roots by commissioning a tartan. Something about the romance of tartan along with its infinite number of pattern and color permutations makes it a covetable symbol of identity. True Scots might deride the newly made up tartans as "bumbee" tartans, but the reality is that they are invented in the same spirit in which those 19th century clansmen sought to reinvent their own histories.

Since the 1970s tartan has become associated with another clan altogether: punks. Much of punk's iconography is a hotchpotch of tribal influences: piercing, tattoos, and, indeed tartan. Malcolm McLaren and Vivienne Westwood first started mixing kilts with bondage pants in a subversive mix of establishment and fetishism. Since then punks have adopted tartan as part of their identity, combined with denim and leather, it is worn as a badge of belonging from Beijing to Bangor.

089 *MacNeil of Barra.*
090 *Robert Innes' image of a punk guitarist in tartan shorts.*

BIG FISH

091
092
094
095
096

091 *MacPherson Dress.*
092 *MacLean of Duart.*
093 and 096 *Punk on Brighton beach taken by Mark Henderson.*
094 *Tartan bondage pants in the USA, seen here by Jennifer Gonzalez.*
095 *Munro.*
097 *MacMillan.*
098 *MacLeod Dress.*
099 *Shredded denim worn over tartan.*
100 *Rosario Lopez Estudillo's Blythe doll, Dresden dressed in punky tartan.*
101 *MacMillan Dress.*
102 *Hannay.*
103 *A Chinese punk on the streets of Beijing.*
104 *A skater punk seen in Vancouver by Martin Ivison.*

Heraldry

In the Middle Ages, when a knight wore his complete armor including metal helmet, it was impossible to identify him in battle. Coats of arms were devised to solve this problem. Heraldry refers to the system of identification by coats of arms, and might be considered an early form of branding—using color, shape, and iconography to communicate identity and create differentiation.

Research into the graphic principles governing coats of arms reveals some fascinating facts. The colors (or "tinctures") used in shields are known by Old French names: vert (green), gules (red), azure (blue), sable (black), or (gold), and argent (silver). The shields are divided into sections, or "fields," in several grid configurations, and the range of combinations of color and pattern within these grids makes for wonderful graphic variety. Patterns—called "furs" (such as ermine or vair)—were also used within the fields. The "rule of tincture" ensures that contrasting colors are juxtaposed to achieve maximum visibility. →

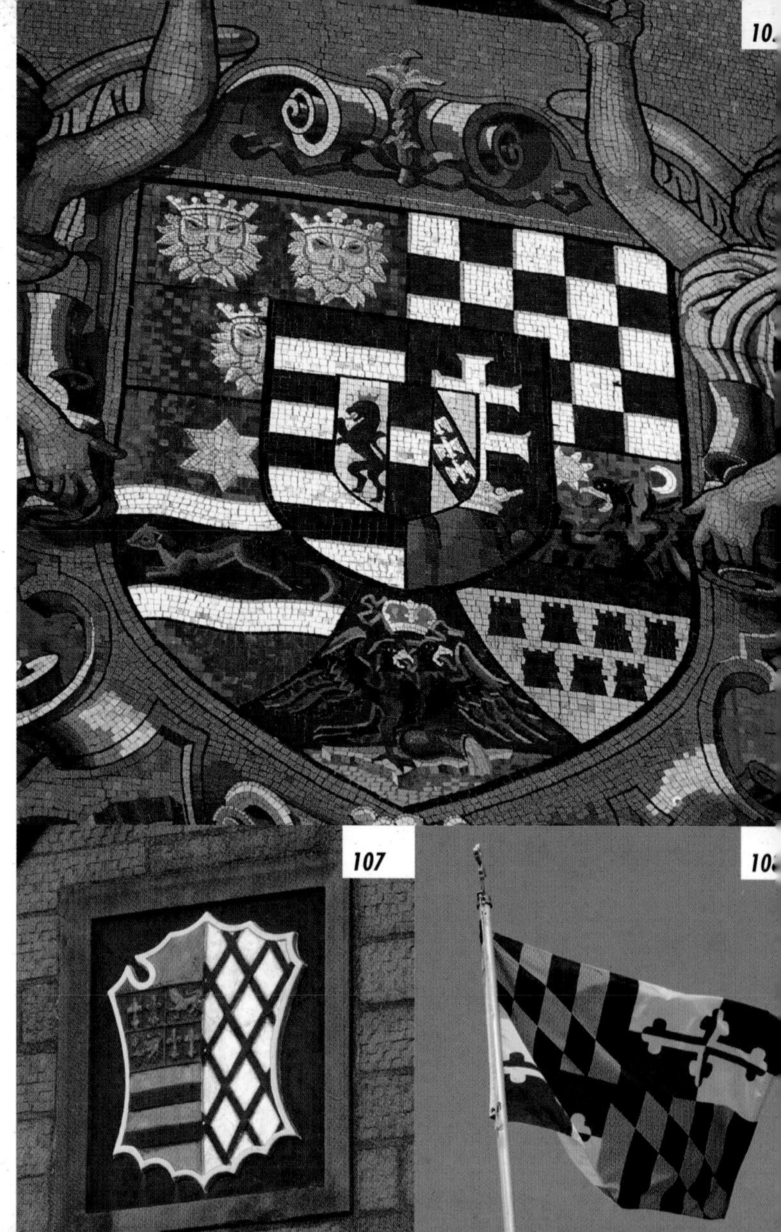

105 *Coat of arms of the kingdom of Hungary, prior to 1918 shown here on the castle in Buda dating from 1880.*
106 *Checkered coats of arms on ships sails.*
107 *Heraldic coat of arms on a market hall in the UK.*
108 *Maryland flag.*
109 *A knight at a Renaissance Faire with heraldic shield.*
110 *Stained glass windows of the cathedral of Tours representing coats of arms.*

106

109

110

→ These constructs of codified shape and color have lost none of their graphic appeal. This is pattern used at its most functional, yet aesthetically engaging. When branding and design consultants Roundel created Railfreight's new brand identity system, they developed a family of heraldic marks inspired by coats of arms and adopting a similar set of visual principles.

The Railfreight brand identity uses high contrast colors in shapes defined by a strict grid. Each "shield" conceals an F, standing for "freight," thus encoding a form of identity into the geometric pattern. The marks were designed to maximize visibility on moving locomotives which, emblazoned with these conspicuous, contemporary coats of arms, take on the appearance of modern day jousting knights.

111–115 *The Railfreight brand identity by Roundel.*

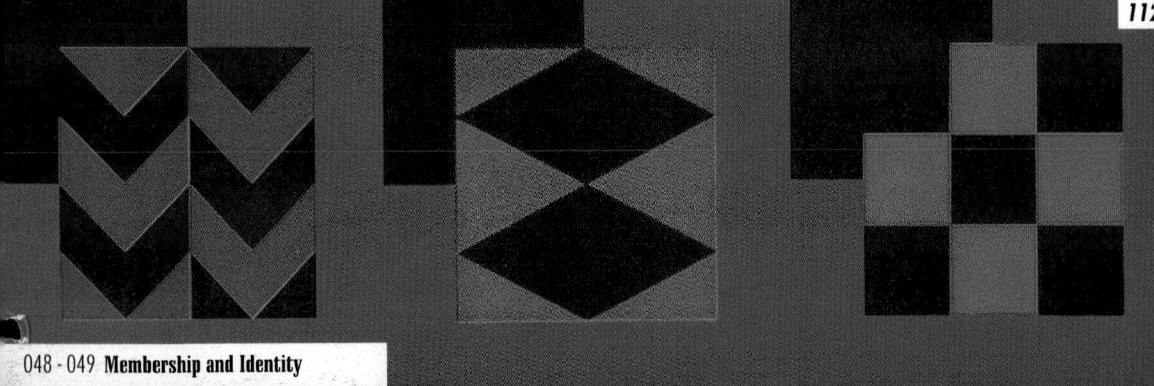

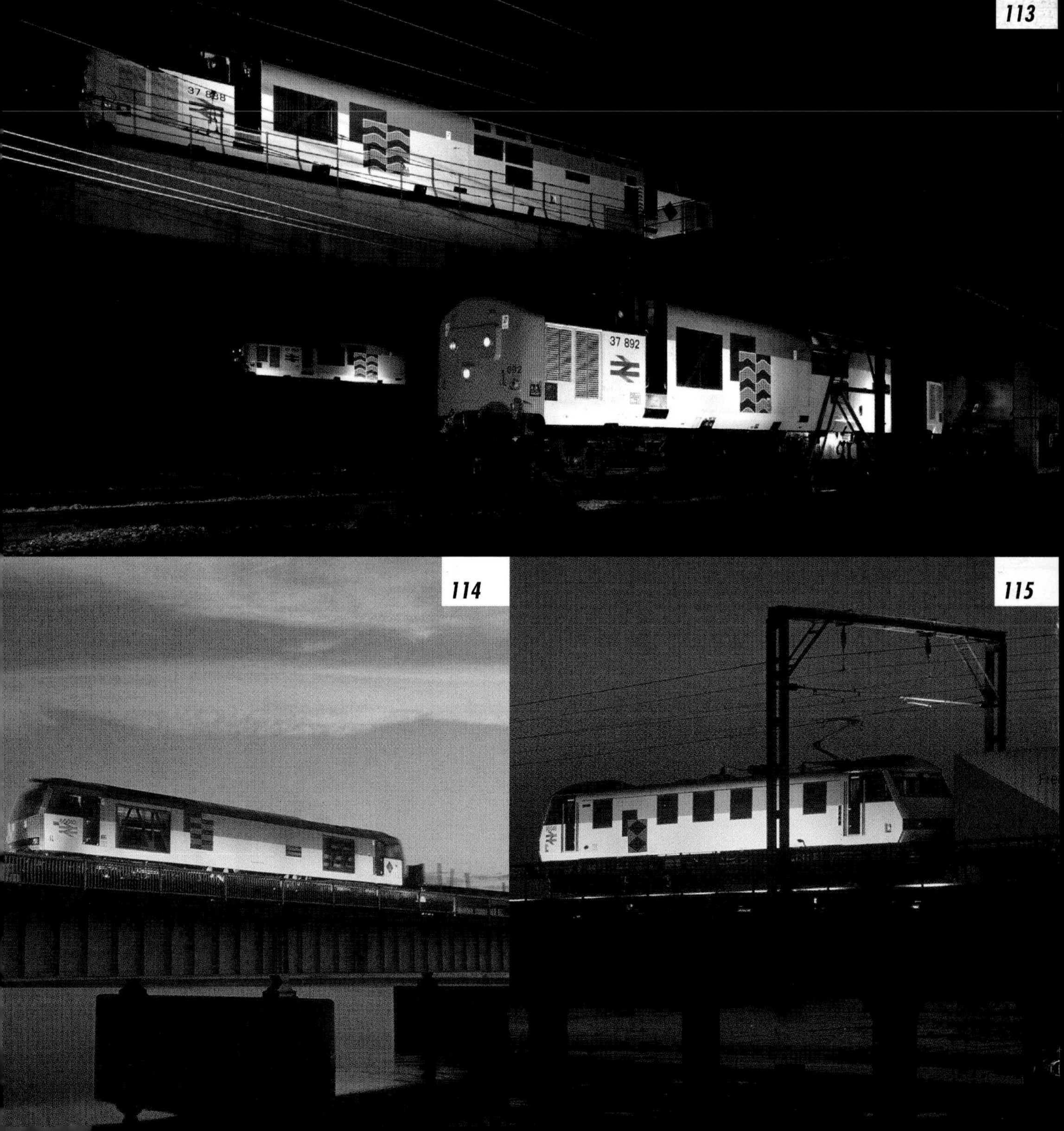
113
37 888
37 892
114
115

Date Plaques

One of the chief clues to a building's identity is the date it was built. Being able to date a building offers valuable insight into the social and historical context within which it was designed, the method of construction and materials used, and even its original purpose.

Buildings from the Victorian period and the early 20th century often display elaborate numerals carved in stone or cast in terracotta. While commemorative plaques are usually circular, applied to the surface of the building (notably the blue English Heritage plaques that celebrate a building's famed inhabitant), date plaques tend to be in more substantial squares, incorporated into the building's fabric. They are usually to be found high up on the facade, sometimes framed within the apex of a gable. Photographer Alan Campbell has documented a wealth of date plaques in and around Glasgow. Seen en masse, a compelling story unfolds of the city's architectural identity.

116–129 *Photographer Alan Campbell's collection of images of date plaques in and around Glasgow.*

AD
1894

124
1909
125
127
BUILT
AD 18
126
THE
McALPIN
NURSING
HOME
1908
128
1890
129
E
A
17
06

Police Uniform

Shortly after becoming the Chief Constable of Glasgow in 1931, Sir Percy Sillitoe conceived the idea for a checkered pattern to be worn by his police force to make them identifiable to motorists who were refusing to stop on country roads. Sir Percy wrote in his journal: “There was no way at all of knowing if one was being halted by a bona fide policeman or a hold-up man. White capes seemed impractical, and white caps would not have been sufficiently distinctive. But the ‘diced band’ of the uniform of the Brigade of Guards would be unmistakable and seemed ideal, so I borrowed it for my men and it became known as Sillitoe’s Tartan.”

Not until 1974 did the checkered pattern become adopted by the entire UK police force. Nowadays it is used as a key component of many police uniforms all over the world—applied to helmets, sweaters, and women’s scarves, and adopted in contrasting fluorescents on the exterior of police cars. Like the stripe (also sometimes used on vehicles), the checkered pattern creates visual “noise” that makes it highly recognizable. Graffiti artist Banksy uses it as visual shorthand in his piece *Snorting Copper*. The checkered band, executed in the two-color stencil method, instantly identifies his subject as a policeman.

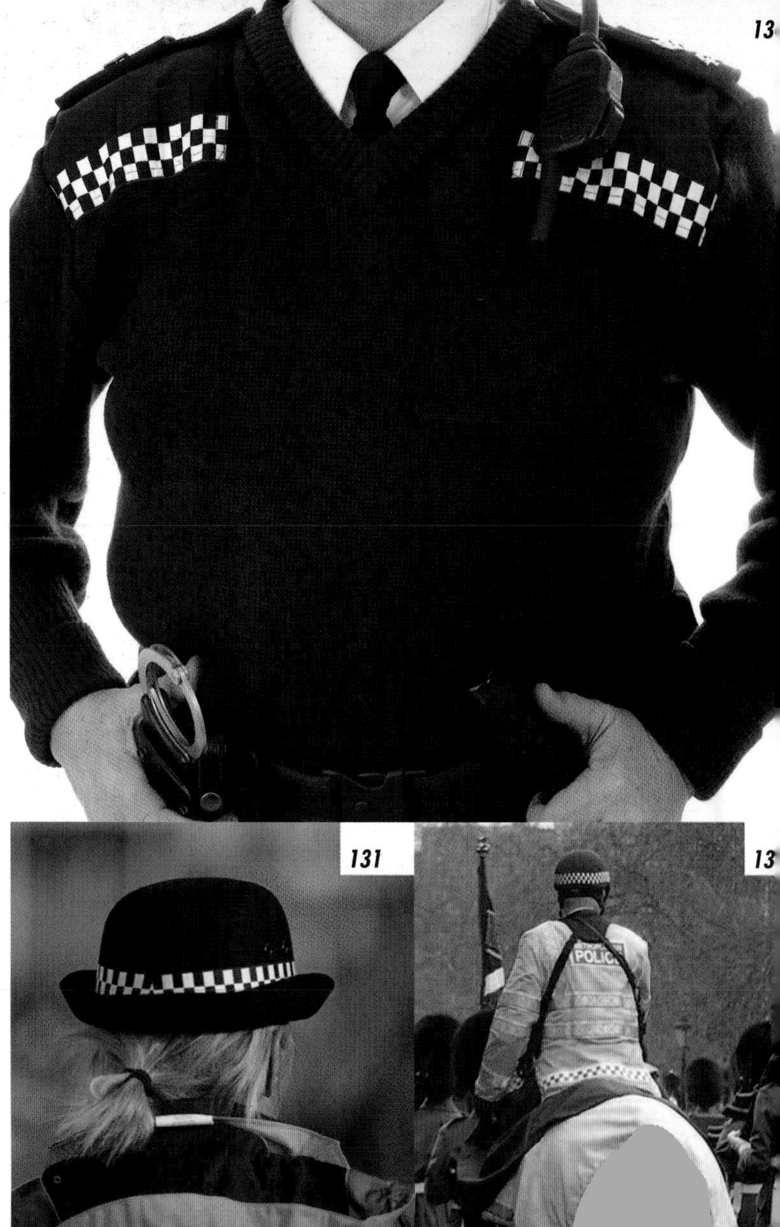

130–132 *UK police uniforms with Sillitoe's Tartan for identification.*
133 *This Bansky image "Snorting Copper," photographed by Martin Bull, has now been removed, but information about it and a similar surviving one is available in his book "Banksy Locations and Tours" or on his website www.shellshockphotos.co.uk*
134 and 135 *UK police vehicles use high contrast checks as an alternative to stripes.*

Harlequin

This diamond-checkered pattern derives its name from the character, Harlequin. In medieval French plays, Hellequin is a messenger of the Devil. Arlecchino is one of the archetypes of the Italian Commedia dell'arte, a form of Renaissance theater improvised by masked players around stock themes such as love, adultery, and jealousy. This later became the Harlequinade in 18th-century England.

His colorful costume, patched from the remnants of richer suits, identifies Harlequin as a servant. Lying, lascivious, yet likable, his chief role is to create confusion. Harlequin was a popular motif in early 20th-century culture. His multicolored costume started to connote festivity and variety. Harlequin became a popular brand name, notably for mid-century plastic kitchenalia and a boxed selection of chocolates. Harlequin enjoyed a return to anarchic form in the hands of punk instigator, Vivienne Westwood.

She used the design for a woman's cat suit in her Voyage to Cythera collection, the transformation into a female character creating a further element of transgression.

136 *John Austen's 1923 illustrations for "The Adventures of Harlequin" by Francis Bickley show how fashionable the character became in this period.*
137 *Poster and promotional material for a performance of Harlequinade by DanceStation, designed by Nora Brown.*
138 *A decorative Harlequin patterned mask.*
139 *Malene Thyssen captured this performance of Harlequinade.*
140 *An illustration of an Arlecchino costume from 1671.*
141 *Harlequin and Columbine from the Voyage to Cythera collection, captured here by Diana Lee at a Vivienne Westwood retrospective.*
142 *What better way to relax than in a harlequin check playsuit? Seen here in a vintage carpet advertisement.*

138
139
140
Arlechino (1671)
141
142

National Identity

Squares, checks, and grids occur less frequently in national flags than the more prevalent stripe, but several flags are based on a simple cross. A diagonal cross like the Scottish flag (the cross of St. Andrew) is known as a Saltire. The Scandinavian countries all use variations of a Nordic cross—where the vertical part of the cross is shifted to the hoist side. Distinguished by its square proportions, the Swiss flag incorporates a white cross on a red base. The flag traditionally stood for Christian faith and honor; modern connotations extend to neutrality, peace, and refuge. It shares its square proportions with only one other national flag—that of the Vatican City, which is also the only state for which Switzerland still permits mercenary service. In 1906 the International Committee of the Red Cross reversed the colors of the Swiss flag to create the Red Cross flag in honor of Swiss native and founder of the humanitarian organization, Henry Dunant.

Symbols of national identity have always evolved throughout history. Croatian designer, Boris Ljubicic's proposal for a new Croatian flag features red, white, and blue squares in a random design. Used as the basic code for the national identity of Croatia, the squares are taken from the historic coat of arms, which appears on the current flag. While the flag has not yet been adopted, it is used for several parallel cultural applications. Boris Ljubicic also uses the square as the basis of a host of brand identities for Croatian businesses and organizations, contemporary in attitude, while reflecting the country's heritage.

143 *Burundi.*
144 *England.*
145 *Faroe Islands.*
146 *Denmark.*
147 *Chile.*
148 *Dominican Republic.*
149 *Guernsey.*
150 *Jamaica.*
151 *Finland.*
152 *Georgia.*
153 *Iceland.*
154 *Madagascar.*
155 *Scotland.*
156 *Sweden.*
157 *Panama.*
158 *Norway.*

144
145
146
148
149
150
152
153
154
156
157
158

159 *Swiss flag flying.*
160 *Flag of Switzerland.*

161

161 *The existing Croatian flag.*
162 *A collection of identities designed by Boris Ljubicic at Studio International, all influenced by the Croatian flag. L/R Top: Product of Croatia; Croatia tourist board; Cro Ski. Middle: Ministry of Culture. L/R Bottom: World Sailing TV Cup, Croatia 1999; Croatia and HRT (Hrvatska Radio Televizija, Croatian Radio Television).*
163 *Alternative Croatian flag designed by Boris Ljubicic incorporating the red, white, and blue squares of the historic Croatian coat of arms.*
164–166 *Croatian Silence fashion project by Boris Ljubicic.*

16.

product of
CROATIA

CROATIA

CRO
SKI

Ministarstvo
kulture
Republika
Hrvatska
Ministry
of Culture
Republic
of Croatia

HRT 2

1 2 3

163
164
165
166

Themes and Moods

Puzzles and Games
Learning
Retro
Automotive
Modernism

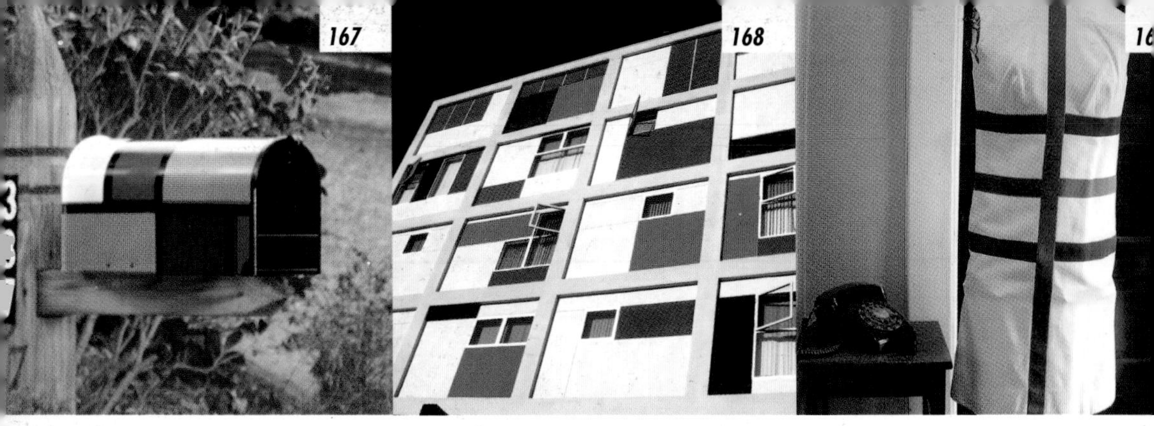

Themes and Moods

Squares and grids have an inherently rational quality that makes them ideal for communicating themes of order and logic. Building blocks are commonly appropriated for concepts of learning and education, while puzzles and games are often constructed on a grid. There are blank squares you fill in and random squares you fit together.

The neutrality of the square means that it has assumed a variety of retro moods, from softly rounded squares in the 1960s to "look sharp" checks of the 1980s ska revival. In motor sports the checkered flag means victory; now it is used to communicate general automotive themes as well as the successful completion of a task, such as downloading software. Honest and functional, the square and the right angle reign supreme in Modernist style: Mackintosh, Mondrian, and Mies van der Rohe all based their aesthetics on its minimalist form.

167 *Artist Chris Hoover created and photographed this Mondrian-inspired mailbox.*
168 *Jennifer Remias captured this Mondrian-style building.*
169 *Amanda Kreuger's vintage "mod"rian dress is no longer worn, but stands as a design centerpiece in her home.*
170 *A miniature board game.*
171 *Hotel Le Corbusier in Marseille.*
172 *Signage for Mackintosh's Glasgow School of Art.*
173 *A snakes and ladders cow.*
174 *The classic Rubik's Cube®.*
175 *A 3D game of noughts and crosses or tic-tac-toe.*
176 *A morning crossword.*
177 *An outdoor game of chess.*

18

184 *The "blümerant" temporary installation on Gendarmenmarkt, Berlin, developed by msk7, seen here by Katja Rostock.*
185 *Puzzle-inspired garment by London fashion art and design collective, Beyond the Valley.*
186 *Puzzle shelving system by Bloq.*
187 and 188 *Crossword-inspired designs for Vans and Converse.*
189 *Revolutionary crossword photographed by Alex Pallent.*

187
VANS
188
E
189
RIOT
VOTE
VILE
REVOLUTION
VIOL
LOOT
RAT
VOLT
RETHMANN
9302•2222

→ The mathematics of the square has a satisfying logic that makes it the ideal vehicle for puzzle setters. The resulting geometry offers graphic appeal that can inspire fashion, furniture, and graphic design. Many games and puzzles have an iconography that lives beyond the game itself. Scrabble is an obvious example. While the crossword is a solitary pursuit, Scrabble creates an opportunity for competition and interaction. Luck plays a part too, in the random choosing of letter tiles with varying scores (rare Zs and Qs score highest, common vowels the lowest). The board—with tantalizing pink and blue squares offering the chance to double or triple your score—is familiar to word puzzle enthusiasts everywhere.

Chess and checkers (also known as draughts) both share the familiar board of 32 black and 32 white squares. Checkers was popular in ancient Egypt, Greece, and Rome. Chess is thought to have originated in India around 1,500 years ago. The game is particularly popular in Russia, home of grandmasters like Garry Kasparov, and was a mark of Soviet pride during the Cold War—up to the end of the Soviet Union, there was only one non-Soviet champion, American Bobby Fischer. Stock market traders play chess to keep their minds agile. In graphics applications, the checkered board and iconic pieces carry connotations of strategy and mental prowess. →

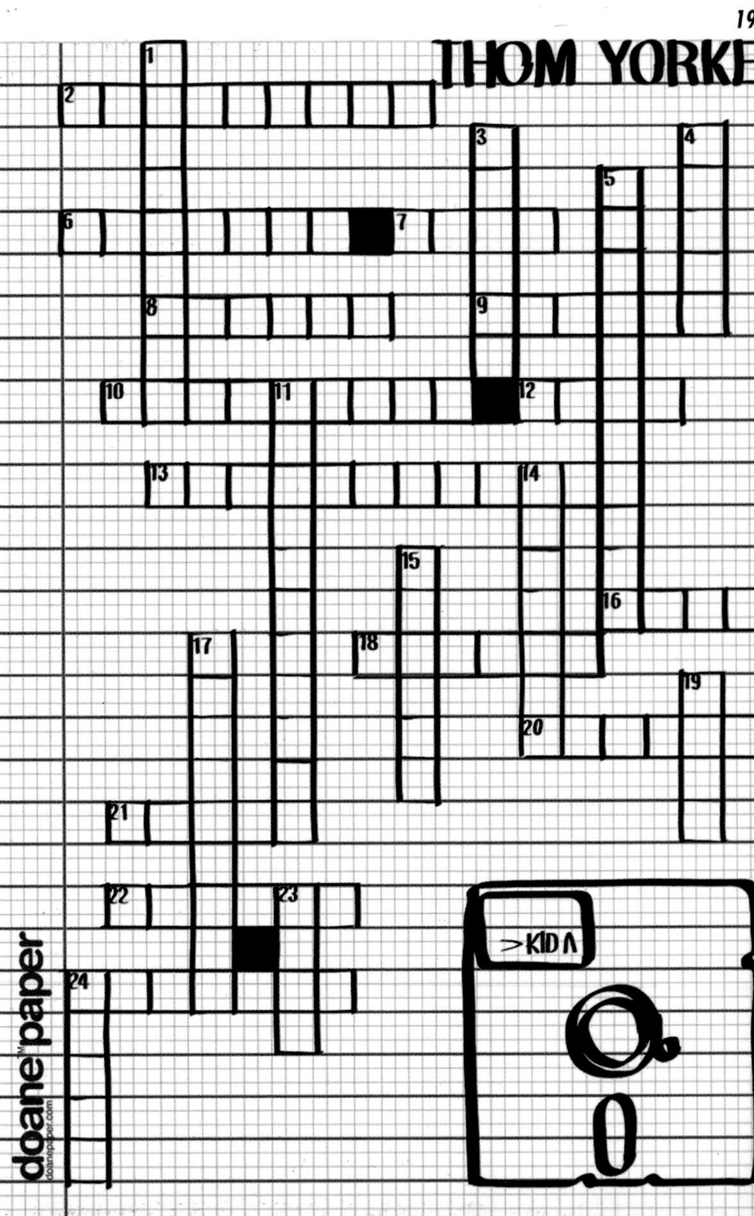

THOM YORKE 2/2

DOWN

1. THESE TWO BROTHERS PLAY LEAD GUITAR AND BASS IN RADIOHEAD
3. HIS DEBUT SOLO ALBUM
4. THIS ARTIST RECORDED AN ACOUSTIC VERSION OF THE SONG KID A AS A B-SIDE
5. HIS FATHER WAS A CHEMICAL ENGINEERING ____________ SALESMAN
11. THIS RADIOHEAD SONG IS PLAYED BY A GUITAR NOT SYNTHESIZERS
14. XL RECORDINGS WAS LAUNCHED BY ________ BANQUET
15. THIS SONG WAS BROUGHT ON BY A CAR ACCIDENT THAT YORKE EXP. IN 1987
17. APPLE PROGRAM USED TO GENERATE THE VOICE IN "FITTER HAPPIER"
19. FAN OF THE BOOK; NO ______ BY NAOMI KLEIN
23. HIS PARTNER AND THE MOTHER OF HIS TWO SONS
24. 30 SECOND FILMS CREATED TO PROMOTE THE RADIOHEAD ALBUM; KID A

ACROSS

2. UNDERWENT OPERATIONS AS A CHILD TO CORRECT A ______ LEFT EYE
6. YORKE HAS FREQUENTLY COLLABORATED WITH THIS VISUAL ARTIST
7. SON TO WHOM THE RADIOHEAD ALBUM "AMNESIAC" WAS DEDICATED
8. CURRENTLY LIVES IN
9. ATTENDED THIS UNIVERSITY
10. "ICE AGE COMING, ICE AGE COMING"
12. THE NAME RADIOHEAD WAS TAKEN FROM THE TALKING HEADS ALBUM "______ STORIES"
13. HIS BROTHER ANDY FRONTED THE BAND; THE ________ TRUTH
16. SOME SAY THE BEATLES SONG "SEXY ______" SOUNDS A LOT LIKE "KARMA POLICE"
18. ON A ____________, RADIOHEAD'S INITIAL NAME
20. PART OF "OK COMPUTER" WAS RECORDED AT THIS ACTRESSES' 15TH CENTURY MANSION
21. RADIOHEAD'S SOPHOMORE ALBUM
22. COLLABORATED WITH THIS DJ FOR PROJECT UNKLE.
24. YORKE'S FALSETTO VOICE HAS BEEN DIRECTLY COMPARED TO THIS DEPARTED ARTIST'S VOICE

doane paper
doanepaper.com

"Doane Paper is a stationery design that I conceived during a lunch break at a product design meeting when I noticed that half the room was using legal pads while the other half were using grid paper notebooks. After the meeting I combined the two stationery designs onto a single sheet. The final product turned out pretty cool.

I was looking for a sound example to demonstrate the qualities of a sheet of Doane Paper and thought that a simple crossword puzzle would do the trick. The puzzle itself works nicely with Doane Paper's grid pattern while the puzzle questions themselves rest on the ruled lines. I'm a big fan of Radiohead and Thom Yorke's initial solo album was being released at the time so I decided to use that as the crossword puzzle's subject."

Chad Doane
Doane Paper

190 and 191 *This Thom Yorke crossword was developed by Doane Paper.*

192
193
19
195
C
N
E
S
19
19

198

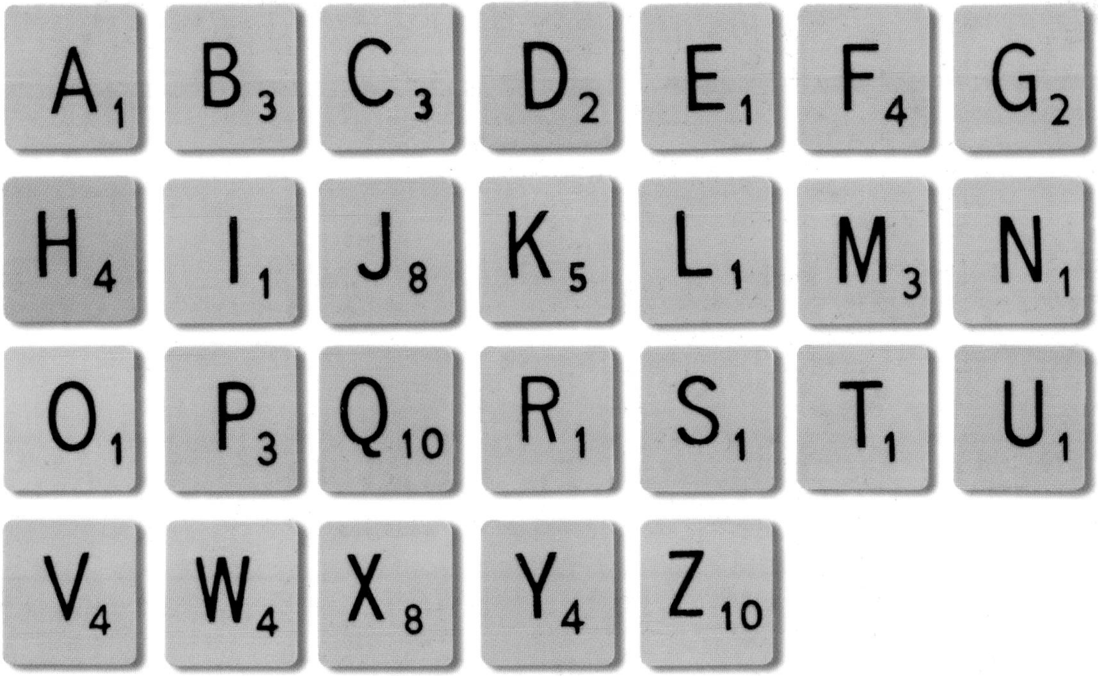

2 A checkerboard building in Brooklyn.
3 Improvised bottle top checkers on an outdoor board.
4 Large-scale outdoor chess game.
5 Croatian National Education Standard (HNOS) design work by
's Ljubicic, Studio International.
6 Snakes and ladders cows.
7 A games board from the Ulster Folk Museum.
8 Leo Reynolds' study of Scrabble pieces.
9 **and 200** A travel version of Scrabble and the original board
pieces.

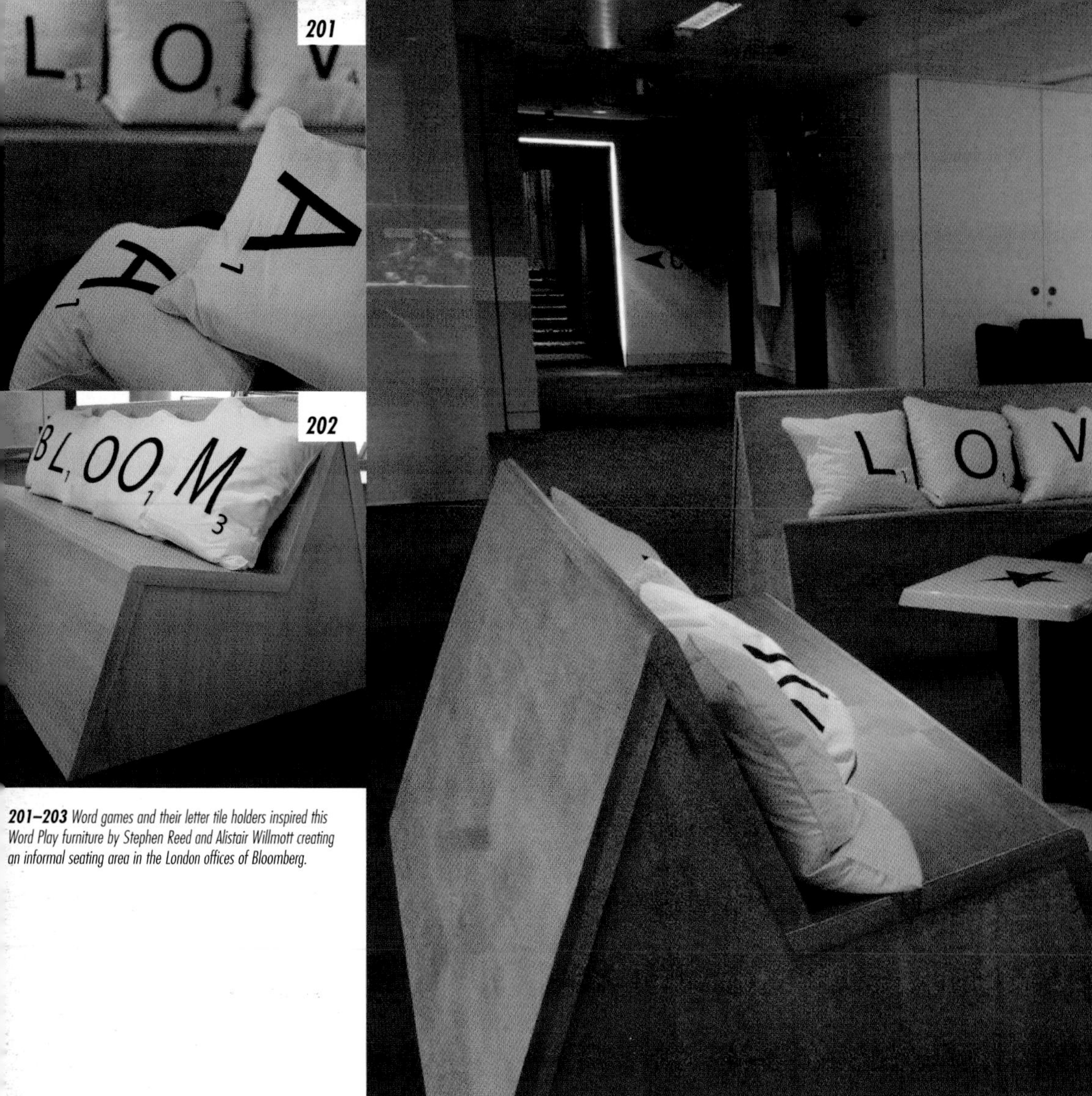

201–203 *Word games and their letter tile holders inspired this Word Play furniture by Stephen Reed and Alistair Willmott creating an informal seating area in the London offices of Bloomberg.*

T1 R1 U1 T1 H4

→ While the square is a symbol of order, puzzles challenge us to create order out of chaos. The sliding tile puzzle has a tactile and interactive quality that makes this an enduring low-tech puzzle whose design influence belies its simplicity. Pentagram has designed an iconic graphic identity system for Saks Fifth Avenue that breaks the rules of conventional branding. The logo is randomly tiled to create a dynamic identity system with an almost infinite number of permutations. →

204 *The Waxwings "Shadows of" CD artwork designed by Tal Brosh, Schnitzel Records.*
205 *Michael Salge created this sliding tile puzzle computer display as a way of exploring the possibility of being able to pixelate a screen physically rather than virtually.*
206 *A traditional sliding tile puzzle square has pieces that reveal an image once solved.*
207 *Although the shapes on this Alba Armoire designed by Russell Pinch are static, the multilevels give a sense of movement and interactivity.*

20

205

20

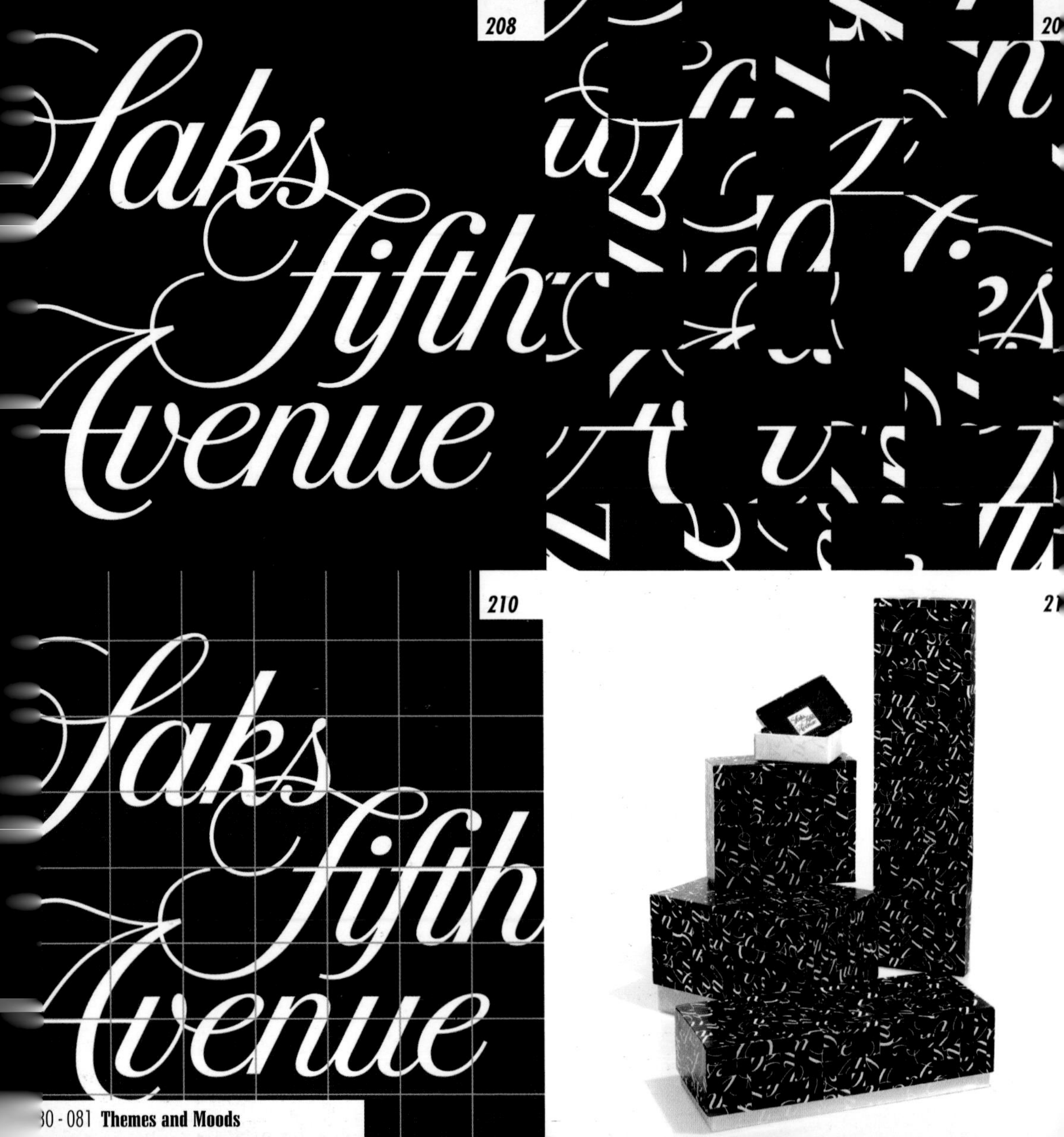
208
Saks Fifth Avenue
210
Saks Fifth Avenue
21

"Saks approached us about designing a new identity for their stores, seeking a graphic program that would encompass signage, advertising, direct mail, online, and, most importantly, packaging. Unlike Tiffany, the store has never had a signature color; unlike Burberry, no signature pattern. On the contrary, examining their history we found the store had used literally dozens of logos since its founding. Of these, one stood out: the logo drawn in 1973 by Tom Carnese. We took the cursive logo, redrew it with the help of font designer Joe Finocchiaro, and placed it in a black square. Then, we subdivided that square into a grid of 64 smaller squares. The 64 tiles can then be shuffled and rotated to form an almost infinite number of variations—the number of possible configurations is nearly 100 googols. Most of the individual logo tiles are quite lovely in their own right, and within the system can be used in various combinations to form still more abstract compositions. The advantage of the program is that it creates recognizable consistency without sameness."

Michael Bierut, Partner, Pentagram

208–212 *Saks Fifth Avenue brand identity by Pentagram. Creative Director: Michael Bierut. Design: Michael Bierut, Jennifer Kinon, and Kerrie Powell. Typography: Joe Finocchiaro.*

213
214
215

213 and 214 *Jigs Up contemporary floor tiles by FLOR.*
215 *Nana jigsaw pattern print by Absolute Zero Degrees. Missing pieces hint at a wooden surface under the puzzle, creating more depth to the design.*
216 *The Jigsaw Pieces wall system by Luke White is made of 95% recycled cardboard laminate jigsaw pieces to create a flexible, updatable wallcovering with integrated CD player, clock, mirror, hooks, and shelves.*

→ Jigsaws have only one solution. There is no deviating from their grid and each piece has to be in the right place for the picture to come together. Introduce flexibility to the grid and you have a modular concept. Modular furniture uses a standard set of components and offers a variety of possible configurations. Multifunctional goes hand in hand with modular: Luke White's Jigsaw Pieces wall system features a clock, mirror, hooks, and CD player, while Bloq's Nest combines the functionality of a table with seating and shelves. →

21

21

217 *This self-promotional piece by Impagination Inc. takes the form of a 3D puzzle cube. A fall-away wrapper reveals a cube with the Impagination credo messages on all sides. The mailer was highly successful, generating a 50% response rate.*
218 *The Takeaway unit by Bloq features a pleasingly puzzle-like configuration of squares.*
219 *Flexible Nest tables by Bloq offer many configurations, each one a successful result.*

220

22

22

→ Various puzzles and games have caused crazes throughout the 20th century, and none greater than the 1980s' obsession with the Rubik's Cube®. Hungarian Erno Rubik was a lecturer in Interior Design in Budapest. Passionately interested in geometry and 3D forms, he often communicated his ideas through models made from paper, cardboard, wood, or plastic. Taking inspiration from classic puzzles like the Tangram, Pentomino, and Soma Cube, he set out to create a 3D object, richer than precedents in configuration variations, that would remain intact while being solved. This proved to be the Cube's unique selling point. After selling for three years in Hungary, the Magic Cube, as it was called, made its debut at international toy fairs in early 1980. With Erno Rubik demonstrating his own creation, it made an immediate impact. The name was changed and the first Rubik's Cubes® were exported from Hungary in May 1980. Over 100 million were sold in 1980–1982.

The puzzle and its iconic design has retained its popularity and found new devotees. Branding consultants Vibrandt created a new positioning and packaging for confectionery brand Poppets® using a series of iconic, retro images from times gone by. The idea was to engage older and younger consumers by appealing to their love for nostalgia. The mint variety proudly features the Rubik's Cube®, complete with an anecdote on the back of pack that reads: "Even now mum thinks it's a paperweight." →

223

224

220, 222, and 224 *The iconic Rubik's Cube® comes in many varieties, from the mini square to 5×5 squares.*
221 *Kevin Minnis captured this puzzle-like installation while on vacation.*

223 *Mint Poppets® packaging by Vibrandt features retro icons including the Rubik's Cube®. Use of the Rubik's Cube® is by permission of Seven Towns Ltd.*
225–227 *Alex Pallent's images of the Melbourne Museum.*

225 226 227

→ A simple grid is all that's required for playing popular children's games like tic-tac-toe, also known as noughts and crosses. The game play of tic-tac-toe is so simple that a winning strategy is easy to master. This results in most games ending in a draw. While we quickly grow out of playing the game, its visual appeal stays with us. It seems that there's something inherently satisfying about filling in the grid and the "x" and "o" symbols even have an emotional quality—lending the game the alternative name "hugs and kisses." The patterns and symbols of the game have varied associations—search flickr.com with "tic-tac-toe" and a wealth of images will appear.

Hopscotch is instant fun requiring no equipment —simply drawn on the playground floor with a stone, the same stone can be used as the marker you throw to play. It was especially popular in Victorian Britain, but originated as a training regimen for Roman soldiers in the Roman Empire. There are versions all round the world including Malaysian "ting-ting" and the French spiral version, "escargot."

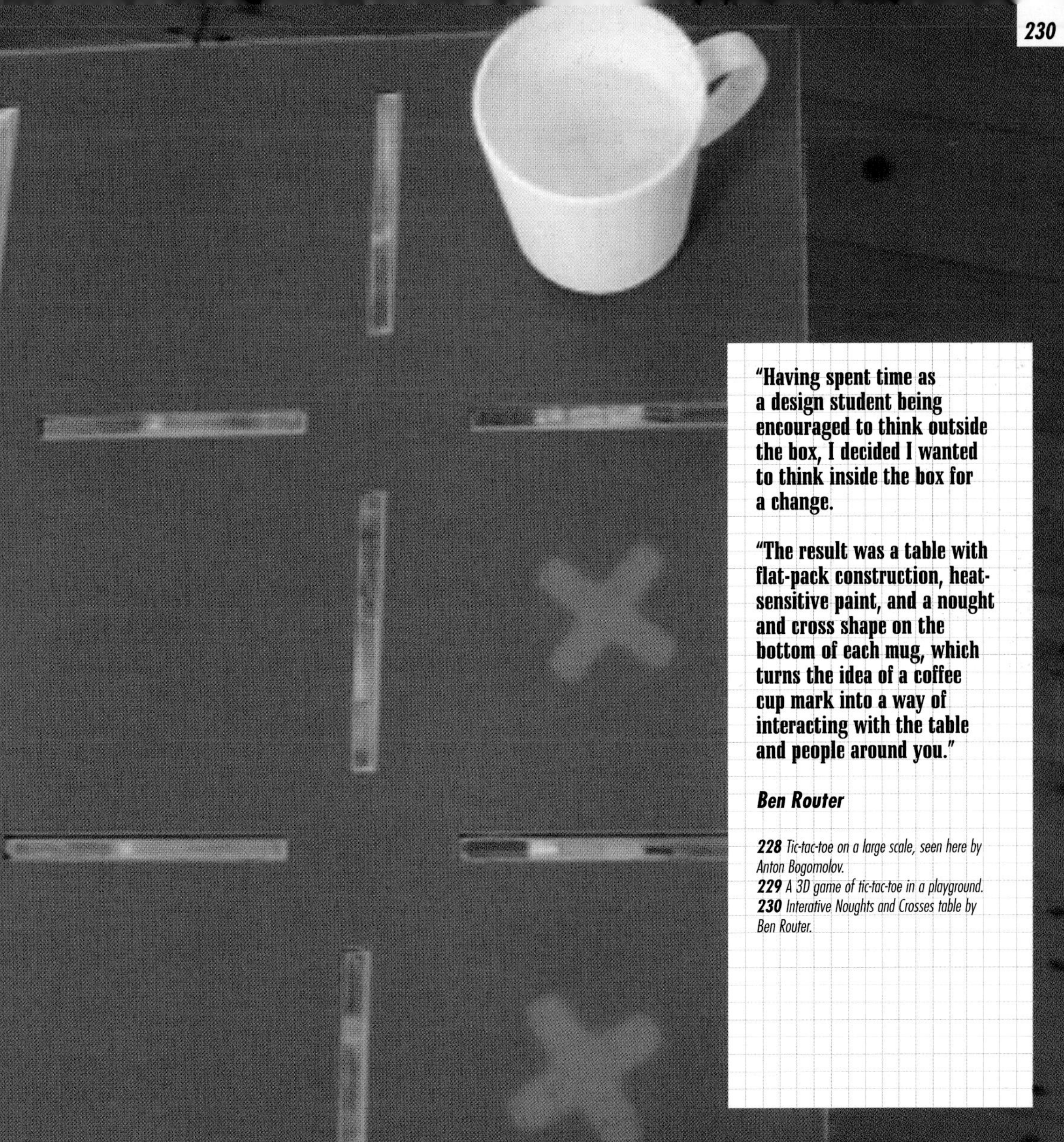

"Having spent time as a design student being encouraged to think outside the box, I decided I wanted to think inside the box for a change.

"The result was a table with flat-pack construction, heat-sensitive paint, and a nought and cross shape on the bottom of each mug, which turns the idea of a coffee cup mark into a way of interacting with the table and people around you."

Ben Router

228 *Tic-tac-toe on a large scale, seen here by Anton Bogomolov.*
229 *A 3D game of tic-tac-toe in a playground.*
230 *Interative Noughts and Crosses table by Ben Router.*

NO NOUGHTS ONLY CROSSES

"This is a conceptual typeface inspired by the words of a child who was playing Noughts and Crosses with his dad on a train journey to London. Fed up with not being able to beat his dad, the boy said, 'let's have another game, but using no Noughts, only Crosses,' guaranteeing his own victory. I drew out a 3 by 3 grid and filled it with crosses. For the remainder of the journey, I sketched out characters using only the lines created by the grid trying to keep the letterforms as square as possible taking away the minimum amount of blank space."

Ric Bell

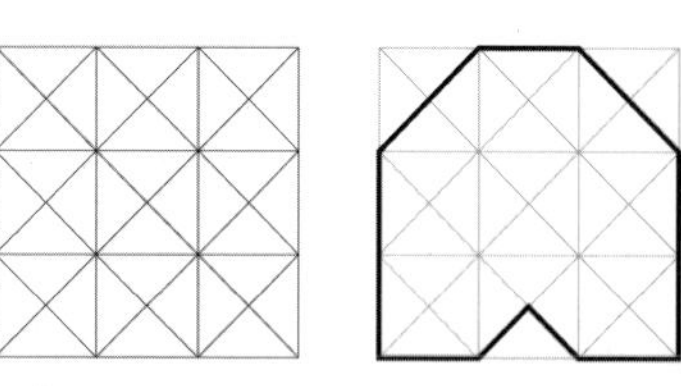

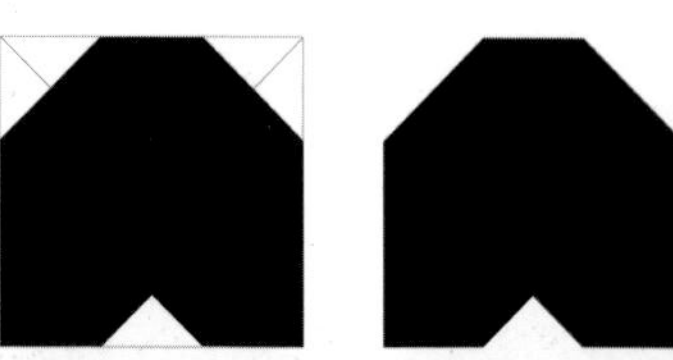

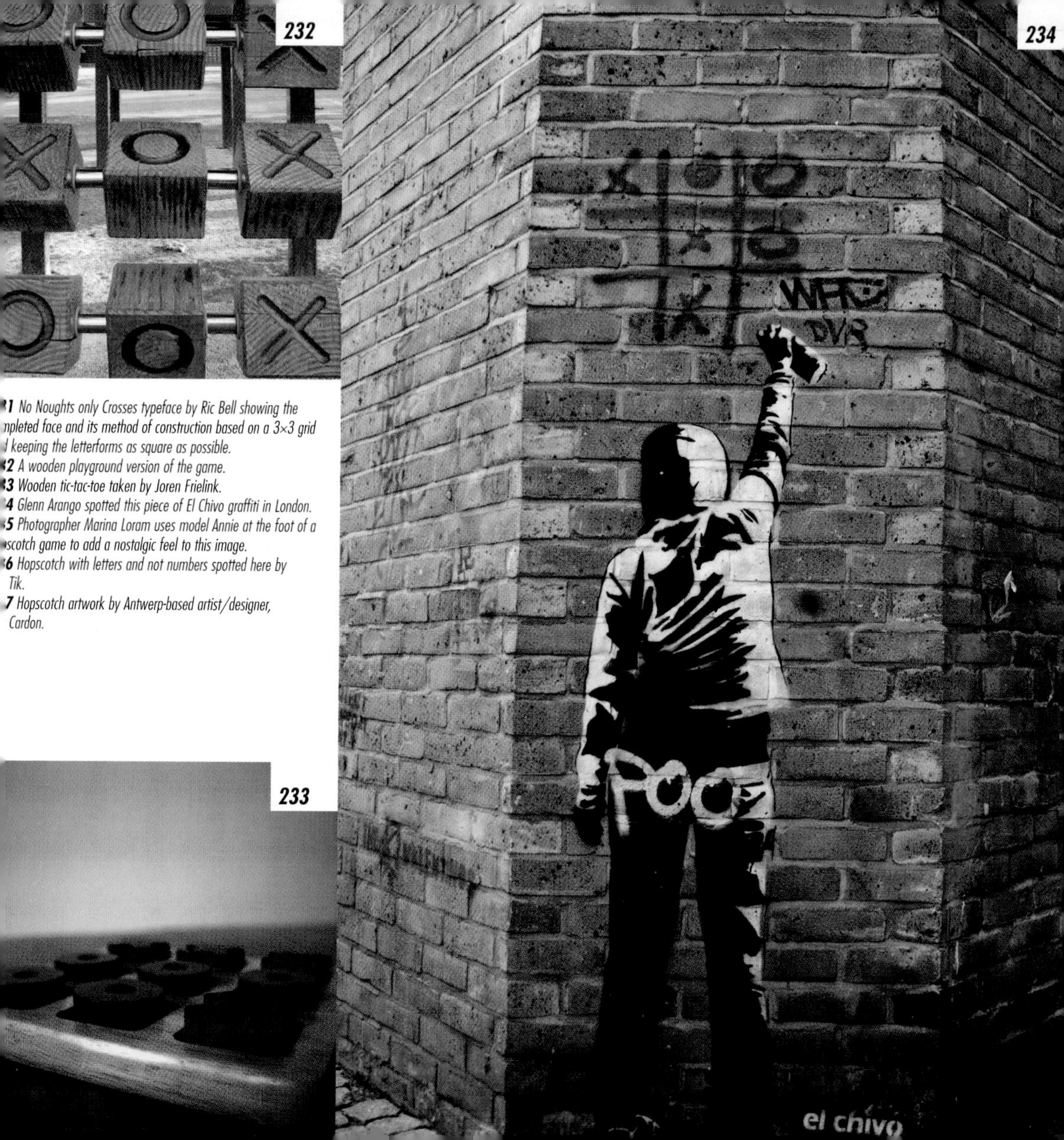

*1 No Noughts only Crosses typeface by Ric Bell showing the
npleted face and its method of construction based on a 3×3 grid
l keeping the letterforms as square as possible.
2 A wooden playground version of the game.
3 Wooden tic-tac-toe taken by Joren Frielink.
4 Glenn Arango spotted this piece of El Chivo graffiti in London.
5 Photographer Marina Loram uses model Annie at the foot of a
scotch game to add a nostalgic feel to this image.
6 Hopscotch with letters and not numbers spotted here by
Tik.
7 Hopscotch artwork by Antwerp-based artist/designer,
Cardon.*

235

Learning

Building blocks help to stimulate a child's imagination. With letters or numbers on each face, they teach elementary literacy and numeracy, and help to develop coordination skills. A group of children sharing a box of Lego will learn social skills too, as they must cooperate with each other over which bricks are needed to complete each individual's project. Building blocks are so much a part of our early development that we instantly relate to them as a metaphor for learning.

Graphically, this offers many opportunities to communicate educational themes—either rendered as squares or cubes. The Holly Lodge Primary School logo and identity system is entirely based on squares; executed in a bold palette of primaries plus green, it evokes the building blocks of early learning. Branding consultancy Roundel has succinctly reflected the school's mission statement, "Building together for the future," with a design solution that appeals to children and speaks to parents.

238 *Bright colored building blocks.*
239 *Holly Lodge Primary School branding and print material by Roundel uses the visual language of building blocks to ground the brand in learning and reflect the idea of building for the future.*

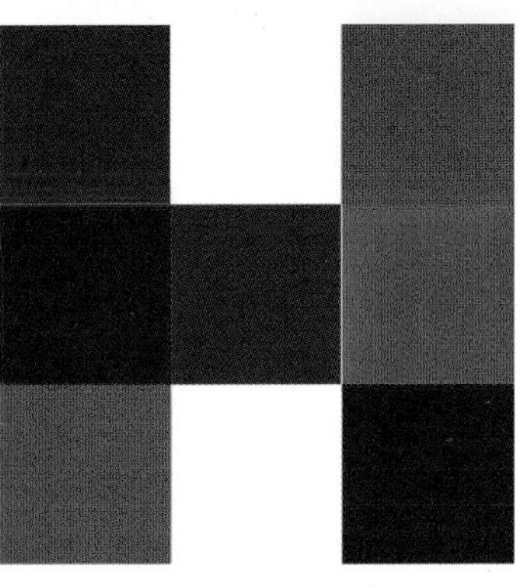

Holly Lodge
Primary School

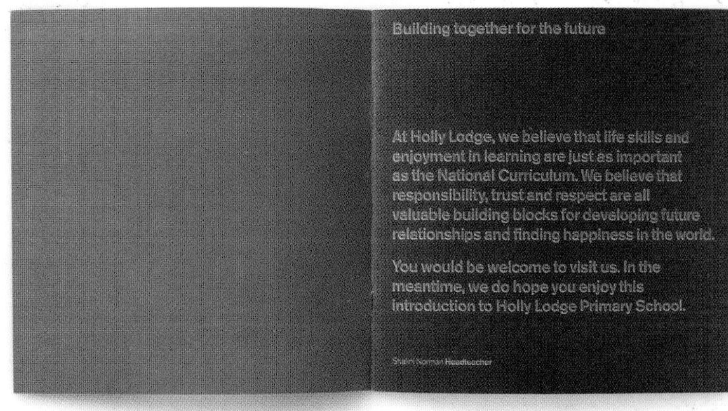

Building together for the future
At Holly Lodge, we believe that life skills and enjoyment in learning are just as important as the National Curriculum. We believe that responsibility, trust and respect are all valuable building blocks for developing future relationships and finding happiness in the world.
You would be welcome to visit us. In the meantime, we do hope you enjoy this introduction to Holly Lodge Primary School.
Shalini Norman Headteacher

"At Holly Lodge we use smarties to help us learn about fractions."
Adam, age 6

"I like games because you can learn to run really fast. I think Holly Lodge is a nice place to be."
Lucy, age 9

"All the teachers help us whatever way they can."
Lauren, age 11

"I like Design Technology because in Year 5 you can make pizza and eat it."
Ryan, age 9

"History is a great subject because you get to find out about all that has happened in the past and I think that's fascinating."
Huw, age 8

"I like having PE - I like doing roly polys on the mat."
Bethan, age 5

"The school is willing to help children naughty or smart."

"I like to learn French at school because if you go on holiday it will be very useful."

"At Holly Lodge we have good school trips."

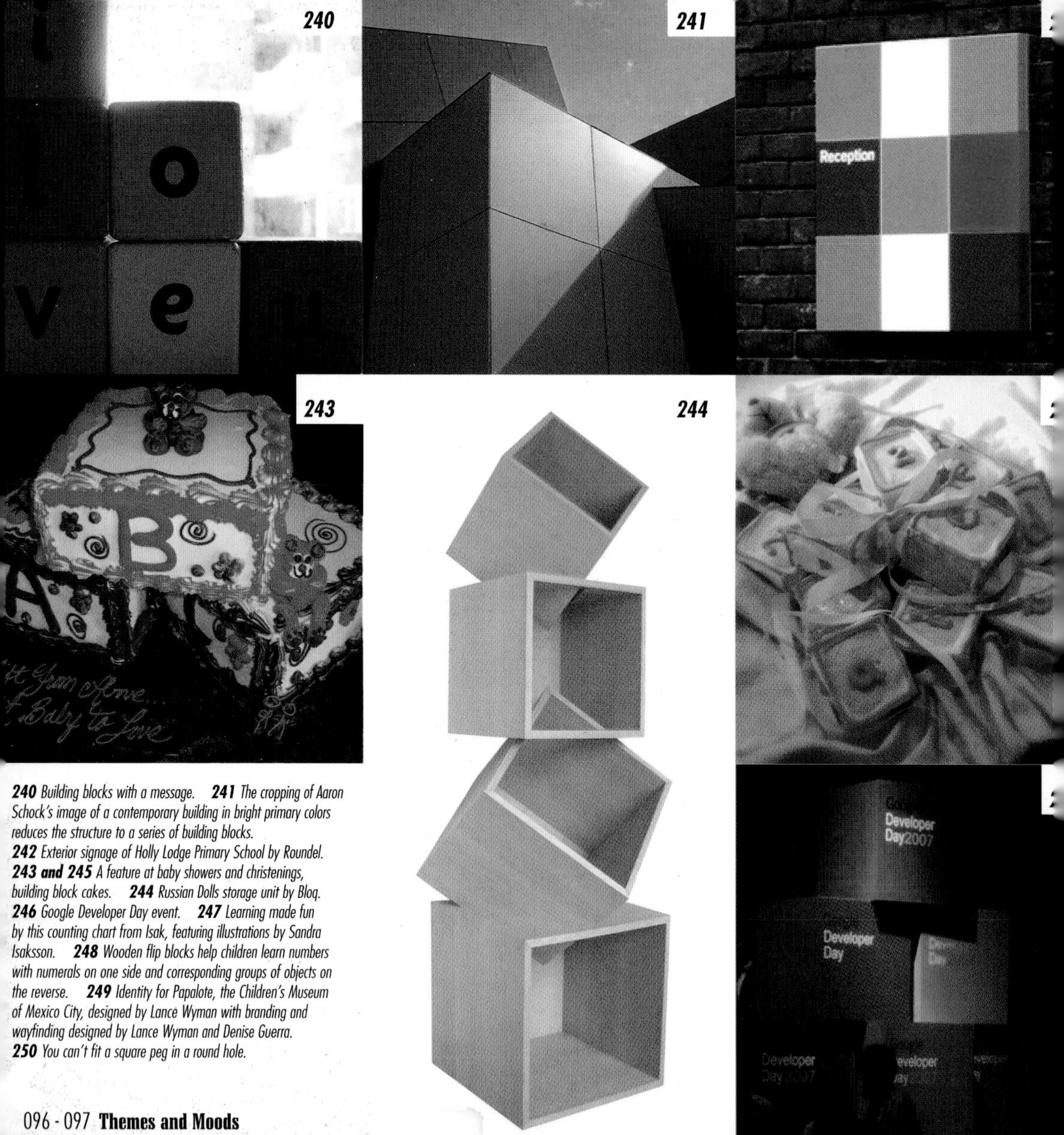

240 Building blocks with a message. **241** The cropping of Aaron Schock's image of a contemporary building in bright primary colors reduces the structure to a series of building blocks.
242 Exterior signage of Holly Lodge Primary School by Roundel.
243 and 245 A feature at baby showers and christenings, building block cakes. **244** Russian Dolls storage unit by Bloq.
246 Google Developer Day event. **247** Learning made fun by this counting chart from Isak, featuring illustrations by Sandra Isaksson. **248** Wooden flip blocks help children learn numbers with numerals on one side and corresponding groups of objects on the reverse. **249** Identity for Papalote, the Children's Museum of Mexico City, designed by Lance Wyman with branding and wayfinding designed by Lance Wyman and Denise Guerra.
250 You can't fit a square peg in a round hole.

247

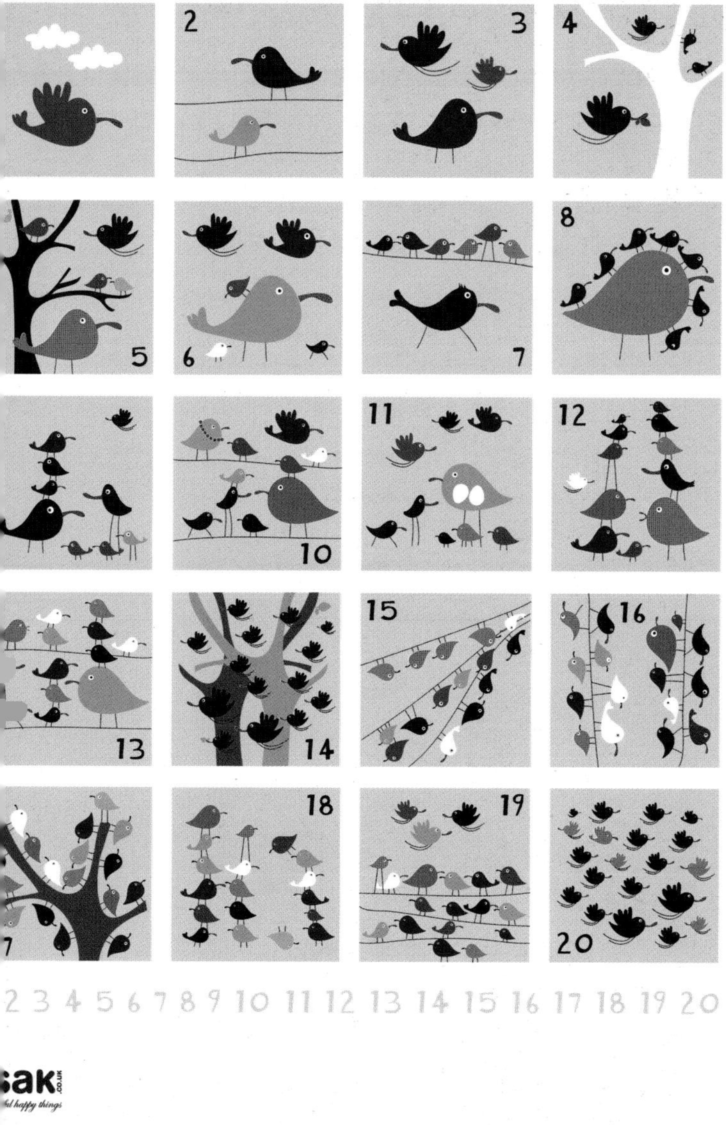

sak.co.uk

248

249

250

Retro

If we accept pattern as a barometer of changing taste, then modifications to the simple square offer useful insights into the graphic mores of the mid-20th century. While the social and cultural events of the 1950s resulted in a prevalence of the atomic circle, squares were often used in an architectural context. The architect's material of choice, concrete was becoming more accepted in mainstream building applications. In the 1950s modern homes and commercial buildings often featured concrete screen blocks, creating a decorative pattern from a simple grid. If you're into the Palm Springs bungalow style and want to recreate it, these blocks are still available from Californian-based company ORCO.

Throughout the 1950s, Josef Albers worked on his series Homage to the Square (see page 7); his asymmetric and concentric configurations continue to evoke the designs of that decade. Moving into the 1960s, squares began to acquire rounded corners. The Eurostyle typeface designed in 1962 by Aldo Novarese typifies this, along with Harri Peccinotti's design for *Nova* magazine—its 1965 launch issue featured a series of round-cornered blocks housing photographs. The style continued through the 1970s until high tech became popular in the 1980s, using squares in graphs and grids to suggest a technical edge. Finally, the 1980s ska music revival resulted in black-and-white checks being used in fashion and graphics to communicate the distinctive 2 Tone style.

2

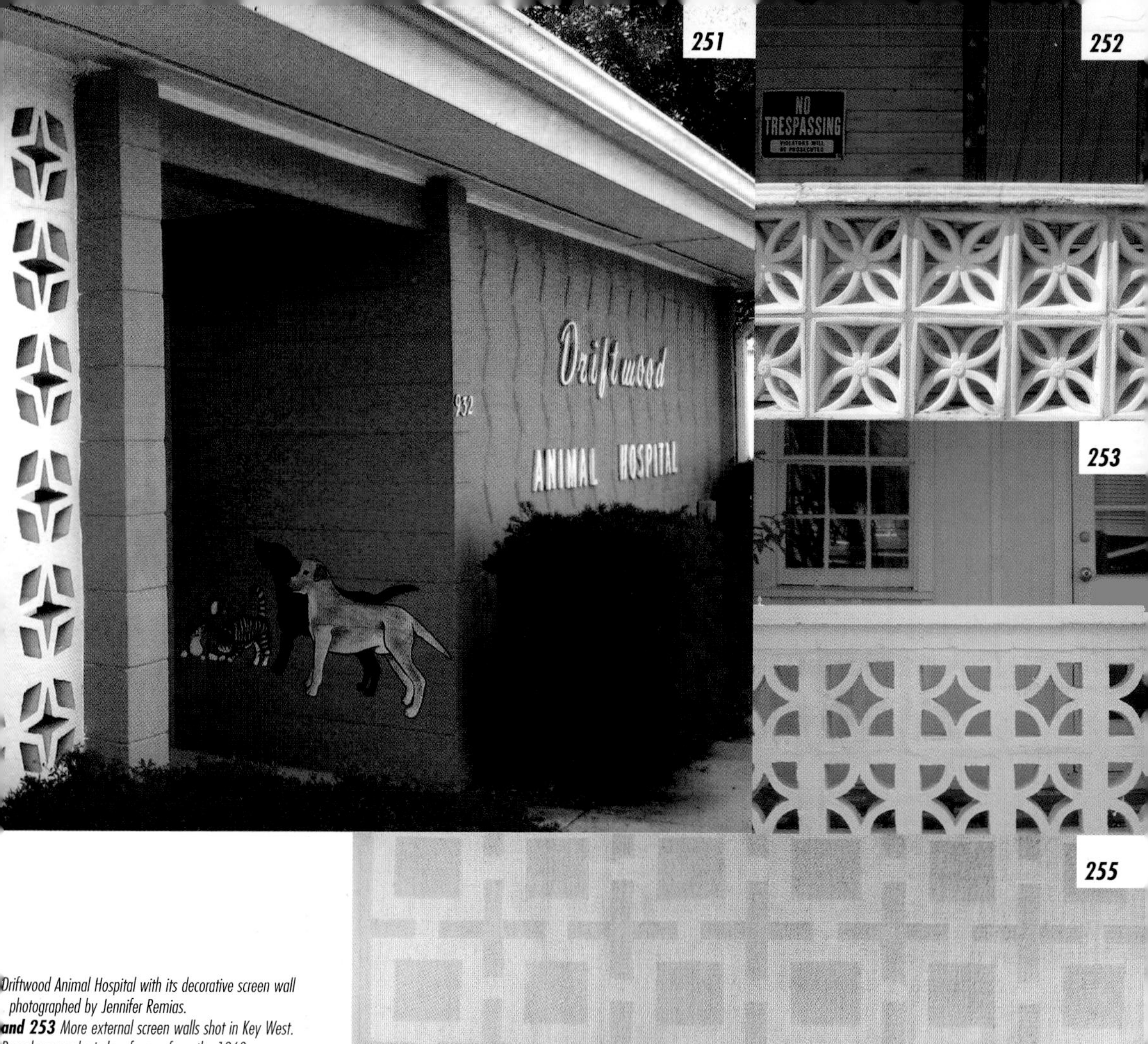

Driftwood Animal Hospital with its decorative screen wall photographed by Jennifer Remias.
and 253 More external screen walls shot in Key West.
Round-cornered window frames from the 1960s.
The name says it all—Richard Nixon rug by an Adler.

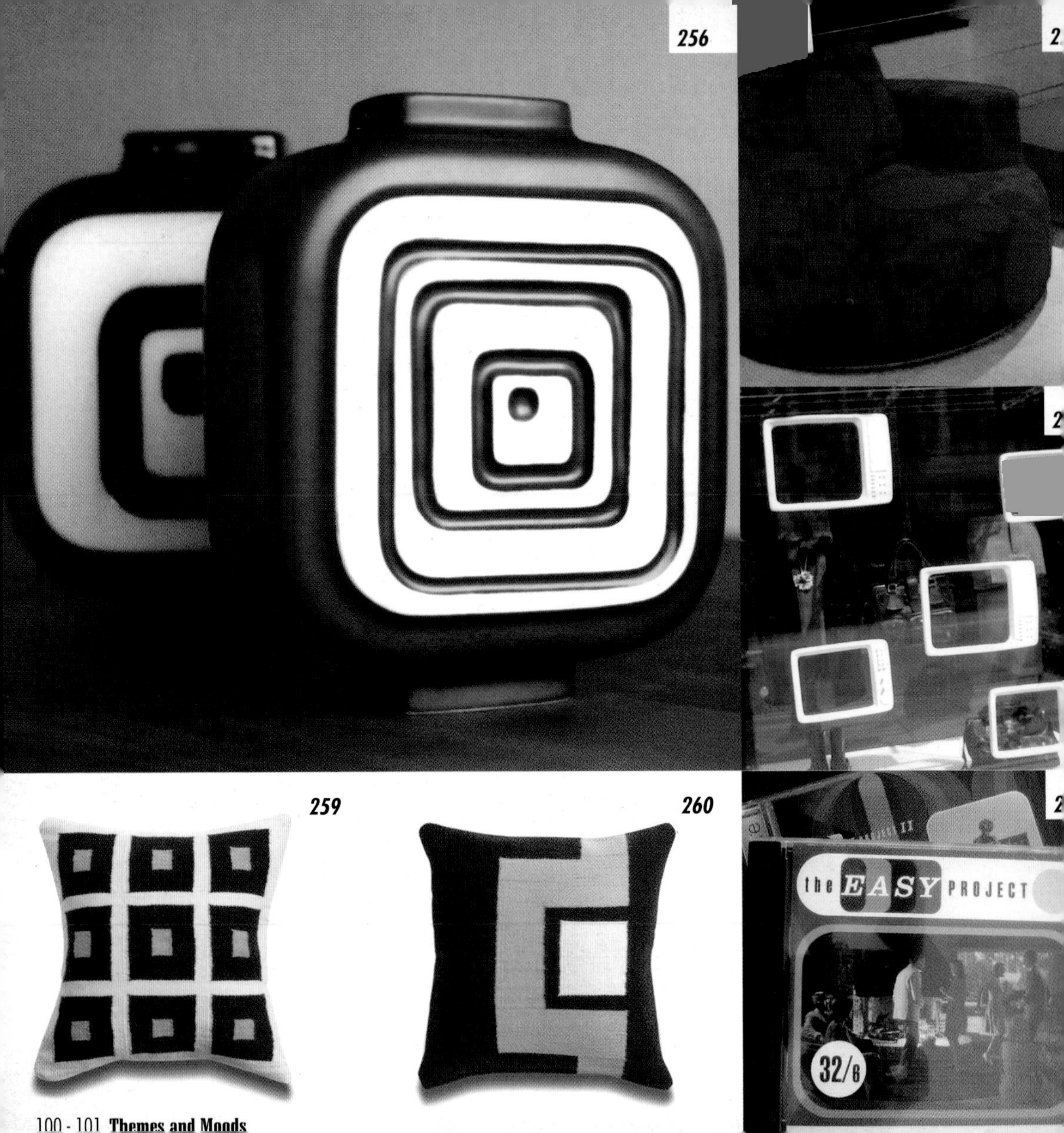
256
2
2
259
260
2
the EASY PROJECT
32/6

262

256 *Squares vases by Scabetti.*
257 *Chair covered in Verner Panton fabric featuring circles within squares.*
258 *Vintage TV screens give this window display a cool retro look.*
259 and 260 *Two graphic cushions: Peter and Butch by Jonathan Adler.*
261 *Compilations of Loungecore music using rounded square shapes for a groovy look.*
262 *Flow 3D wallpaper tiles by Mio.*

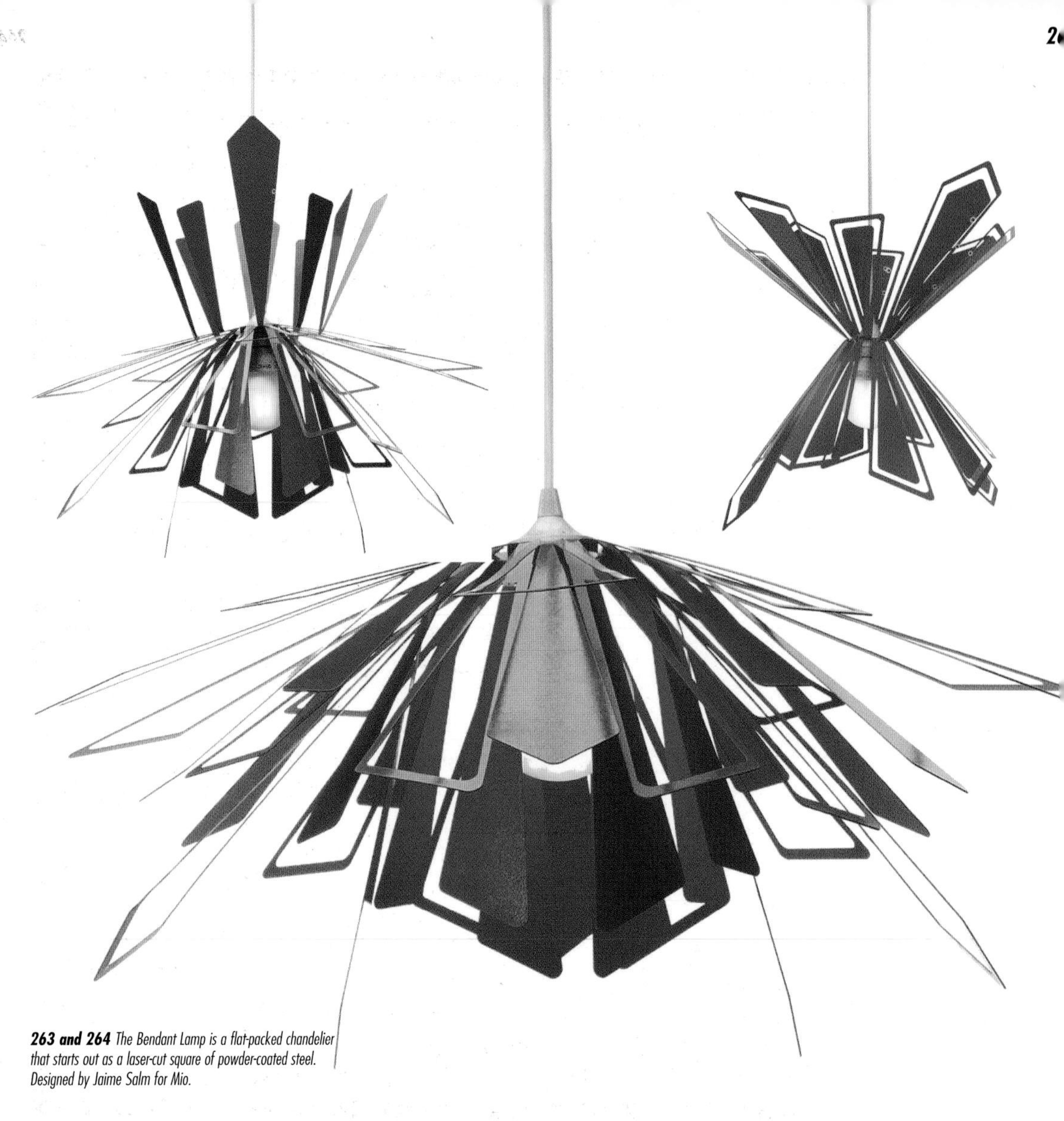

263 and 264 *The Bendant Lamp is a flat-packed chandelier that starts out as a laser-cut square of powder-coated steel. Designed by Jaime Salm for Mio.*

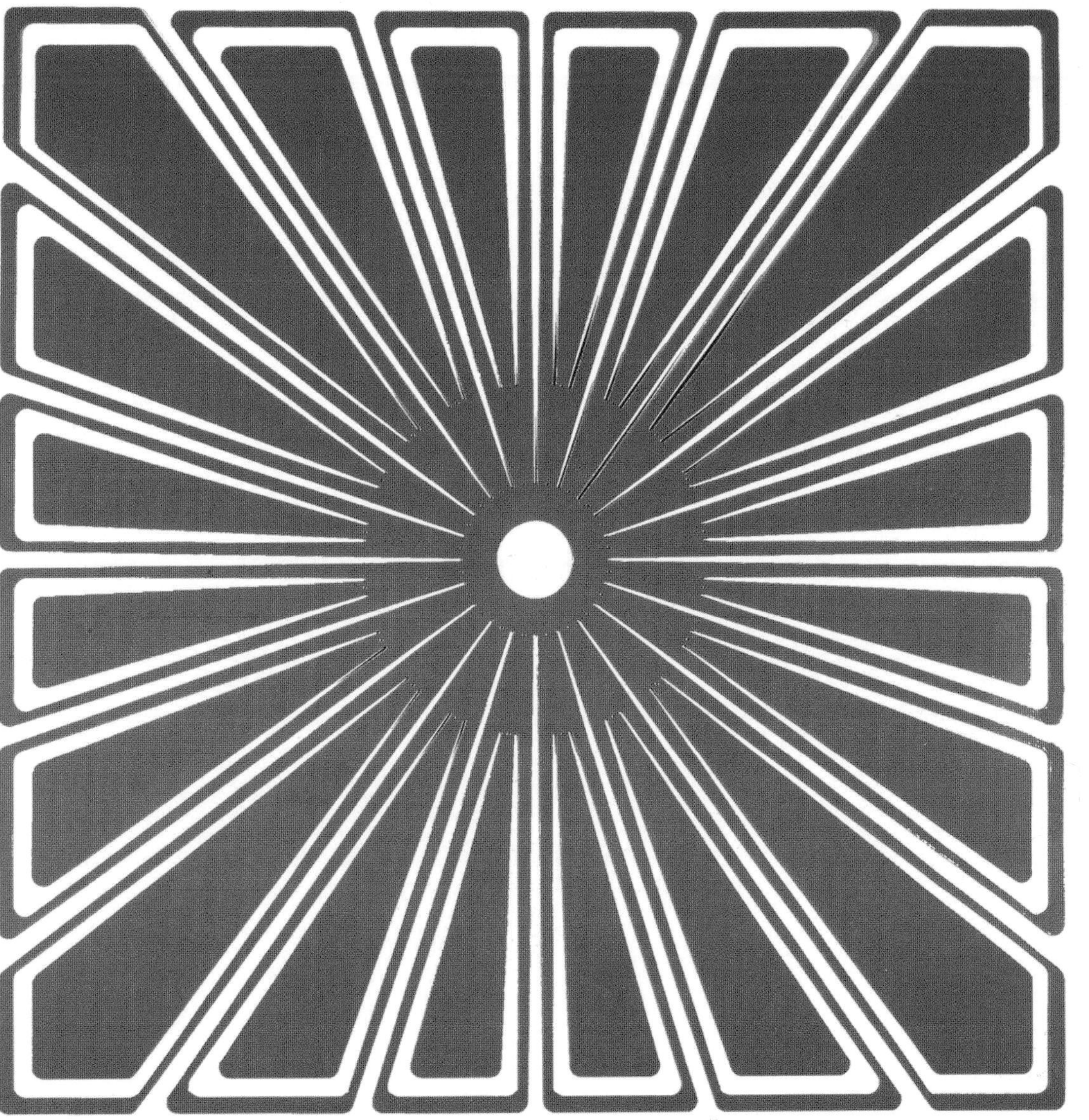

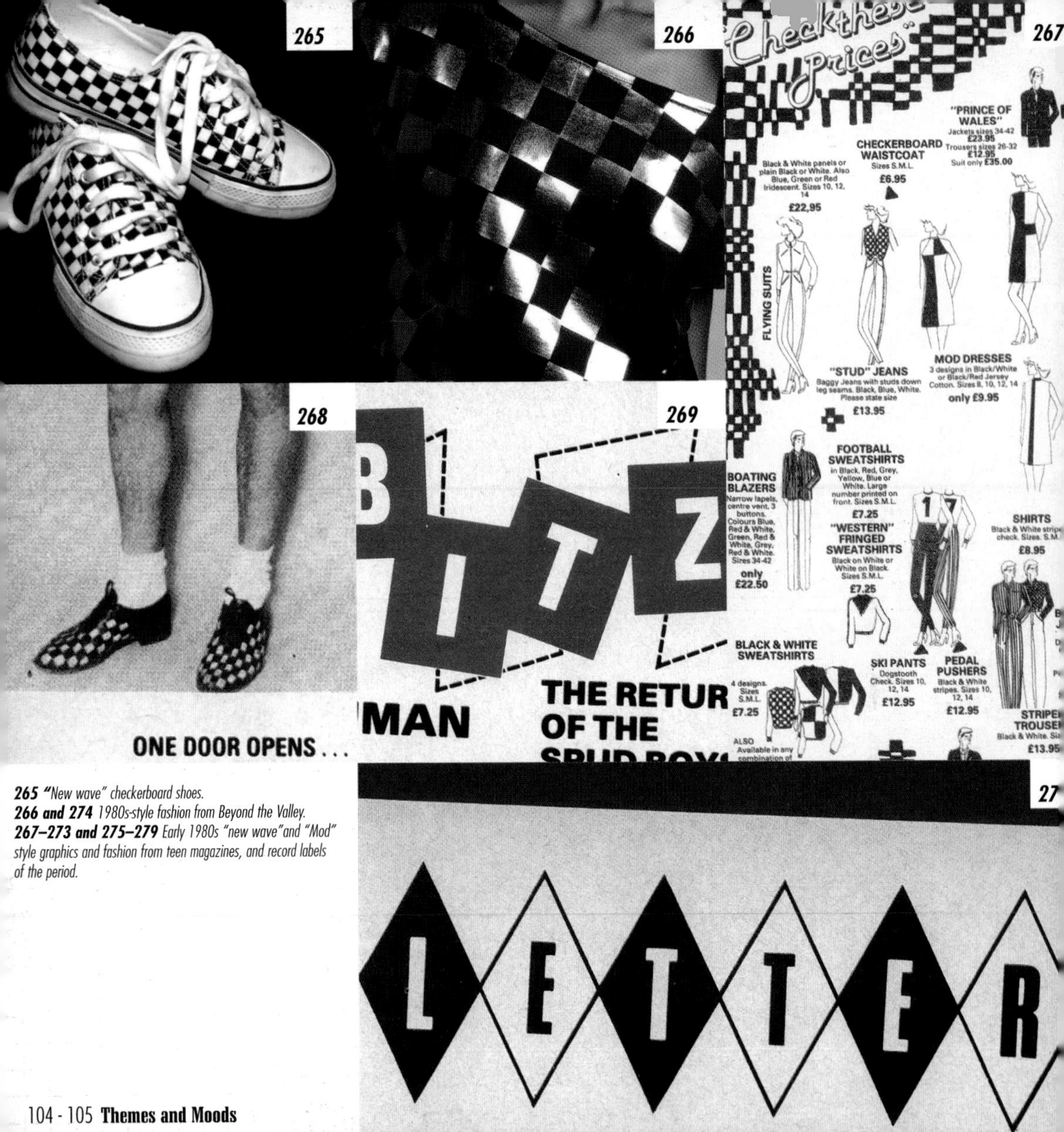

***265* "**New wave" checkerboard shoes.
266 and 274 *1980s-style fashion from Beyond the Valley.*
267–273 and 275–279 *Early 1980s "new wave" and "Mod" style graphics and fashion from teen magazines, and record labels of the period.*

271
CHS TT17
MARKETED BY CHRYSALIS RECORDS LTD
272
DISC
TOP 40
TWO WEEKS AGO
TITLE/ARTIST
LABEL
BPM
THE GROOVE RODNEY FRANKLIN
CBS 109
ATLANTIC 117
273
DANCE CRAZE
274
275
BITZ
276
REV
277
.dindisc
278
279
3.99

Automotive

The black-and-white checkered flag is waved to signal victory at the end of motor races. The benefits of its design are clear: black-and-white squares offer high contrast visibility, so this flag is the most conspicuous way to signal to drivers (originally driving on dusty dirt tracks) that the race has ended. The flag's origins are variously attributed to tablecloths, cycling shirts, and sailing, but racing historian Fred Egloff asserts in his book, *Origin of the Checker Flag: A Search for Racing's Holy Grail*, that the flag's checks were used to mark "checking stations" along the 1906 Glidden Tour from Buffalo to Bretton Woods, New Hampshire. The first recorded use of the flag to end a race was at the 1906 Vanderbilt Cup.

Used on vehicles or incorporated into brand marks, these checks succinctly connote motoring themes. Between 1948 and 1966, Goodwood Motor Circuit ranked alongside Silverstone as the UK's leading racing venue. During this time it hosted Formula One, the famous Goodwood Nine Hours race, and the celebrated Tourist Trophy sports car race. Now, for three days each September, the circuit stages the Goodwood Revival—a historic race meeting for the kind of cars and motorcycles that would have competed at Goodwood during its active years. In racing green and silver, and incorporating the checkered flag, its identity reflects this historic motoring period.

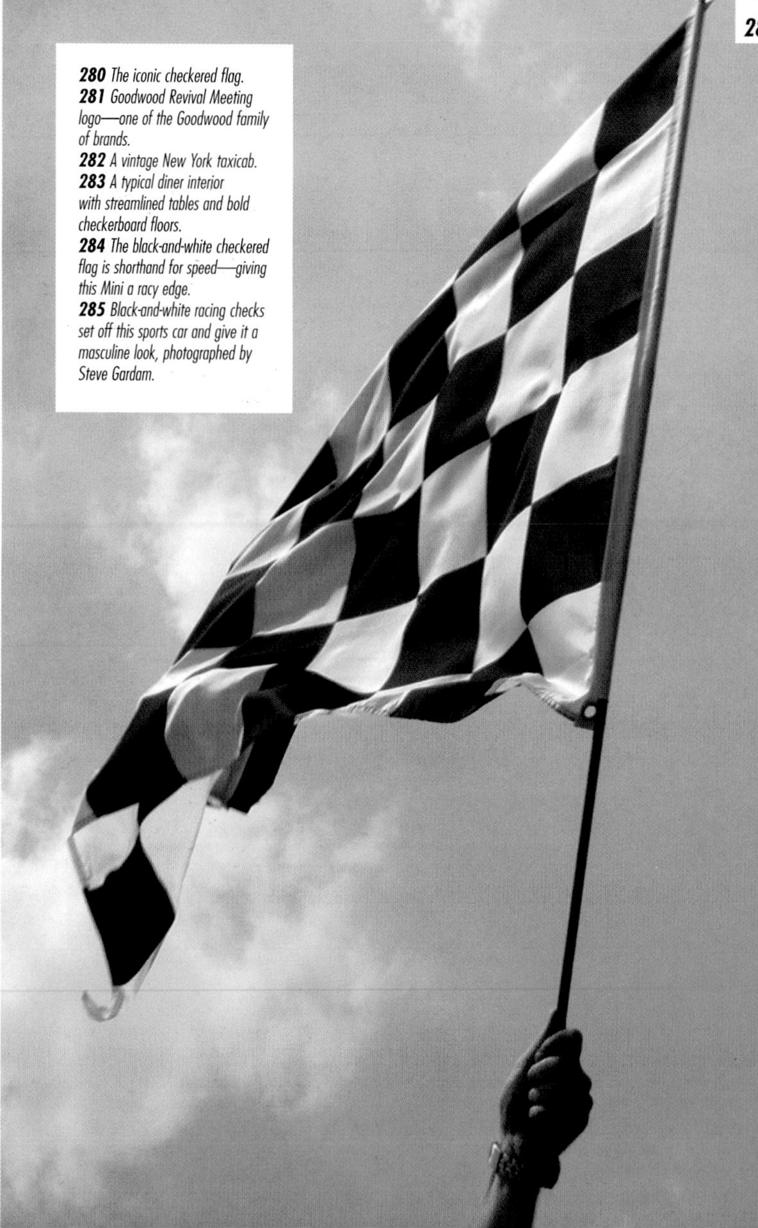

280 *The iconic checkered flag.*
281 *Goodwood Revival Meeting logo—one of the Goodwood family of brands.*
282 *A vintage New York taxicab.*
283 *A typical diner interior with streamlined tables and bold checkerboard floors.*
284 *The black-and-white checkered flag is shorthand for speed—giving this Mini a racy edge.*
285 *Black-and-white racing checks set off this sports car and give it a masculine look, photographed by Steve Gardam.*

281
GOODWOOD
GOODWOOD ROAD RACING COMPANY
REVIVAL MEETING
©
282
283
284
285
PEUGEOT FINANCEMENT
NIKKO

Modernism

Modernism embodies the work of several groups and movements of people working in art, architecture, craft, music, and literature in the late 19th and early 20th century. Embracing the potential of technology and the machine, they looked to a better future transformed by design and art. The British Arts and Crafts movement is often considered politically and aesthetically the start of Modernist thinking. One of its key exponents was Charles Rennie Mackintosh. He rejected Victorian fussiness in favor of geometric shapes and unadorned surfaces—a philosophy of functionality that came to epitomize the Modernist style. While an apprentice architect, Mackintosh attended art evening classes at the Glasgow School of Art where he met his wife Margaret Macdonald, her sister Frances, and Herbert McNair. Together they laid the foundations of "the Glasgow Style," which exhibited in Europe and influenced the Viennese Art Nouveau movement around 1900.

Like his US contemporary Frank Lloyd Wright and Italian Gio Ponti a few decades later, Mackintosh's vision was all encompassing—he specified the decoration and furnishing of many of his buildings. His square block motif acts like a signature on furniture, signage, and masonry. Home to most of his buildings, drawings, and designs, Glasgow is a destination for Art Nouveau enthusiasts. The building that helped to make his international reputation is the Glasgow School of Art. Its austere rectangular framework, pared-down detailing, grid-like ironwork, and block signage all pay tribute to the square.

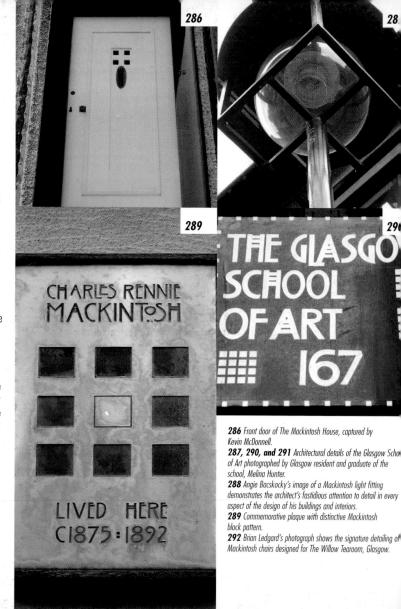

286 *Front door of The Mackintosh House, captured by Kevin McDonnell.*
287, 290, and 291 *Architectural details of the Glasgow School of Art photographed by Glasgow resident and graduate of the school, Melina Hunter.*
288 *Angie Bacskocky's image of a Mackintosh light fitting demonstrates the architect's fastidious attention to detail in every aspect of the design of his buildings and interiors.*
289 *Commemorative plaque with distinctive Mackintosh block pattern.*
292 *Brian Ledgard's photograph shows the signature detailing of Mackintosh chairs designed for The Willow Tearoom, Glasgow.*

288
291
292

293 and 295–298 *A selection of Mackintosh architectural details from the Glasgow School of Art—windows and lampposts in particular feature squares as the key form of decoration.*
294 *The back door of The Hill House by Mackintosh, built in Helensburgh in 1902. Photographed by Cherry Welsh.*
299 *Mackintosh appropriated graphics on a Glasgow address plaque.*
300 *Checkered pattern on the facade of Mackintosh's Scotland Street School, captured by Alan Campbell.*
301 and 302 *Graphic details from The Willow Tearoom in Glasgow.*

298
299
137
CARRICK
COURT
300
301
No
217
302
THE
WILLOW
TEAROOM

→ Dutch-born Piet Mondrian associated with Braque and Picasso when he moved to Paris in 1911 where he was influenced by some of the principles of Cubism. While Cubism sought to challenge the representation of 3D objects on a 2D surface, emphasizing form and volume, Mondrian reduced the subject to mere lines and color. He called this abstract style Neo-Plasticism and restricted himself to primary colors: red, blue, and yellow, and to a grid of black vertical and horizontal lines on a white ground. Occasionally, gray features. In this way, he felt his work took Cubism to its "logical conclusion." Along with Theo van Doesburg, Mondrian contributed to the central ideas of De Stijl (The Style) movement, which advocated pure abstraction, believing that simplification of visual composition to the square, cube, and right angles could create spiritual harmony and order.

Always striving for asymmetry, the works achieve equilibrium through deceptively simple compositions. The distinctive combination of color and shape has inspired the creative community for nearly a century. When Yves Saint Laurent created the Mondrian dress in 1965, it was one of the first appropriations of art in the fashion world. The simplicity of the style perfectly sums up Saint Laurent's innovative approach and demonstrates how fresh Mondrian's work continued to appear, well after the artist's death. →

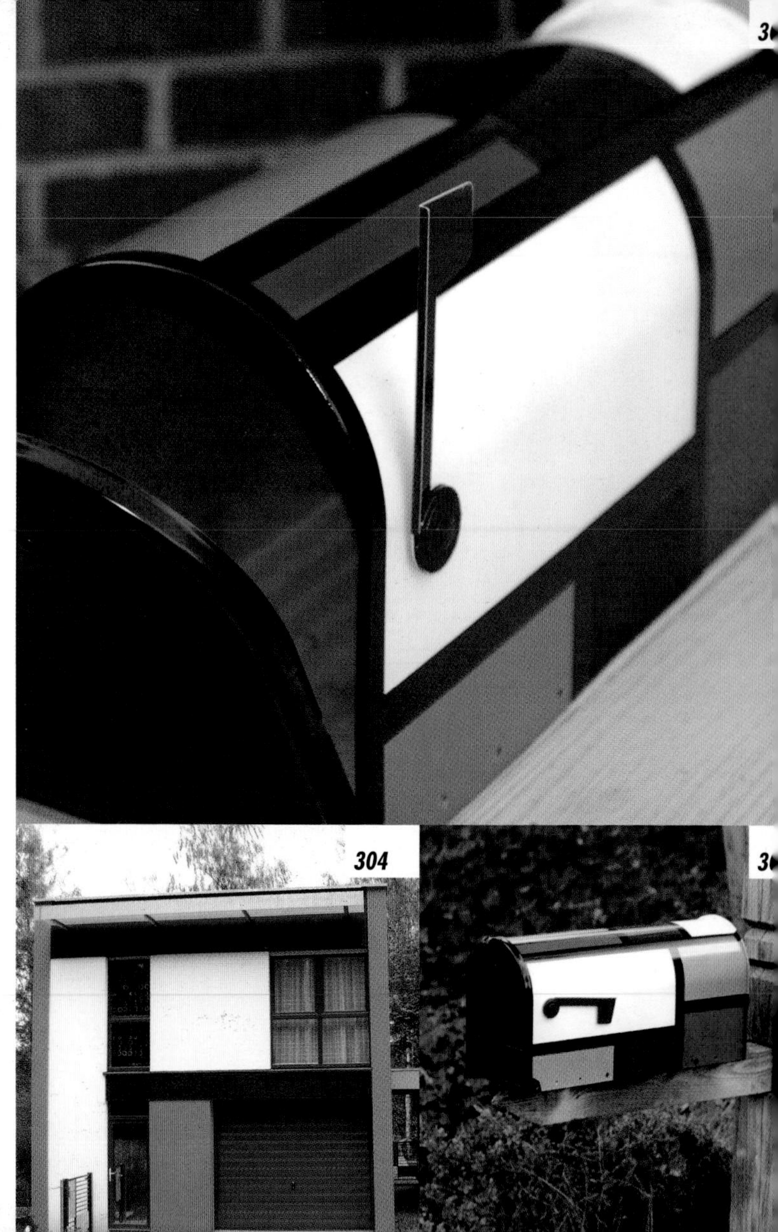

306

303 and 305 *Artist Chris Hoover created his own homage to Mondrian using the medium of a mailbox.*
304 *A contemporary house in Chemnitz uses the colors and proportions of a Mondrian piece of art.*
306 *The 1965 Mondrian dress by Yves Saint Laurent still looks modern today. V&A Images/Victoria and Albert Museum.*

308

309

307 *Mondrian-style garage door, seen by Bruce Grant.*
308 *Homage to Mondrian by Seattle artist little bird.*
309 *Neil Crocodile captured little bird's sticker artwork pasted up in the Capitol Hill neighborhood of Seattle. Seen above it is a piece by Starheadboy.*

310 *Austin Cross captured this shot of artist Emily Duffy's Mondrian Mobile on Solano Avenue in Albany.*
311 *The various facades of these buildings come together in a composition reminiscent of Mondrian. Photographed by Olivier Bareau.*

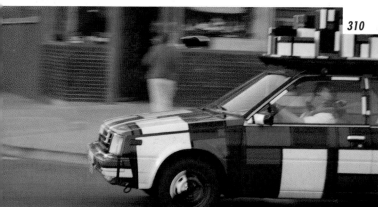

310

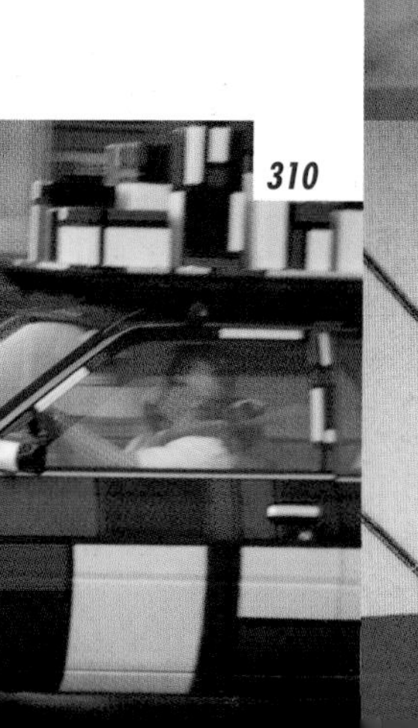

311

→ "Mondrian" has now become a loose term for many graphic styles involving blocks of color and defined grids. Modern day artists, architects, and designers pay homage to the color and composition of Mondrian's classic paintings in a variety of applications. It is ironic that, while there are several examples of architecture that came out of the De Stijl movement, it is Mondrian's canvases that are more frequently emulated on building facades; they seem to lend themselves perfectly to the modern built environment. But while Mondrian's later New York pieces (like the Boogie-Woogie pictures) introduced greater freedom and dynamism into his work, he never bent his own rules as far as some appropriators do. Can secondary colors really be used in a "Mondrian-inspired" context? You decide. →

312, 315, 316, and 318 *Mondrian paintings have influenced the facades of these buildings, either in color or form, or both.*
314 *The Challenger Mondrian kite, photographed by Mascia Serafini.*
313 and 317 *"Come on get happy"—the Partridge Family bus seen by Gail Dedrick*

→ Completed in 1924, the Rietveld Schröder House is the only building created entirely according to De Stijl principles. Its facade is a collage of intersecting lines and rectilinear forms in different planes. Each component has its own position and color: white and gray for surfaces, linear elements in primaries, and black for window frames.

The use of intersecting planes is also fundamental to the influential Club (Wassily) Chair by another key Modernist and member of the Bauhaus, Marcel Breuer. Its square tubular profile emphasizes how great a departure this piece of furniture represented from its bulky ancestors. →

319, 323, and 324 *The Rietveld Schröder House conforms in its construction to De Stijl principles. The interior of the house embodies the maxim "form follows function," since the inner walls can be moved and the rooms reconfigured to the inhabitant's liking. Built by Gerrit Rietveld, it has been named a UNESCO World Heritage site.*
320–322 *Le Corbusier's Unité d'Habitation in Marseille was constructed in béton brut (rough-cast concrete) which inspired the term "brutalist" architecture.*
325 *The square frame tubed Wassily Chair No B3, designed in 1925 by Marcel Breuer. Courtesy of Knoll International.*

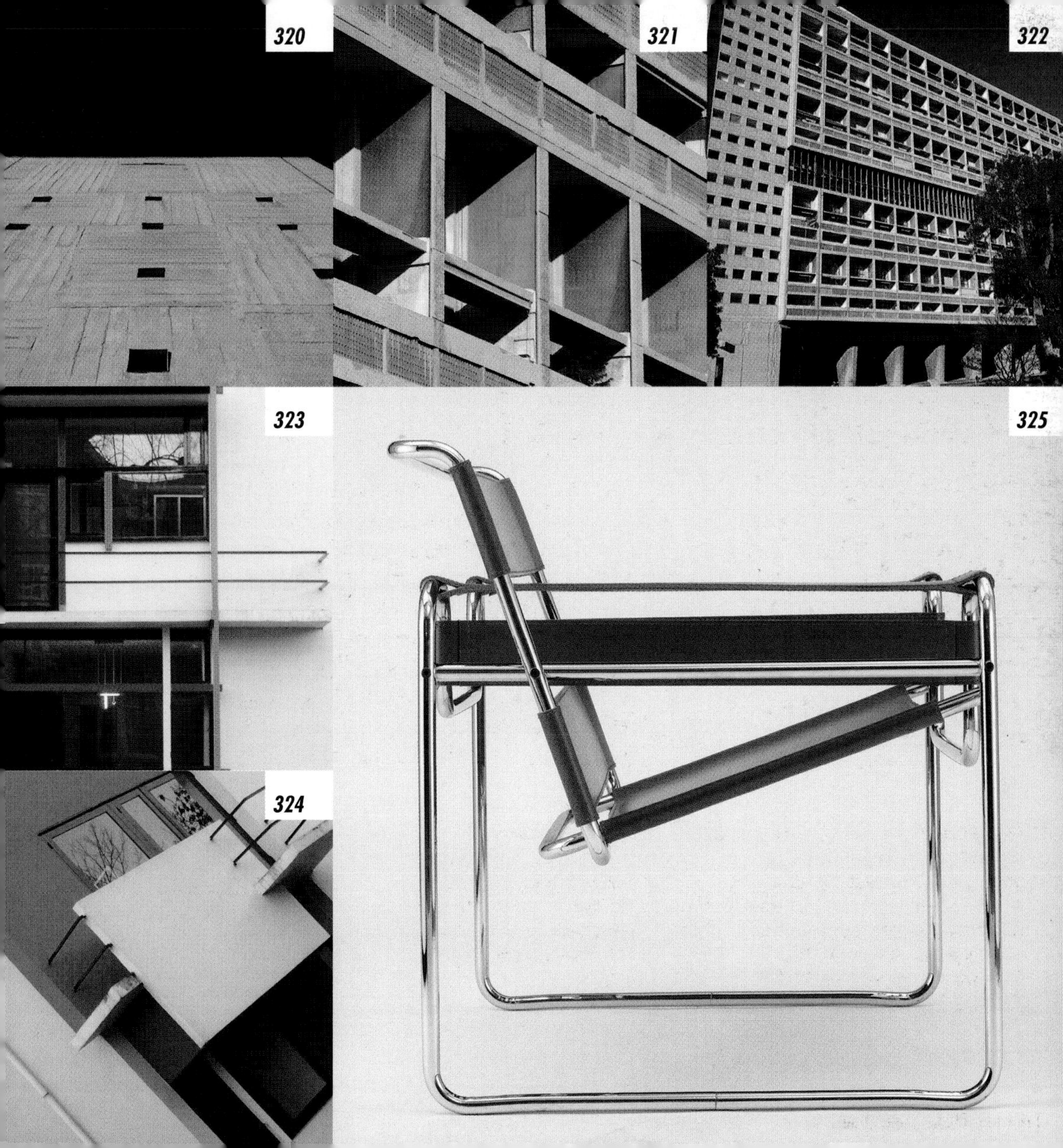
320
321
322
323
324
325

→ Another proponent of De Stijl was Mies van der Rohe, who became the third and final director of the Bauhaus—the German school of art, design, and architecture founded in 1919 by Walter Gropius. He coined the term as an inversion of "Hausbau"—meaning house construction—a metaphor for the way the school turned traditional design wisdom on its head. Exemplified by the Bauhaus building in Dessau, constructed in 1925 based on designs by Gropius, Bauhaus style is characterized by its economic, geometric design and honest use of materials. The Bauhaus influence can be traced from architecture to typography and even modern teaching methods—it introduced the art foundation course. The critic Wolf von Eckhardt summed up the Bauhaus influence thus: "it helped to invent modern architecture; it altered the look of everything from the chair you are sitting in to the page you are reading now."

After WWII Europeans like Ernö Goldfinger maintained the Modernist ideal. Strongly influenced by Le Corbusier's Vers une Architecture, Goldfinger's raw concrete buildings took the principles of rationality and functionality to the extremes of Brutalism. Poor urban planning and build quality meant that Modernism fell out of favor in the latter half of the 20th century, but popular interest is growing once more: Goldfinger's Trellick Tower is protected by English Heritage. Technological advances in construction techniques and materials have made the Modernist aesthetic more achievable in the 21st century. Many international architects once again cite Modernist principles as the driving force behind their designs.

326 Hans Munk's photographs of the Bauhaus school in Dessau.
327 Poster in the Bauhaus Museum café. Designed by Fritz Schleifer in 1923, it reduces the face to a series of bold geometric shapes with a square eye. This image was later used as iconic branding for 1980s "goth" band Bauhaus.
328–330 Haus am Horn 61 in Weimar. Designed by Georg Muche in 1923, it is the only Bauhaus building constructed in Weimar.
331 Master's house at the Bauhaus school in Dessau.
332 Balconies of the student accommodation at the Bauhaus school in Dessau.

"Ernö Goldfinger was key in the implementation of the aims and ideas of the Modern movement and his use of golden section geometry in the construction of Trellick Tower illustrates this perfectly."

Hannah Dipper
People Will Always Need Plates

333–335 and 337 *Alexander Fleming House, London, designed by Ernö Goldfinger, 1963.*
336 and 338–339 *Trellick Tower, London, designed by Ernö Goldfinger, 1967–1972.*
340 *Trellick Tower roller blind design by People Will Always Need Plates.*

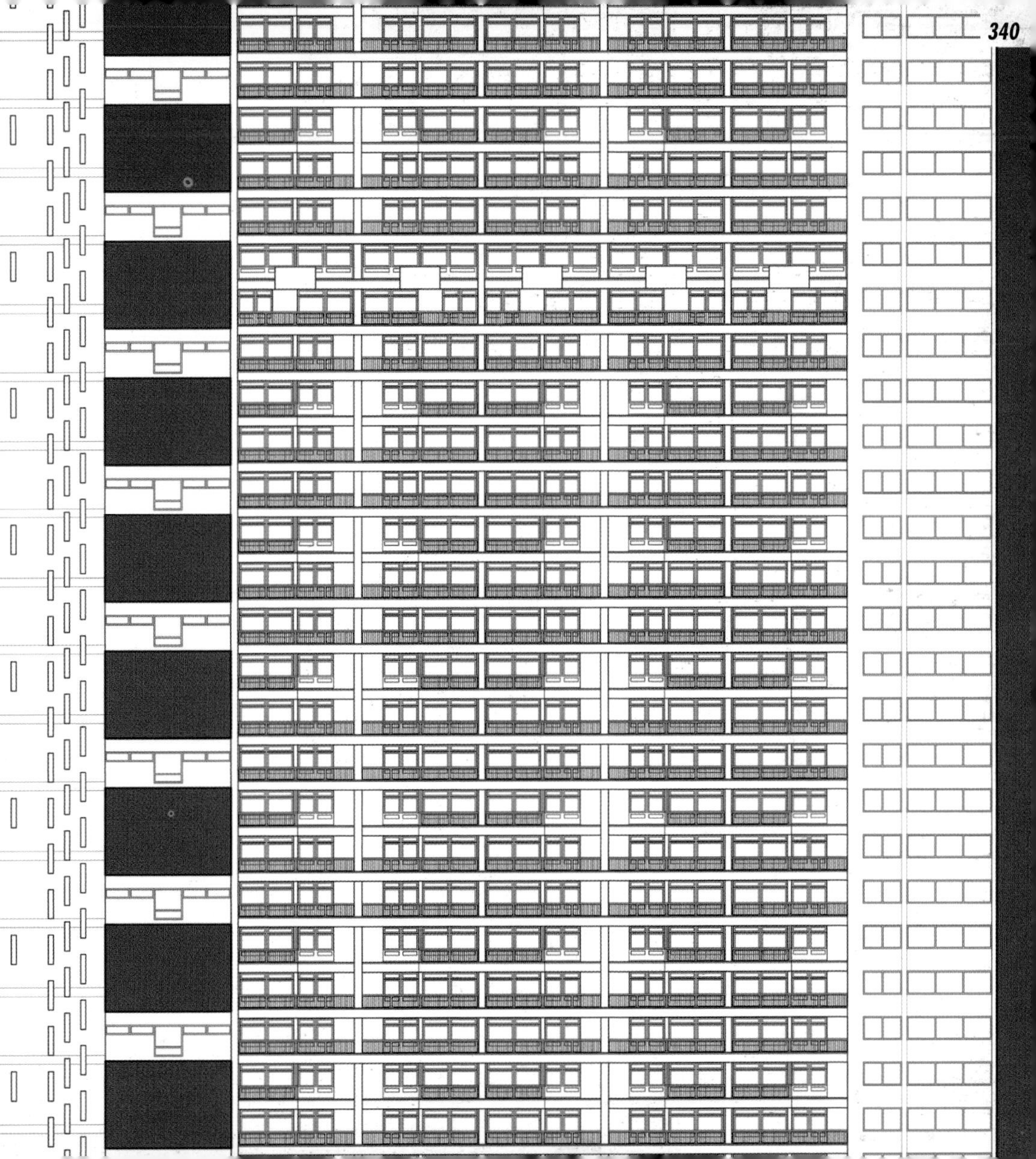

All part of the Commune by the Great Wall project in China:
341 Distorted Courtyard House designed by Rocco Yim.
342 See and Seen House by Cui Kai.
343 Cantilever House by Antonio Ochoa.
344 Shared House by Kanika R'kul.
345 The Clubhouse by Seung H-Sang.

"Quad designs and builds Future Classics—enduring architecture characterized by the bold use of honest materials and attention to detail. Our designs combine strong modernist lines with finishes of the highest quality, making imaginative use of glass, timber, concrete, and stone."

Nuggy Lianos
Quad

346–348 *Award-winning architecture: Edge Apartments by the river Thames, London. Designed by Quad.*

Signals and Information

Warning Signs
Pixels
Periodic Table
Keyboards
Optical Effects
Grids and Graphs

Signals and Information

Squares are a valuable graphic device in the communication of signals and information. We type on square keys to compile, store, and exchange information. International signage systems use diamonds to create standout on highways and hazardous chemical containers. Graphs and grids order information, just as the Periodic Table tabulates chemical properties in an easy-to-digest format. Squares can deceive too—used to create optical effects that distort color and shape, and create false perspective.

In the digital age, pixels are fundamental to conveying visual information. These digital "building blocks" hold a fascination for a generation of artists and designers who fondly remember the low-tech appeal of the original Space Invaders game. Pixelated "bit-mapped" graphics are celebrated here, along with informative, warning, and systemizing squares.

349 *Pixel artwork by Scott Blake.*
350 *Minipops Mystery Inc—the Scooby Doo gang by Craig Robinson.*
351 and 362 *Graph paper.*
352 *Coaster by Frank.*
353 *Mosaic space invader in Paris.*
354 *A sign warning motorists to watch out for pedestrians.*
355 *Pixel Christmas Tree toast created with ZUSE, designed by Inseq Design.*
356 *Artwork by little bird and The Chicken Kid.*
357 *Tiles with a perspective pattern.*
358 *5 A Day identity by Identica.*
359 *Pixel corner unit by Bloq.*
360 *Toy hazard signs.*
361 *Detail of a portrait by Ken Knowlton, using keys from a vintage computer.*
363 *Hazardous materials warning sign.*

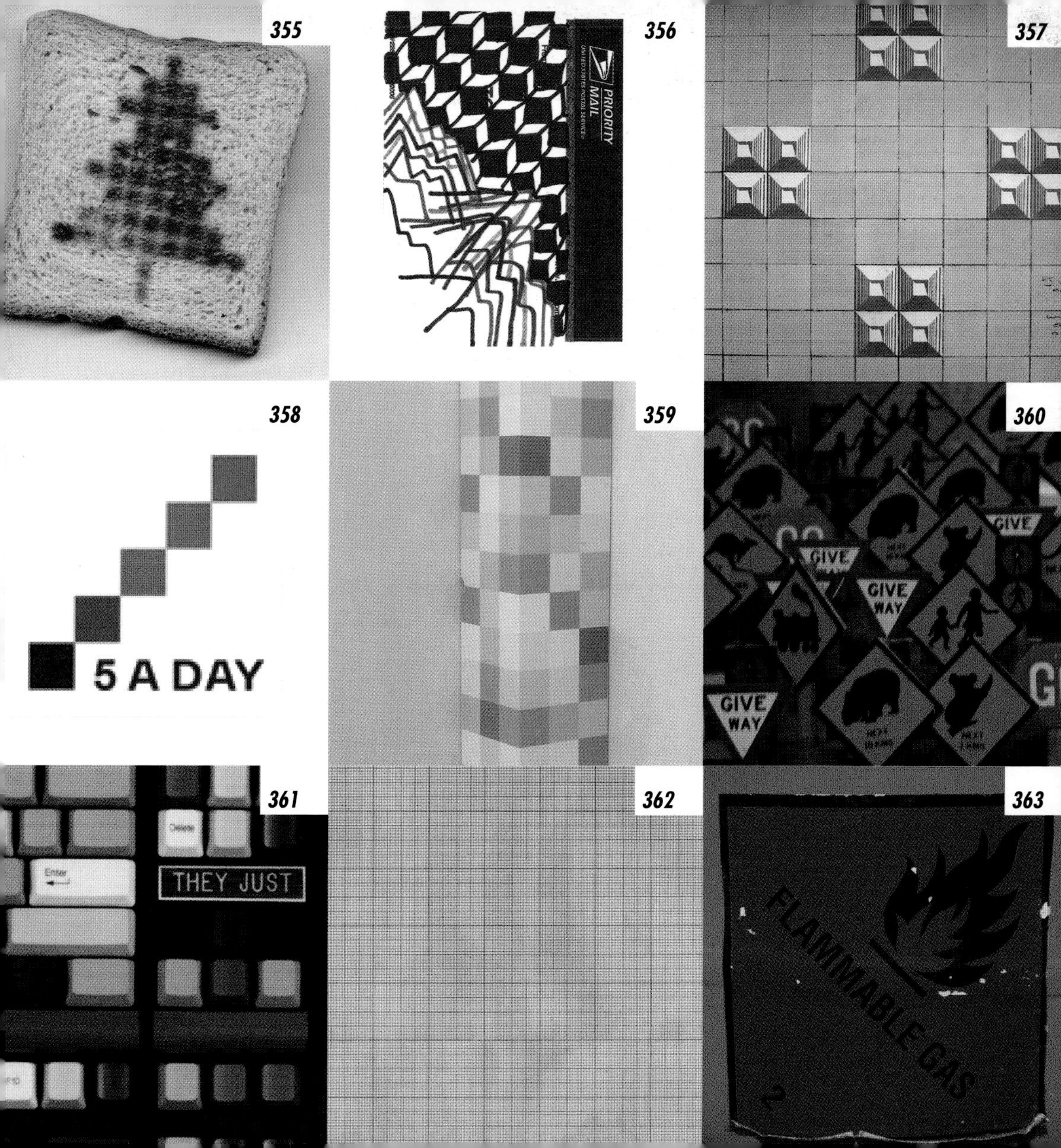
355
356
PRIORITY MAIL
UNITED STATES POSTAL SERVICE
357
358
5 A DAY
359
360
GIVE WAY
GIVE WAY
GIVE WAY
GIVE
361
Delete
Enter
THEY JUST
362
363
FLAMMABLE GAS
2

Warning Signs

Used as public signage, the square is a benign shape. In the UK it is generally used for guidance and information: less arresting than either the warning triangle or prohibitive circle. But turn a square 45 degrees and it becomes a diamond with double the impact. The US road signage system employs a variety of shapes including circles, trapezoids, pentagons, and octagons. Diamonds signify warning, in yellow for motorists and green for cyclists. Orange is reserved for temporary signs. Whether conveying official or more individualized road information, the shape is always eye-catching.

Color-coded squares are also the basis for systems of labeling hazardous chemicals such as the US National Fire Protection Association "fire diamond," used to identify quickly the levels of risk posed by hazardous materials. Each of the four quadrants displays a color to refer to the type of risk: red for flammability, blue for health, yellow for reactivity, with the white quadrant reserved for special hazard information. It stands out as a particularly succinct and effective communication device. European hazard symbols are also in squares and rectangles, using graphic symbols in distinctive black and orange.

364 *Left lane ends ahead.*
365 *Bump ahead.*
366 *Men working temporary sign.*
367 *Pedestrians crossing.*
368 *Temporary roadworks ahead.*
369 *Dead end.*
370 *A homemade Mexican road sign—the cow doesn't look as if it's going to be moved.*
371 and 372 *Two pieces of graffiti using the hazard sign as a canvas, spotted by Neil Crocodile.*
373 *Roundabout.*
374 *Warning—kangaroos ahead.*

375 *International hazard symbols use squares in different ways. The US system shown below, developed by the National Fire Protection Association (NFPA), adopts a color-coded, numerical system for indicating the health, flammability, and reactivity hazards of chemicals. The European hazard symbol system shown on the right uses pictorial icons to convey information.*
376 *The diamond configuration makes the square more arresting, used for hazard signs on potentially dangerous substances.*
377 and 378 *Hazard signs in use.*

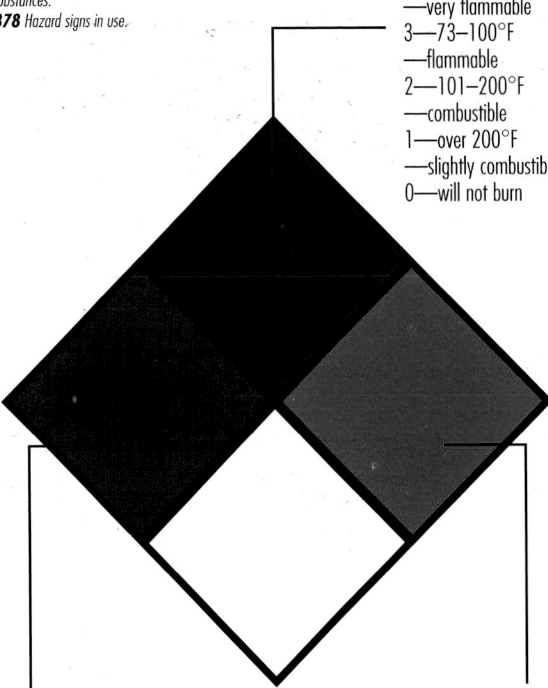

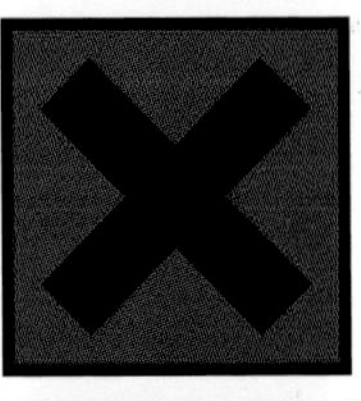

376

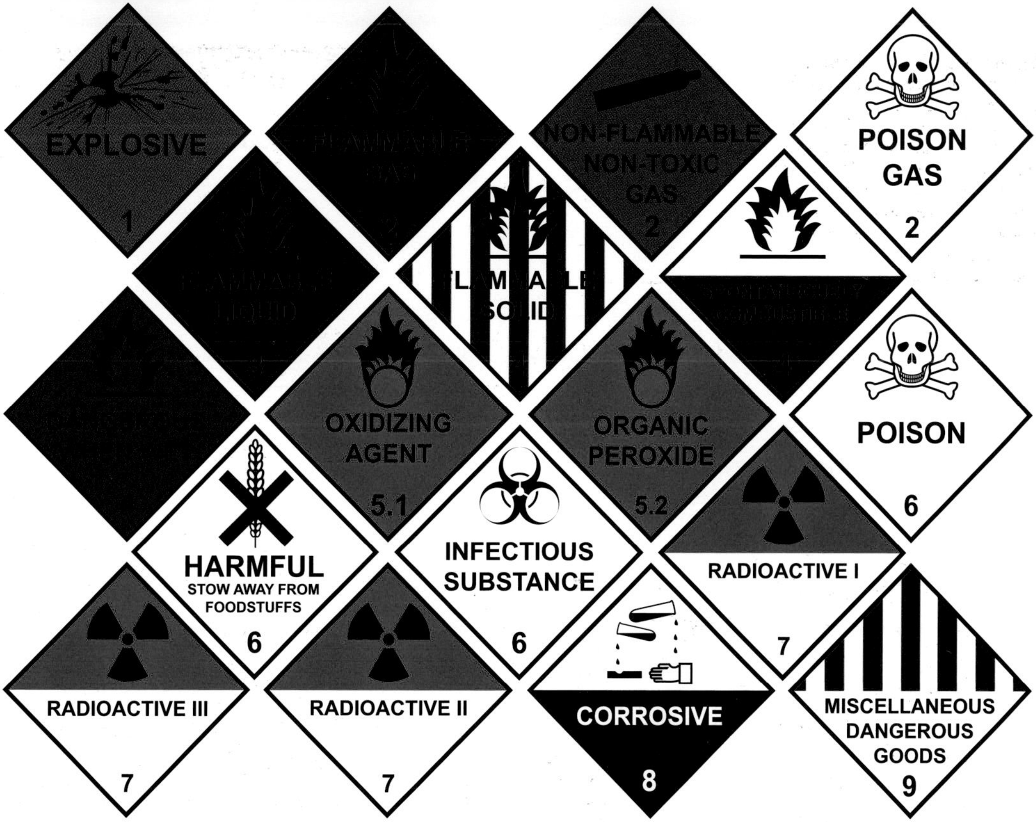

EXPLOSIVE
1
NON-FLAMMABLE
NON-TOXIC
GAS
2
POISON
GAS
2
OXIDIZING
AGENT
5.1
ORGANIC
PEROXIDE
5.2
POISON
6
HARMFUL
STOW AWAY FROM
FOODSTUFFS
6
INFECTIOUS
SUBSTANCE
6
RADIOACTIVE I
7
RADIOACTIVE III
7
RADIOACTIVE II
7
CORROSIVE
8
MISCELLANEOUS
DANGEROUS
GOODS
9

377

DROSULFITE
NTANEOUSLY
OMBUSTIBLE

378

POISON
6

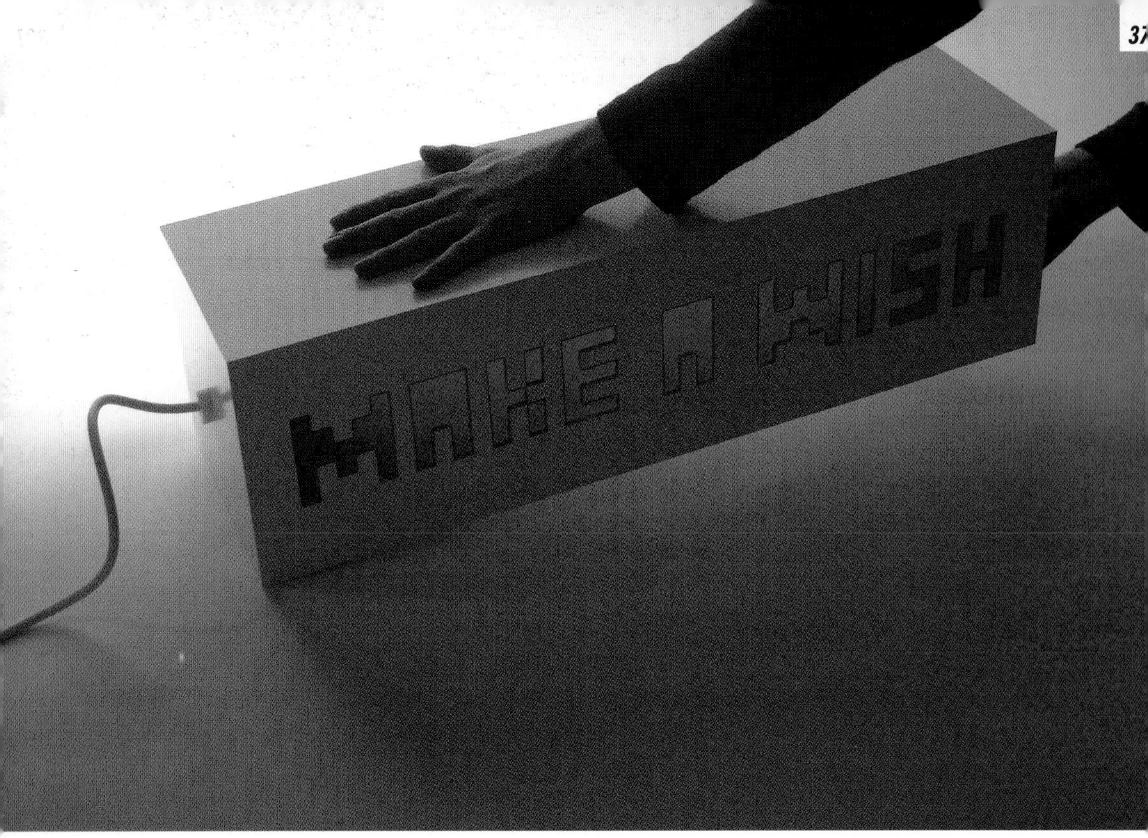

Pixels

In 2005 Alex Tew had an idea for raising money to fund a business management course at Nottingham University. He set up milliondollarhomepage.com to sell advertising space in the form of pixels costing a dollar each. For a minimum purchase of $100, participants could purchase a 10×10 square to hold their logos or messages. Clicking the square would take you to the advertiser's website. Within four months he had sold every pixel, exceeded his financial goal, and become a media star in the process. Some call the completed home page art, others, just a really clever money-spinner. It proves that the pixel has currency in the digital economy.

Pixels are the building blocks of digital information. An abbreviation of pic-ture el-ement, a pixel is a single point in a graphic image—technically, neither a square nor dot, but an abstract sample of information. Pixels act like individual tiles in a digital mosaic, yet pixel-inspired design isn't confined to the digital medium. →

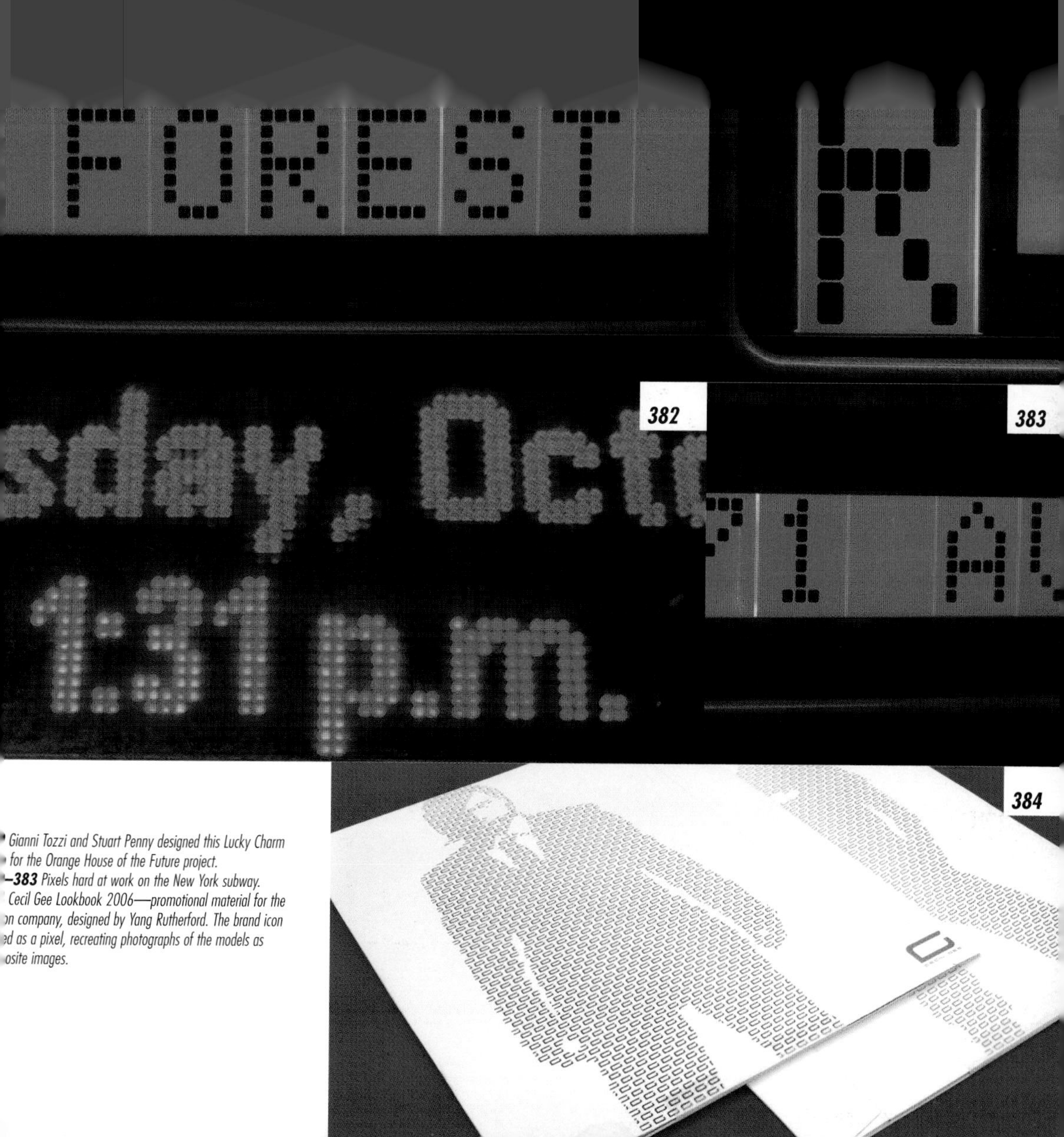

Gianni Tozzi and Stuart Penny designed this Lucky Charm for the Orange House of the Future project.
*–**383*** *Pixels hard at work on the New York subway.*
Cecil Gee Lookbook 2006—promotional material for the on company, designed by Yang Rutherford. The brand icon ed as a pixel, recreating photographs of the models as osite images.

"Minipops sound dull when you try to explain them—'they're small drawings of popstars; about 25 pixels high'—but somehow they seem to have caught people's attention. Making them has been a joy, a challenge, infuriating, hard work, and a lesson. It's made my website—flipflopflyin.com—more popular than I could possibly have imagined. I owe Minipops a lot."

Craig Robinson

385 *Minipops Yoda*
From Top Row 1, L/R: The Simpsons; Mystery Inc.—Velma, Scooby Doo, Shaggy, Daphne, and Fred; The Beatles—Sgt Pepper's Lonely Hearts Club Band.
Row 2, L/R: Darth Vader and Yoda; R2-D2 and C-3PO; The Incredible Hulk; Super Furry Animals.
Row 3, L/R: The White Stripes; The B-52's; The Human League.
Row 4, Outkast (Hey Ya video).

386

38

38

386 *Karl Lagerfeld pixel portrait by Boy Bastiaens at Stormhand.*
387 *Painted pixel heart by Scott Blake.*
388 *I (heart symbol) Pixels T-shirt by Scott Blake.*
389 *Interior of the Kapok hotel in Shanghai. The name of the hotel is spelled out "pixel fashion" by black books in a grid of backlit white bookshelves, creating a dramatic feature overlooking a reading area of the lobby.*

390

```
C:\kt>tracert -d www.endfile.com

Tracing route to endfile.com [209.123.115.77
over a maximum of 30 hops:

  1     2 ms     3 ms     2 ms  192.168.0.1
  2   127 ms   139 ms   139 ms  217.32.137.2
  3   160 ms   157 ms   139 ms  217.32.137.1
  4   189 ms   145 ms   140 ms  217.32.137.2
  5   123 ms   139 ms    72 ms  194.159.246.
  6   199 ms    72 ms   148 ms  194.70.98.6
  7   284 ms   278 ms   275 ms  195.66.224.9
  8   217 ms   294 ms   209 ms  209.123.11.2
  9   276 ms   289 ms   201 ms  209.123.115.

Trace complete.
```

391 392 39

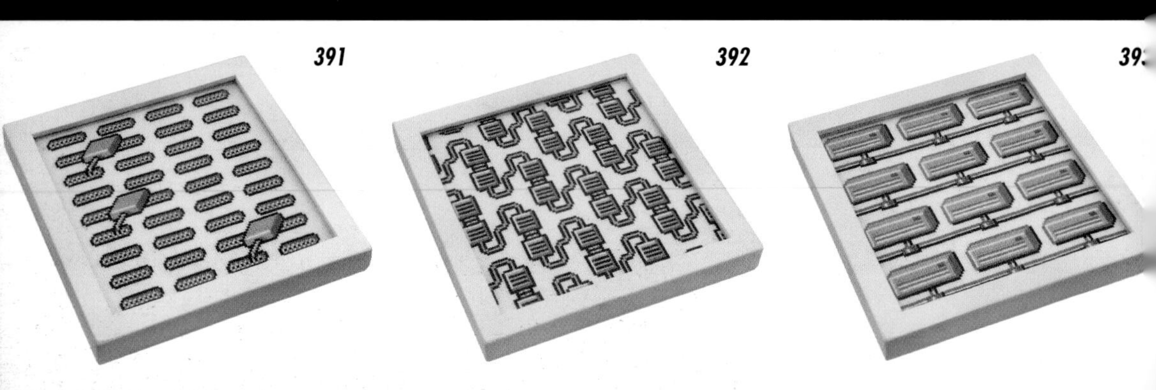

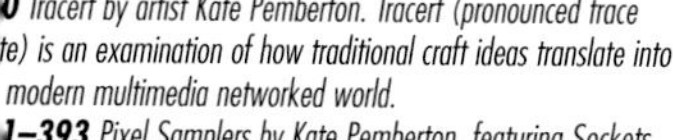

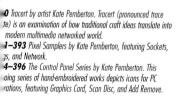

0 *Tracert by artist Kate Pemberton. Tracert (pronounced trace te) is an examination of how traditional craft ideas translate into modern multimedia networked world.*
1–393 *Pixel Samplers by Kate Pemberton, featuring Sockets, gs, and Network.*
4–396 *The Control Panel Series by Kate Pemberton. This oing series of hand-embroidered works depicts icons for PC rations, featuring Graphics Card, Scan Disc, and Add Remove.*

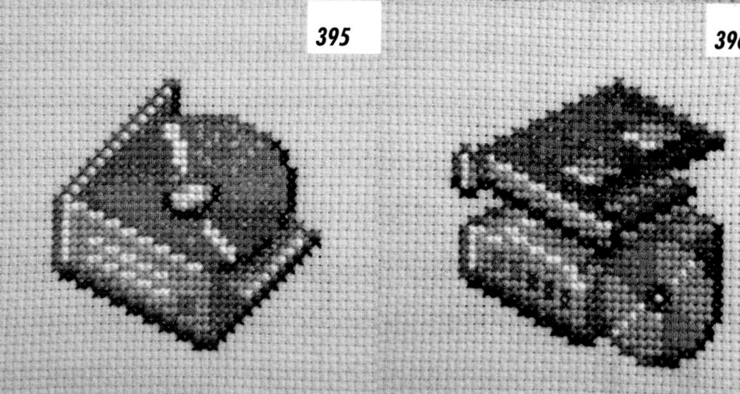

"Pixels are a big part of our home life, whether on personal computers or HDTV. Our Pixel wallpaper in calming warm colors is perfect for any room."

Gerardine Hemingway
Hemingway Design

397 *Hemingway Design's Pixel wallpaper for Graham and Brown.*
398 and 400 *Pixel credenza with internal square shelving compartment by Bloq.*
399 *Pixel shelving by Bloq.*
401 *Pixel wall-mounted corner unit by Bloq.*
402 *Pixel graphic styled mosaic exterior with integrated window captured by Alex Pallent.*

398
399
400
401
402

→ Artists and designers appropriate the pixel aesthetic to create works on diverse themes. Craig Robinson's book of Minipops reduces celebrities down to their pixelated essence, yet they remain instantly recognizable. At the other extreme, supersized pixels adorn graphic wallpaper by Hemingway Design and practical storage by Bloq. Rendering pixels in natural materials creates an intriguing juxtaposition of low and high tech—evidenced by the eco-intelligent cork ModuTiles by Jaime Salm and Hannah Berkin-Harper for Mio.

Artist Kate Pemberton observes: "cross-stitch preceded pixels by quite a few hundred years, though both are based on the principle of generating small squares of color to build up an image." Her work represents symbols of the digital world through traditional crafts: a sampler is cross-stitched by hand from a transposed graphic of a tracert DOS command to create her Dos-Stitch works. →

403 *Cork ModuTiles by Jaime Salm and Hannah Berkin-Harper for Mio.*
404 *The Cloud Bed is an updated version of a Ming Dynasty era Chinese alcove bed. The overall form is pierced with a pixelated pattern derived from digital photographs of clouds taken on a trip to Patagonia. Created by Courtney Skott.*

Market Express
BARBER SHOP

' Poster for the Ivan Meštrovic Foundation by Boris Ljubicic
udio International.
• This promotional poster for Sappi Magno paper by Curious
a composition of individual images and is designed to be hung
corner with a 45 degree angle.
' Portrait of Robert T. Wainwright who solved the "partridge
pear tree" puzzle, packing a 78×78 square with one 1x1
e, two 2×2s, three 3×3s, etc… up to 12 12×12s, with no
apping squares. Ken Knowlton pays homage to this by creating
ortrait using 12 sets of: six 1x1 squares, five 2×2s, four
, three 4×4s, two 5×5s, and one 6×6.

→ Digital technology fills our world with pixels, with the popularity of gaming contributing to the pixel vernacular. Self-styled "godfathers of pixel" eBoy produce graphic design rooted in popular culture, presented as 3D isometric illustrations filled with robots, cars, and guns.

As gaming gets more sophisticated, designers and artists are increasingly drawn to the look and feel of retro games like the original Space Invaders—the forerunner of modern video gaming. Created in 1978 by Toshihiro Nishikado, the game was based on one of his earlier electromechanical games called Space Monsters. When Japanese company Taito released the game, it quickly became its best-selling title. Today, Space Invaders is one of the most duplicated, bootlegged, and hacked arcade games. Meanwhile, the simple graphic construction of the characters makes them infinitely replicable—knitted on sweaters, toasted on bread, fret cut into furniture, and, in a neatly cyclical twist, rendered as mosaics on the walls of the world's metropolises.

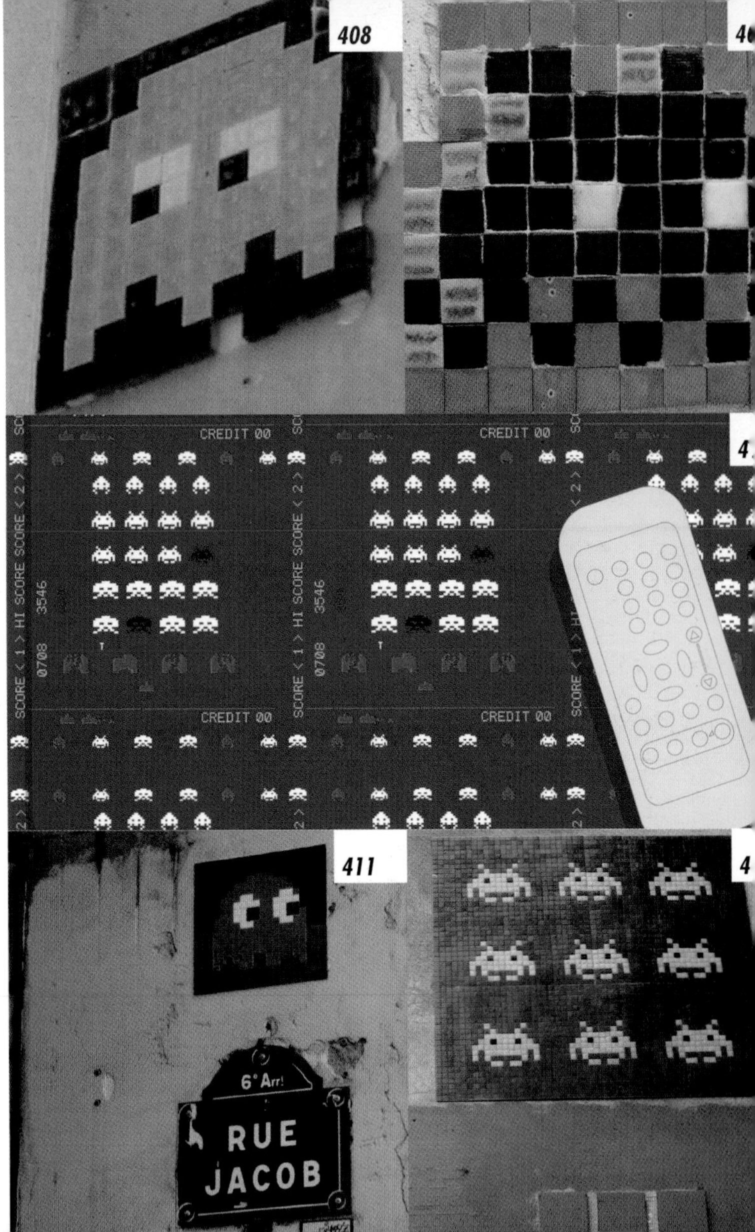

408, 409, 411, 412, and 414–416 *Mosaicked space invaders from around the world.*
410 *Darren tray design by Absolute Zero Degrees.*
413 *Place Invaders™ space invader–inspired coasters by Art Meets Matter.*

413
414
415
416

"ZUSE doesn't see itself merely as a compact toasting device, but more like a printmaker of the traditional kind. Inspired by the early matrix printers, it now engages in burning black-and-white pictures with 12 by 12 pixel resolution into the toast by diligently marking line by line. With its candid intention of providing happiness to its owner, ZUSE can randomly draw from its repertoire of images encoded in its memory chip. ZUSE custom-toasts for a fresh start of the day."

Jakob Illera
Inseq Design

417 and 418 *ZUSE pixel toaster by Inseq Design.*

419 *Jonathan Stilts photographed this large-scale space invader, created by him and his friends for Google Earth's flyover of Wentworth Park, Sydney, on Australia Day 2007.*
420 *Interlocking Place Invaders™ coasters by Art Meets Matter.*
421 *Ryan Popoff spotted this large-scale invader in Manchester.*
422 *Space Invaders even get onto your clothes.*
423 *Beau Wade created this image by cloning windows on an existing image he had taken of New York.*

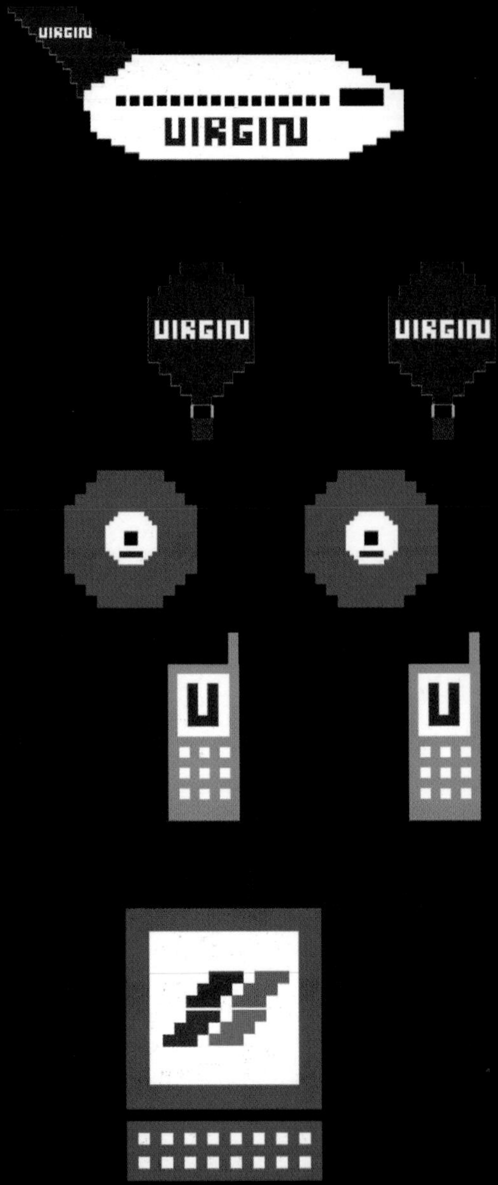

424 *Knitted space invaders.*
425 *Stills from a short film made by Sarah Chanter at Edinburgh College of Art entitled "race to space." This one-day project, designed to encourage spontaneous thinking, was set by Jane Stockdale and Ryan Joiner, former students from ECA, with the brief to create a visual fight. Sarah chose the subject of Bill Gates and Richard Branson fighting it out to be the first in space and used space invader style visuals to express it.*
426 *MXL_Inka by eBoy was created for the Exposif wallpaper collection by Maxalot. eBoy build 3D illustrations of imaginary landscapes filled with robots and cars. They simultaneously have achieved cult status among fellow graphic designers as well as great commercial success with a list of prestigious clients. Max Akkerman and Lotje Sodderland of Maxalot showcase graphic design as a contemporary art form, commissioning and producing graphic wallscapes created by the cream of graphic society, and inviting industry leaders and pioneers of graphic style and technique to exhibit in shows which are free from the boundaries of their client work.*

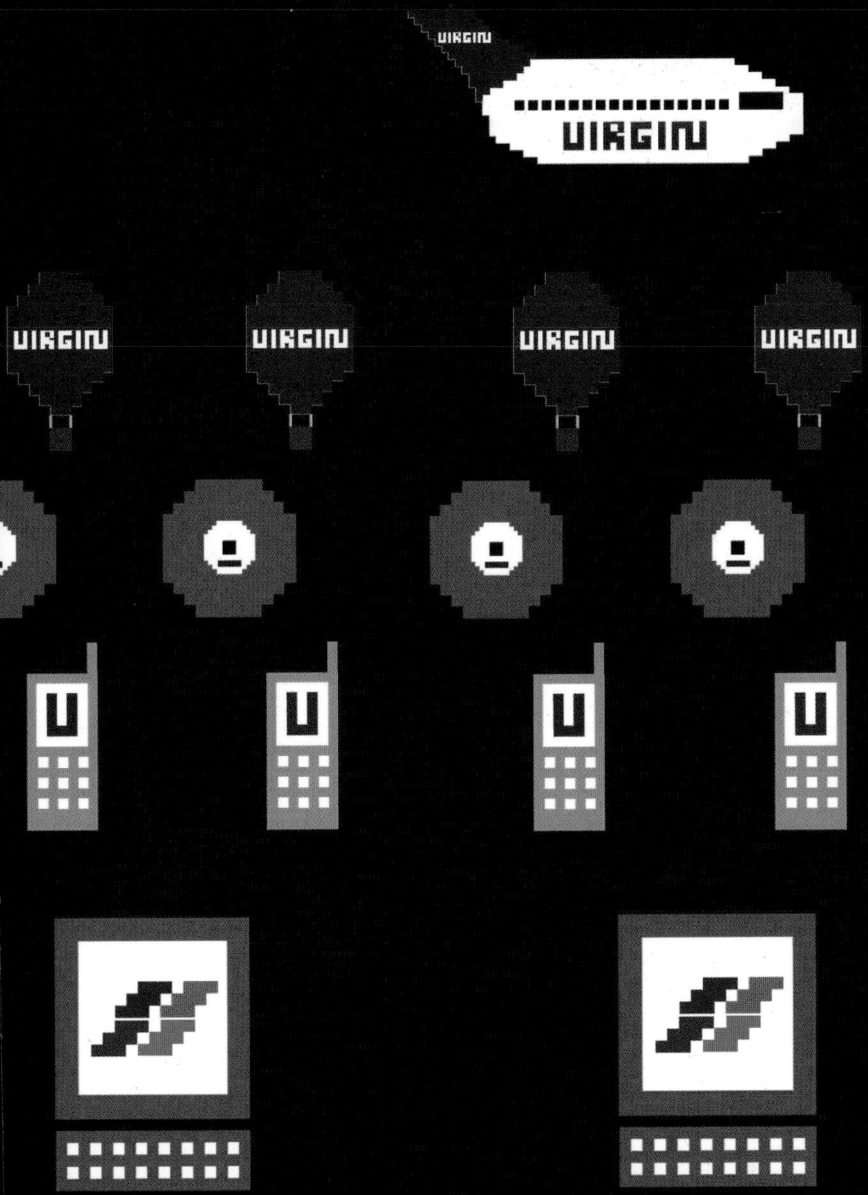

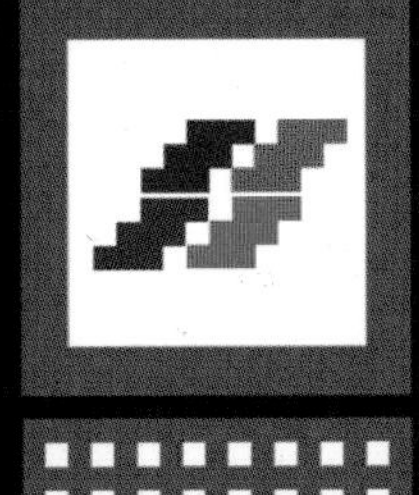

Sup
er
Bronco

"The hand-stitched High Church of Gaming kneelers explore parallels between religious ceremony and digital gaming culture. While inspired by religious ideas, they incorporate pixel imagery taken from games such as Super Mario, Sonic the Hedgehog, and Zelda where each pixel has been replaced with a stitch."

Kate Pemberton

427 *Computer gaming—the new religion?*
The High Church of Gaming is an art piece by Kate Pemberton, using pixel gaming iconography on traditional prayer kneelers.

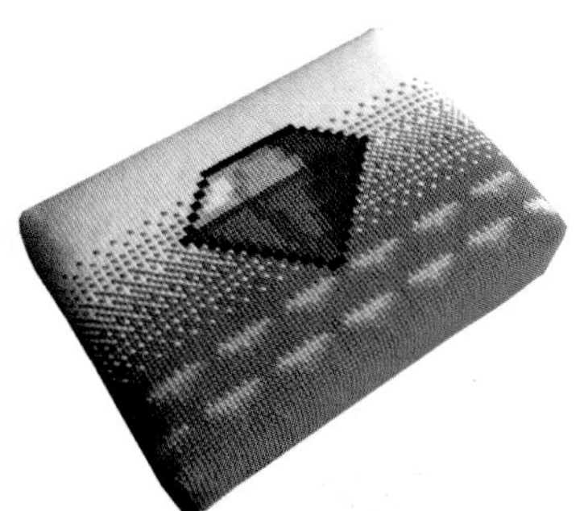

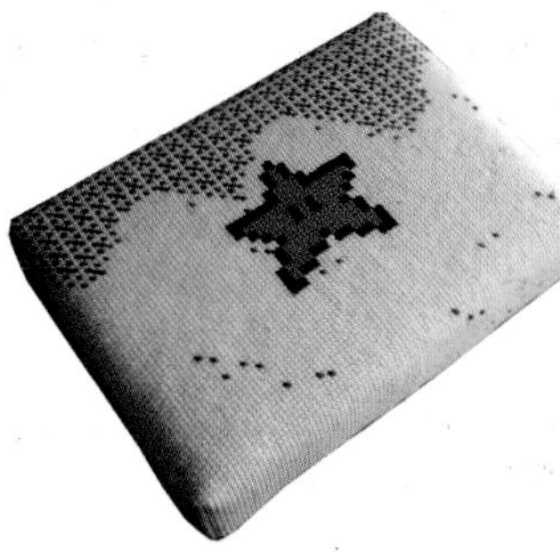

Periodic Table

Known to every chemistry student courtesy of the big poster on the science lab wall, the Periodic Table owes its existence to Russian chemist Dmitri Mendeleev. Formalized in 1869, the table was intended to illustrate recurring (thus, "periodic") trends in the properties of the elements. Its grid format is a practical solution to the presentation of so much detailed information. It offers a framework to classify and compare the different forms of chemical behavior, and can also be updated as new elements are discovered.

The table holds a fascination that goes beyond the realms of science and into the world of art and design. In his piece The Periodic Table of British Elements, Tom Rothwell deconstructs British culture into categories including Regional Stereotypes, Very British Traits, Cuisine, and Celebrities. Rothwell explains, "The periodic table was a perfect structure to use, because it's split up into distinct sections, and, although they house many disparate elements, they are linked together by their very nature." The table is categorized using color-coded squares; gold is fittingly reserved for the Queen and her mother.

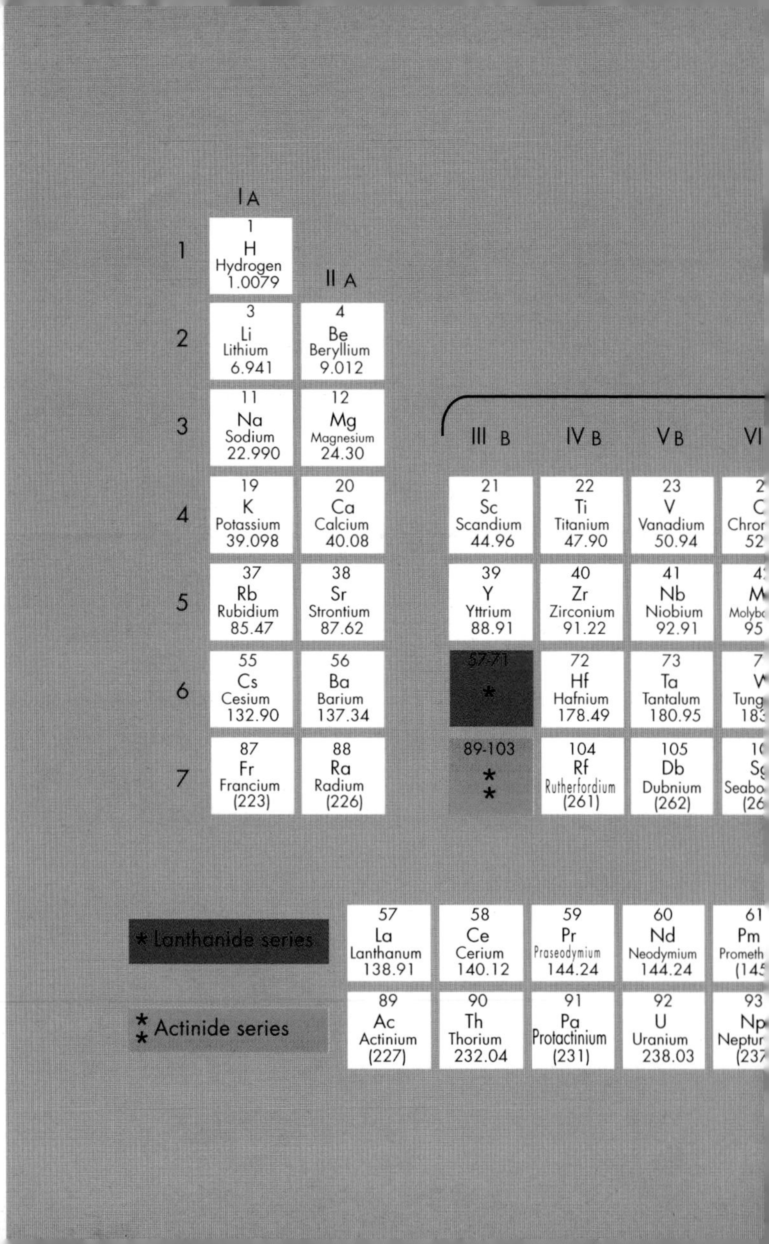

428 *The Periodic Table.*

	IA	IIA	III B	IV B	V B	VI
1	1 H Hydrogen 1.0079					
2	3 Li Lithium 6.941	4 Be Beryllium 9.012				
3	11 Na Sodium 22.990	12 Mg Magnesium 24.30				
4	19 K Potassium 39.098	20 Ca Calcium 40.08	21 Sc Scandium 44.96	22 Ti Titanium 47.90	23 V Vanadium 50.94	2 C Chror 52
5	37 Rb Rubidium 85.47	38 Sr Strontium 87.62	39 Y Yttrium 88.91	40 Zr Zirconium 91.22	41 Nb Niobium 92.91	4 M Molyb 95
6	55 Cs Cesium 132.90	56 Ba Barium 137.34	57-71 *	72 Hf Hafnium 178.49	73 Ta Tantalum 180.95	7 W Tung 18
7	87 Fr Francium (223)	88 Ra Radium (226)	89-103 **	104 Rf Rutherfordium (261)	105 Db Dubnium (262)	1 Sg Seabo (26

* Lanthanide series	57 La Lanthanum 138.91	58 Ce Cerium 140.12	59 Pr Praseodymium 144.24	60 Nd Neodymium 144.24	61 Pm Prometh (14
** Actinide series	89 Ac Actinium (227)	90 Th Thorium 232.04	91 Pa Protactinium (231)	92 U Uranium 238.03	93 Np Neptur (23

Metals

Semimetals

Nonmetals

TRANSITION ELEMENTS

	VIII			I B	II B	III A	IV A	V A	VI A	VII A	VIII A	
											2 He Helium 4.003	1
						5 B Boron 10.81	6 C Carbon 12.011	7 N Nitrogen 14.007	8 O Oxygen 15.9994	9 F Flourine 19.00	10 Ne Neon 20.179	2
						13 Al Aluminum 26.98	14 Si Silicon 28.09	15 P Phosphorus 30.974	16 S Sulfur 32.064	17 Cl Chlorine 35.453	18 Ar Argon 39.948	3
5 ın anese .94	26 Fe Iron 55.85	27 Co Cobalt 58.93	28 Ni NIckel 58.70	29 Cu Copper 63.55	30 Zn Zinc 65.38	31 Ga Gallium 69.72	32 Ge Germanium 72.59	33 As Arsenic 74.92	34 Se Selenium 78.96	35 Br Bromine 79.904	36 Kr Krypton 83.80	4
3 etium 7)	44 Ru Ruthenium 101.1	45 Rh Rhodium 102.91	46 Pd Palladium 106.4	47 Ag Silver 107.868	48 Cd Cadmium 112.40	49 In Indium 114.82	50 Sn Tin 118.69	51 Sb Antimony 121.75	52 Te Tellurium 127.60	53 I Iodine 126.90	54 Xe Xenon 131.30	5
5 e ium 5.2	76 Os Osmium 190.2	77 Ir Iridium 192.2	78 Pt Platinum 195.09	79 Au Gold 197.0	80 Hg Mercury 200.59	81 Tl Thallium 204.37	82 Pb Lead 207.2	83 Bi Bismuth 208.98	84 Po Polonium (209)	85 At Astatine (210)	86 Rn Radon (222)	6
07 n ium 54)	108 Hs Hassium (265)	109 Mt Meitnerium (268)	110 Uun Ununnilium (269)	111 Uuu Unununium (272)	112 Uub Ununbium (277)							7

um 35	63 Eu Europium 152.0	64 Gd Gadolinium 157.25	65 Tb Terbium 158.93	66 Dy Dysprosium 162.50	67 Ho Holmium 164.93	68 Er Erbium 167.26	69 Tm Thulium 168.93	70 Yb Ytterbium 173.04	71 Lu Lutetium 174.97
um)	95 Am Americium (243)	96 Cm Curium (247)	97 Bk Berkelium (247)	98 Cf Californium (247)	99 Es Einsteinium (254)	100 Fm Fermium (257)	101 Md Mendelevium (258)	102 No Nobelium (259)	103 Lr Lawrencium (260)

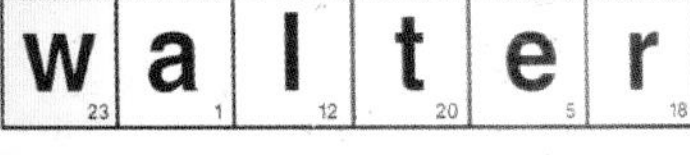
w 23
a 1
l 12
t 20
e 5
r 18

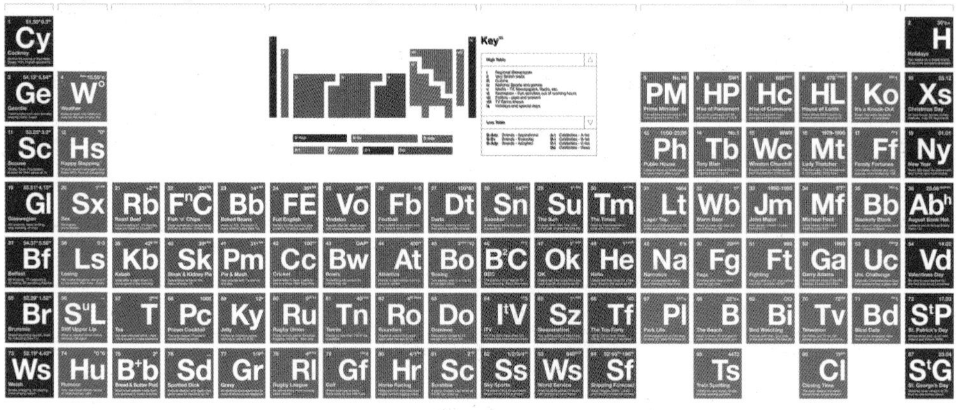
Periodic Table of British Elements

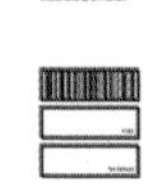

432

433

434

429 *Exterior signage of walter, the Antwerp flagship store of designer Walter Van Beirendonck. The lettering is given a periodic table style by placing each letter in a square and including the number of its position in the alphabet—W 23, etc.*
430 *Using the windows of the Daley Center, Chicago, as a framework for a huge format periodic table.*
431 *Periodic Table of British Elements by Tom Rothwell.*
432 *A 3D periodic table at the Griffith Observatory, Los Angeles. Taken by Jonathan Tony Lau.*
433 *Based on the standard periodic table, this set of eight elemental drink mats allows you to send coded messages to your guests—arsenic for your love rival, gold for the object of your desire. Designed by Frank.*
434 *Brian Kennedy spotted this periodic coffee table in the staff offices at the Oregon Museum of Science and Industry (OMSI).*

Keyboards

Ray Tomlinson sent the first e-mail in 1971. The message, sent to another computer in his office, read QWERTYUIOP—the letters of the top row of the keyboard. Odd that he couldn't think of anything more interesting to write, but in those days our lives weren't filled with keyboards as they are now. With the ubiquitous use of PCs, cellphones, and a host of other personal organizers, pundits suggest that the art of handwriting is dying out. Now we depend on the functional keyboard grid for all our communication requirements.

So what about that message? It stems from the invention of the QWERTY keyboard, designed by the man responsible for the first typewriter, Christopher Sholes. The letters were originally arranged in alphabetical order, but speed typing on mechanical machines caused the metal letter bars to become entangled. The solution was to split up the commonly used letters to different sides of the keyboard, alternating letters between left and right hands. The QWERTY keyboard has long been the standard for all English language users. Anticipating the need for a more adaptable keyboard, designer Michael Salge was inspired by the Rosetta stone to create a multi-linguistic keyboard whose keys can be freely reconfigured by the user.

437

438

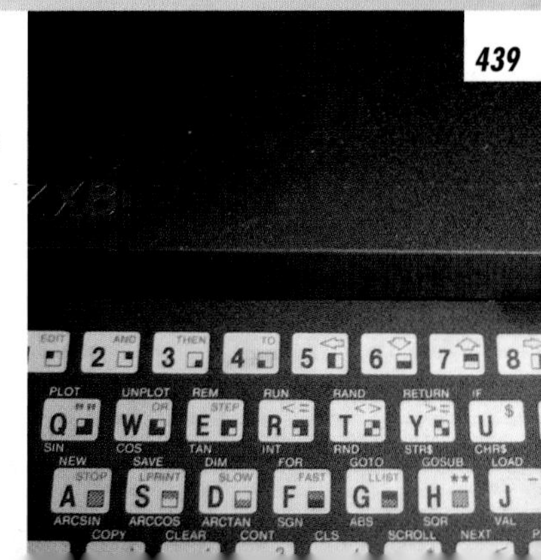

439

435 *"Old coders never die, they just fade away." Portrait of Bertram Herzog commissioned as a tribute for his retirement from the position as Editor-in-Chief of "Computer Graphics and Applications." Created by Ken Knowlton using vintage computer keys in black and beige.*

436 and 438 *Keyboards immediately connote online activity. Add headphones and the image suggests music downloads. A customized key—such as the shopping cart—immediately communicates online shopping.*

437 *Michael Salge's conceptual keyboard reconfigures the keys.*

439 *"Old school" technology—the iconic ZX81, from Sinclair Research, 1981.*

Optical Effects

Since squares, grids, and graphs help us to impose order on the world around us, it seems a betrayal of our trust that the square should also play a part in some of the most disorienting optical effects. Squares can deceive the eye in several ways. The classic is the Hermann grid illusion. Nobody can come up with a definitive theory why we see dots at the intersections of the squares. A regular grid can appear to warp and curve as a result of strategically placed black-and-white squares or diagonal lines. Orientation affects visual perceptions too: a diamond of the same proportions as a square seems larger because the eye focuses on its longer diagonal axis.

Juxtaposed squares can alter our color and spatial perception, and even help to camouflage an object. Dazzle camouflage was painted on ships during WWI to deceive the enemy's visual rangefinders; it confuses rather than conceals. John Morgan employs a version of dazzle camouflage using pixel-style squares in his designs for Polish bus and tram liveries. →

***440** The Hermann grid illusion informs the brand identity and packaging for Coca-Cola TaB Energy.*
Design: Turner Duckworth.
Creative Directors: David Turner and Bruce Duckworth.
Designers: Sarah Moffat and Chris Garvey.

4

4

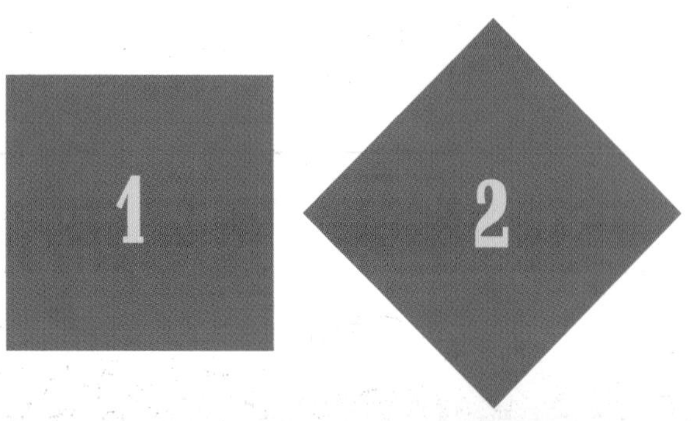

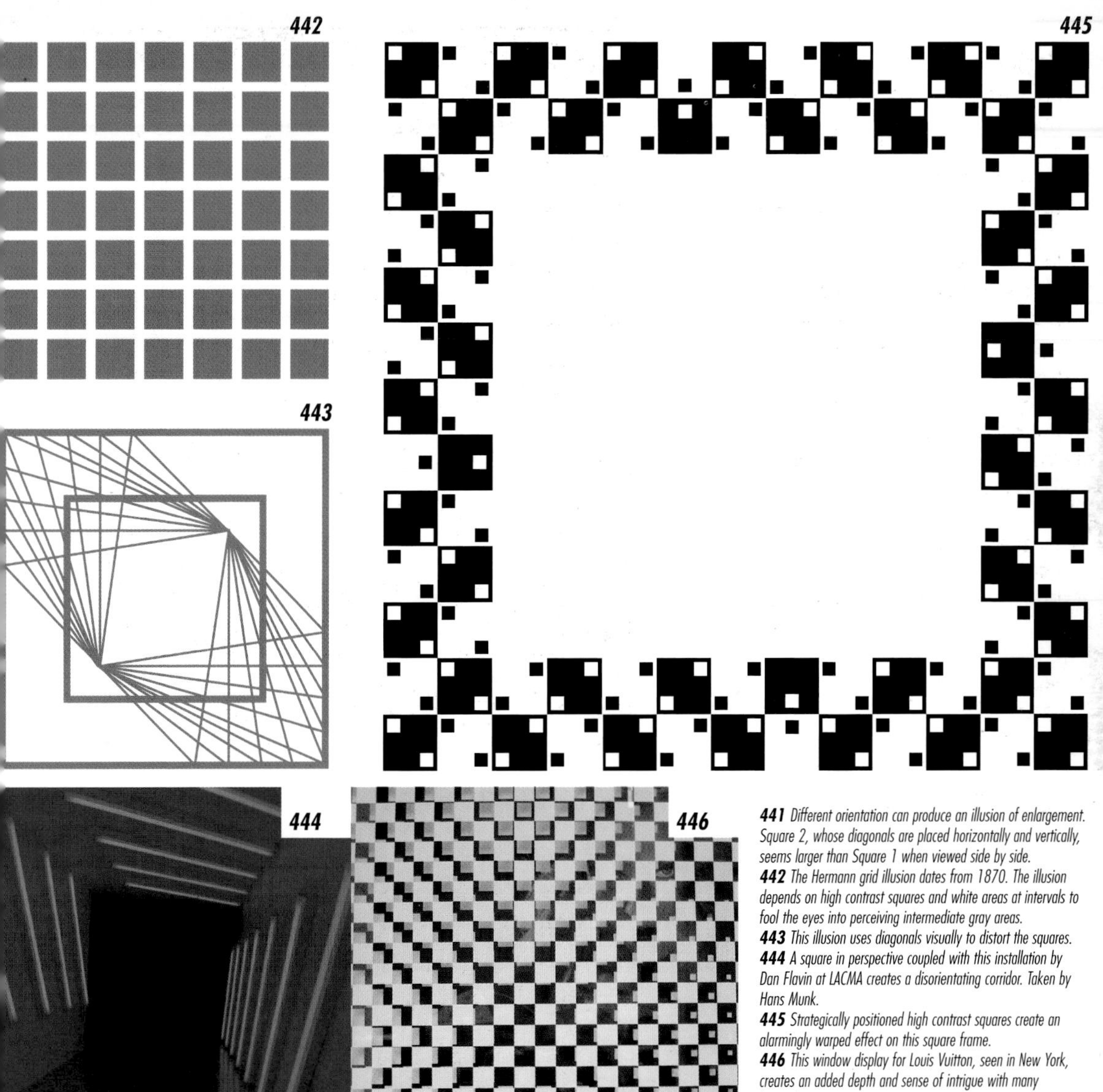

__441__ Different orientation can produce an illusion of enlargement. Square 2, whose diagonals are placed horizontally and vertically, seems larger than Square 1 when viewed side by side.
__442__ The Hermann grid illusion dates from 1870. The illusion depends on high contrast squares and white areas at intervals to fool the eyes into perceiving intermediate gray areas.
__443__ This illusion uses diagonals visually to distort the squares.
__444__ A square in perspective coupled with this installation by Dan Flavin at LACMA creates a disorientating corridor. Taken by Hans Munk.
__445__ Strategically positioned high contrast squares create an alarmingly warped effect on this square frame.
__446__ This window display for Louis Vuitton, seen in New York, creates an added depth and sense of intrigue with many layered squares.

447 *The design for Polish buses and trams by John Morgan Studio, inspired by dazzle camouflage. Unlike camouflage that tries to conceal through techniques of blending or mimicry, dazzle camouflage is disruptive—making a single thing appear to be a hodgepodge of unrelated items.*

44

449

450

448 *This color illusion appears to contain two shades of pink square. In fact, the pink squares are all the same shade, but appear darker due to the juxtaposition with green squares instead of white.*
449 *A disorientating ceiling pattern taken by Alex Pallent in Melbourne.*
450 *"How to disappear completely"—John Morgan Studio applied black-and-white dazzle camouflage to the Polish tram system.*
451 *Albatros Air identity by StormHand.*
452 and 453 *Checkered Past™ by FLOR is an op art–inspired floor tile covering, seen here in laurel and lime.*

451

452

453

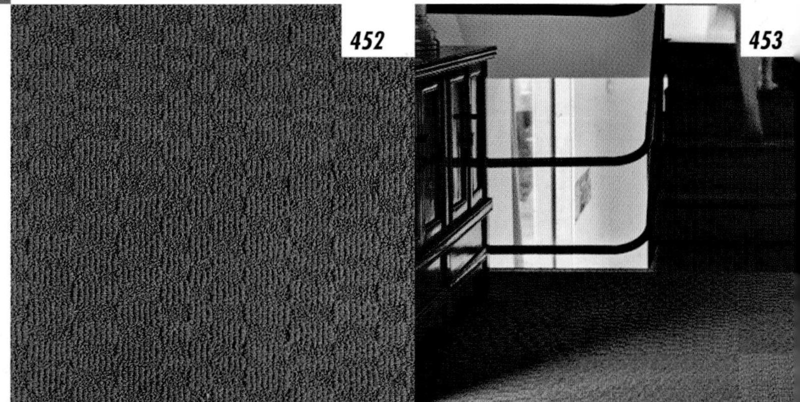

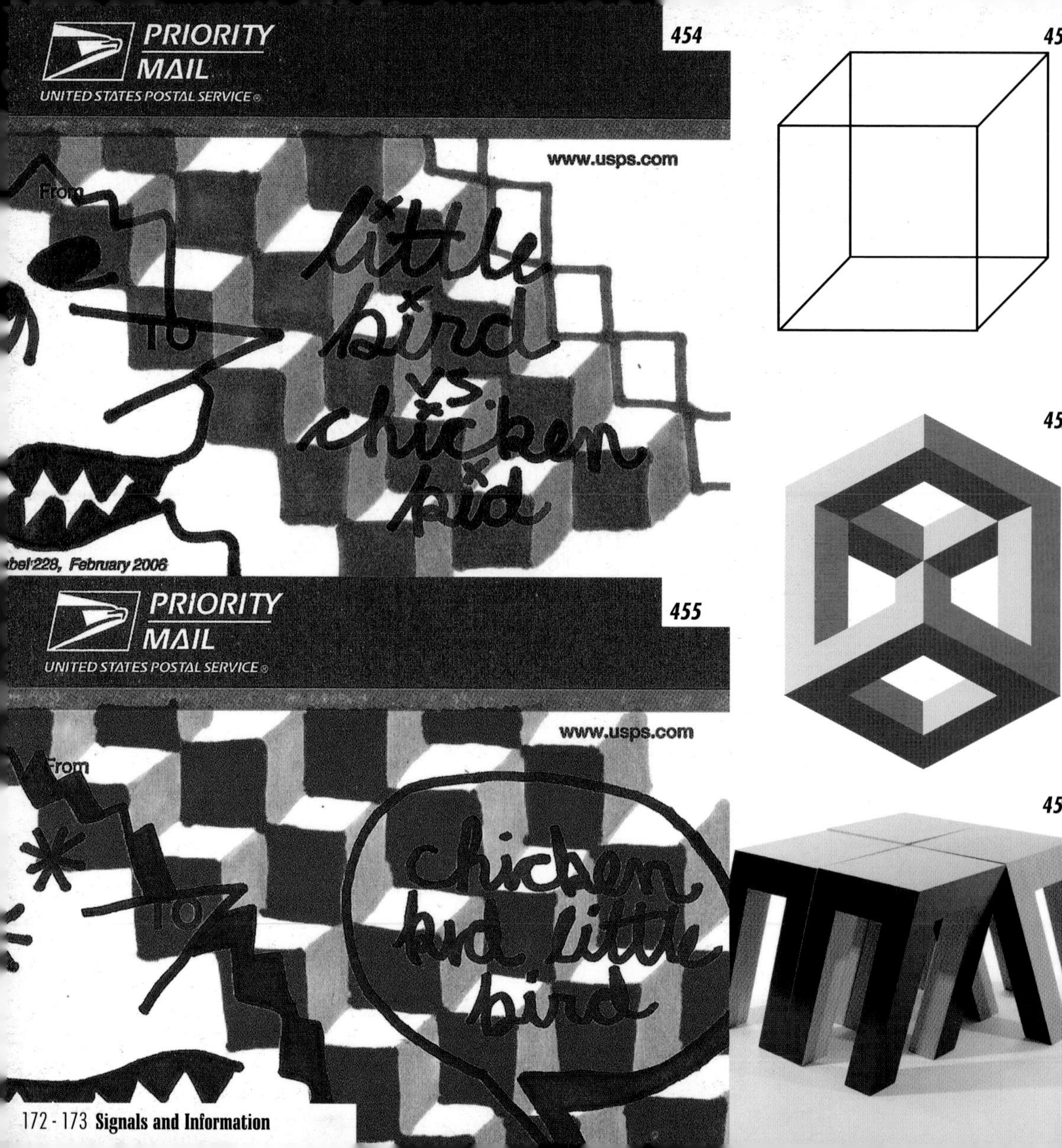
454
PRIORITY MAIL
UNITED STATES POSTAL SERVICE ®
www.usps.com
From
To
little bird vs chicken kid
bel 228, February 2006
455
PRIORITY MAIL
UNITED STATES POSTAL SERVICE ®
www.usps.com
From
To
chicken kid little bird
45
45
45

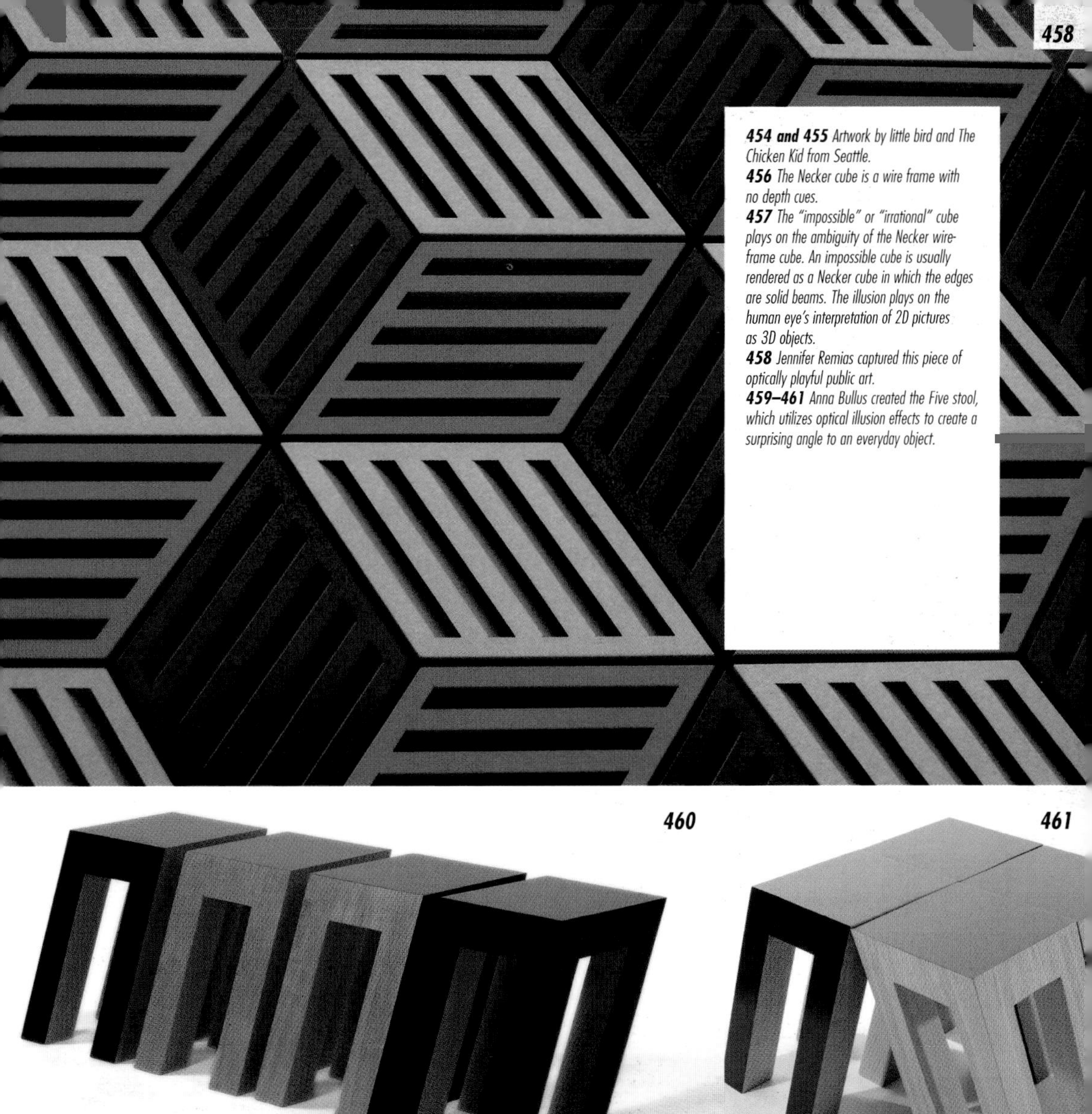

458

454 and 455 *Artwork by little bird and The Chicken Kid from Seattle.*
456 *The Necker cube is a wire frame with no depth cues.*
457 *The "impossible" or "irrational" cube plays on the ambiguity of the Necker wire-frame cube. An impossible cube is usually rendered as a Necker cube in which the edges are solid beams. The illusion plays on the human eye's interpretation of 2D pictures as 3D objects.*
458 *Jennifer Remias captured this piece of optically playful public art.*
459–461 *Anna Bullus created the Five stool, which utilizes optical illusion effects to create a surprising angle to an everyday object.*

460

461

→ Squares help to communicate perspective and, by the same token, can create false 3D illusions. The Necker Cube is a wire-frame drawing of a cube in isometric perspective. Created in 1832 by Swiss crystallographer Louis Albert Necker, it has helped scientists understand the way the human visual system works. Staring at the cube, the brain alternates between two different interpretations of the cube, depending whether the lower or upper square is perceived as the front face.

Artists and designers use false perspective to create visual tension or look for ways to introduce 3D playfulness to everyday objects. Two notable examples are: Anna Bullus's Five —a set of four optically challenging stools; and Claire Stevens' hand-cut wallpaper, inspired by the repetitious structures of organic forms abstracted into geometric arrangements through the manipulation, cutting, and folding of paper.

462 *3D Orange Squares wallpaper by Claire Stevens.*
463 and 464 *Using tone within a square can create an effect of depth and perspective.*
465 *Tiles with a false perspective printed on the surface.*
466 *Hannah Broadhead toys with perspective in this art piece. The image itself is 3D, including a perspective view through a 2D door and completed with a distorted perspective frame.*
467 and 468 *This optical illusion makes something special out of an everyday concrete floor, spotted by Elisa Renouard.*

463
464
465
466
467
468

Grids and Graphs

Every graphic designer knows the benefits of the typographic grid as a formatting tool for the layout of type and pictures. A typographic grid is basically a structure of intersecting vertical and horizontal axes on which designers can organize content in a more easily digestible manner. This book's grid is set out here. It is a three-column grid that allows up to nine images per page. Type can work in columns or rows.

The grid divides opinion: helpful tool or constraining tyrant? Post WWII interest in modernist design theory expounded by influential designers like Jan Tschichold led to several key graphic designers creating a flexible system to help with page layout, culminating in the widespread uptake of the grid—largely attributed to the Müller-Brockmann book, *Grid Systems in Graphic Design*. In the 1960s Anthony Froshaug wrote: "To mention both typographic, and, in the same breath/sentence, grids, is strictly tautologous." He asserted that typography is in itself a grid. In the 1980s the use of Macs meant designers had greater control of typographic layout and many rebelled against the grid in favor of a freer approach to layout. Recently, typographic grids have become popular among web designers, exemplified by Khoi Vinh's work for the *New York Times*. →

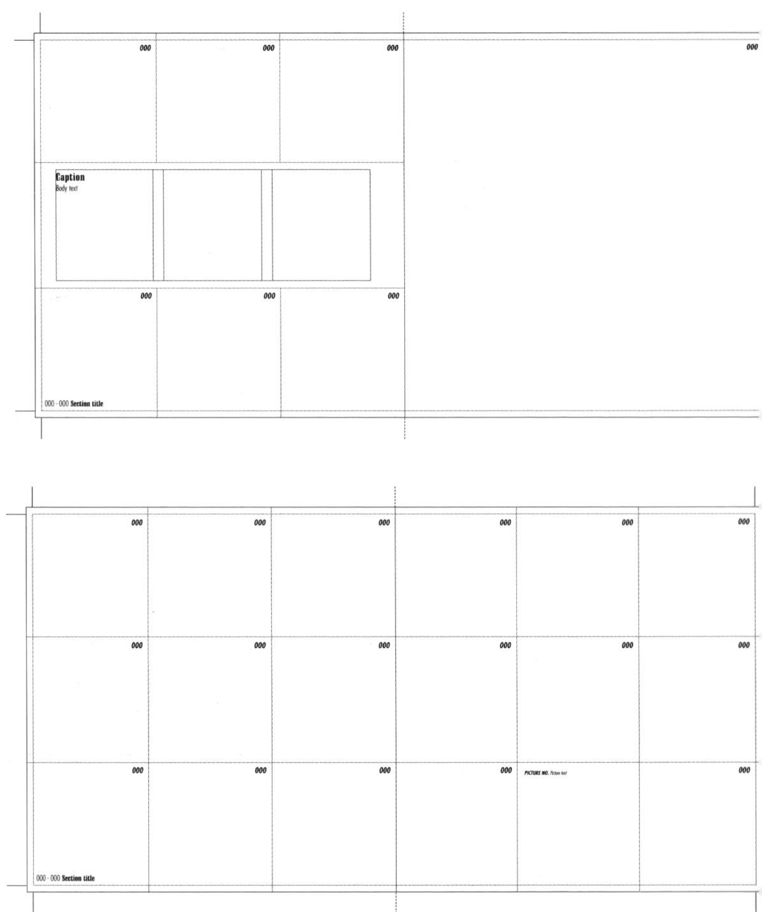

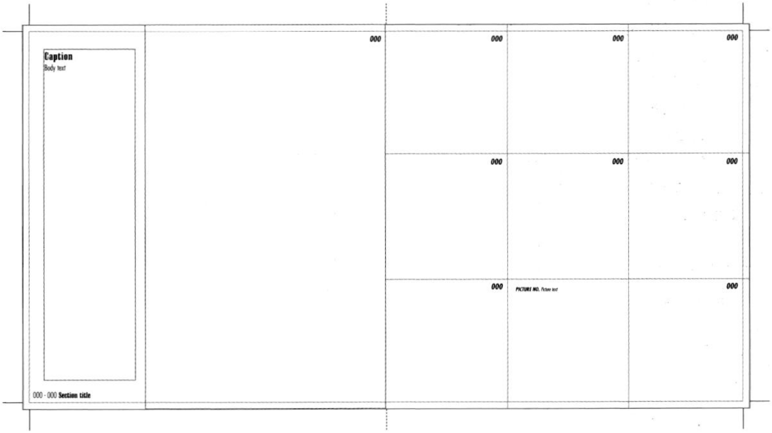

Caption
Body text

000

000 000 000

000 000 000

000 **PICTURE NO.** Picture text 000

000 - 000 **Section title**

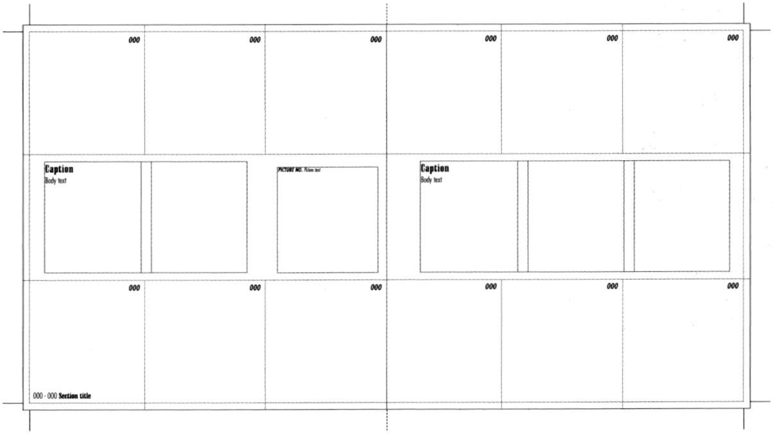

000 000 000 000 000 000

Caption
Body text

PICTURE NO. Picture text

Caption
Body text

000 000 000 000 000 000

000 - 000 **Section title**

→ A fascination with grids has compelled designer Astrid Stavro to create her Art of the Grid range of notepads and shelves based on the grids that have changed the history of design. From the Bible to *The Guardian* newspaper, Astrid pays tribute to the grid as an essential tool without which, "our lives would be messier, uglier, and more confusing places."

If grids represent an inherent human instinct to impose order on a chaotic world, graphs and charts represent another achievement: the ability to represent complex scientific information in a simple and easy-to-digest format. Plotted against horizontal and vertical vertices, a graph represents the relationship between two or more variables. The visual language of the graph is employed to solve many communication problems—from the ascending bars of a graphic equalizer expressing differing levels of volume or intensity to the simple set of ascending blocks used by the UK's 5 A Day scheme, which endorses fruit and vegetable produce to encourage healthier eating.

Ric Bell's Lunar Phase Calendar represents the Moon's phases by converting the amount of the Moon's surface showing in each phase into a percentage of black. The result is a pattern of squares fading from white (when there is a full moon) to black (when there is no moon to be seen). →

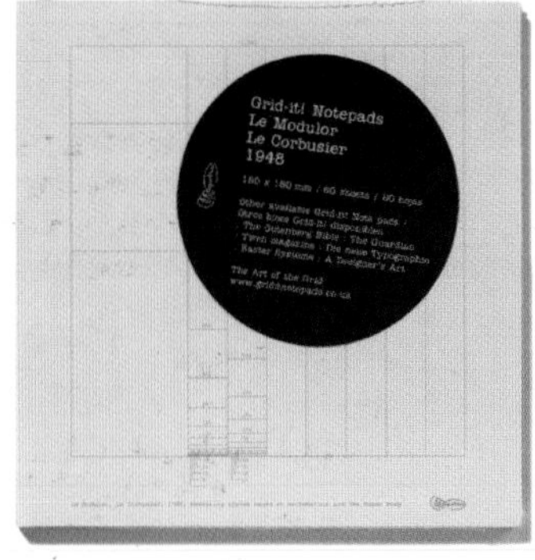

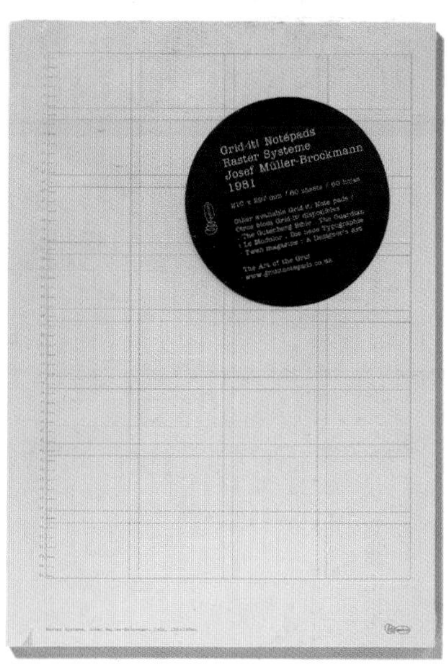

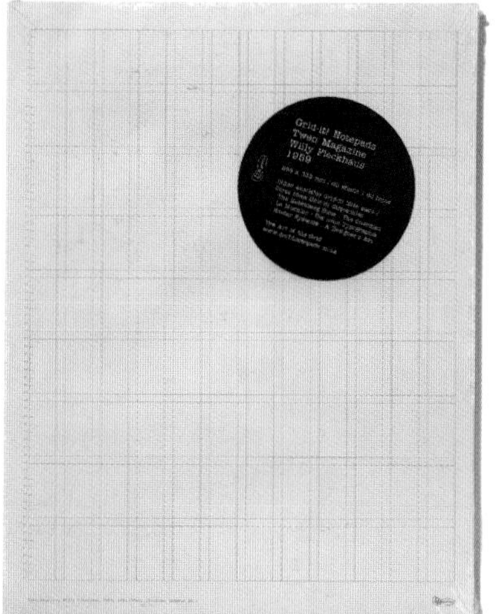

"Grid-it! Notepads are notepads based on the layout grids of famous publications. These grids played an historic role in the development of design systems and cover a wide spectrum of classic and contemporary design."

Astrid Stavro

469 *Grid-it! Notepads designed by Astrid Stavro.*
Publication grids: Opposite Top L/R "The Guardian" newspaper grid by David Hillman, 1988. The Bible by Johannes Gutenberg, 1455. Opposite Bottom L/R "Le Modulor" by Le Corbusier, 1948. "Die neue Typographie" by Jan Tschichold, 1928. This Page Top L/R "Raster Systeme" by Josef Müller-Brockmann, 1981. "A Designer's Art" by Paul Rand, 1985. Bottom "Twen Magazine" by Willy Fleckhaus, 1959.

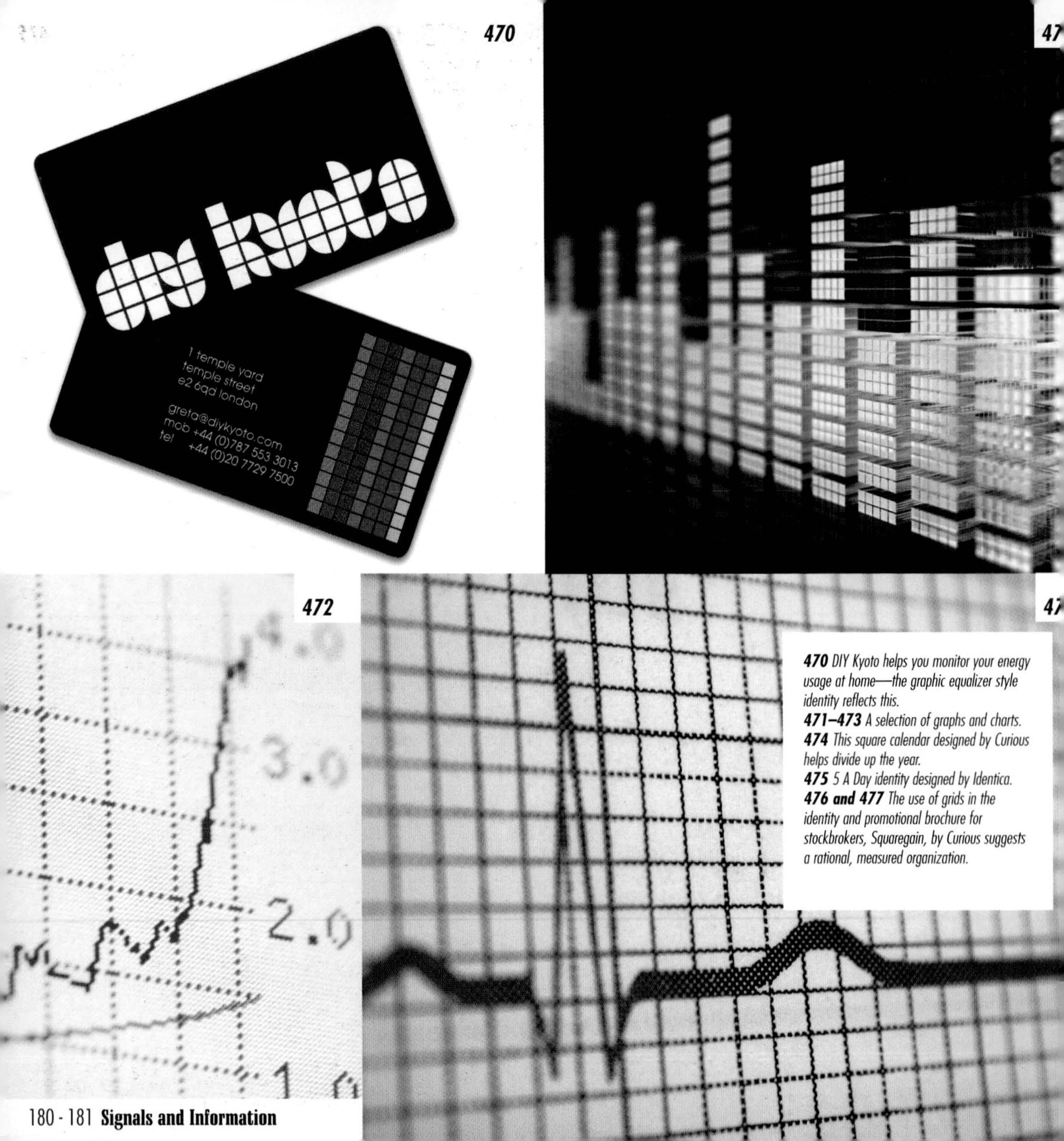

470 *DIY Kyoto helps you monitor your energy usage at home—the graphic equalizer style identity reflects this.*
471–473 *A selection of graphs and charts.*
474 *This square calendar designed by Curious helps divide up the year.*
475 *5 A Day identity designed by Identica.*
476 and 477 *The use of grids in the identity and promotional brochure for stockbrokers, Squaregain, by Curious suggests a rational, measured organization.*

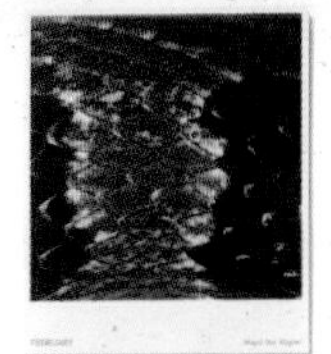

474

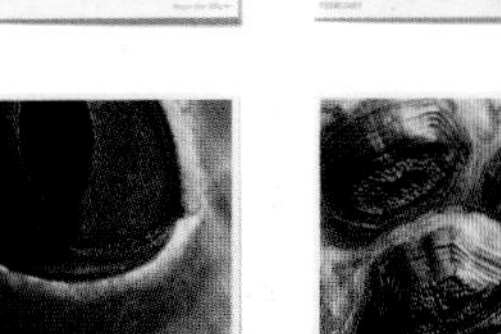
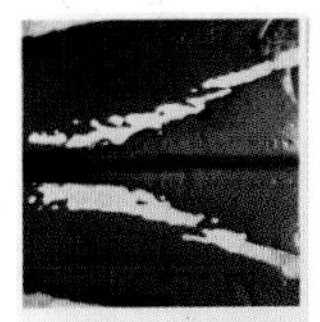
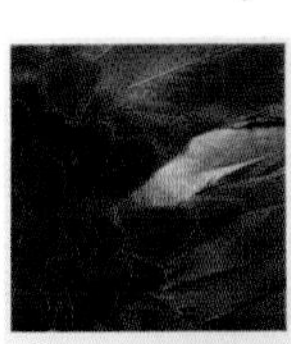
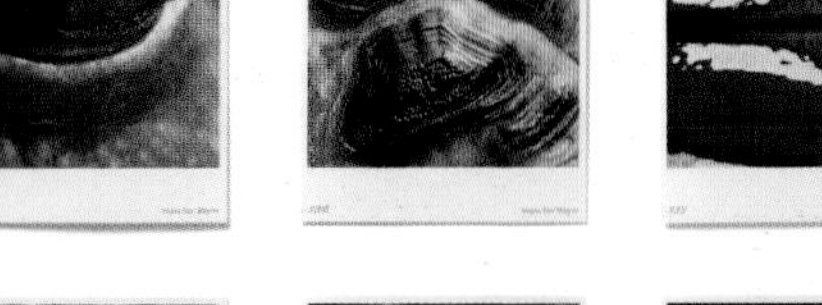
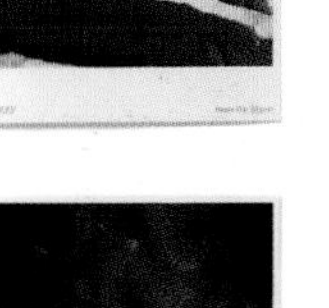

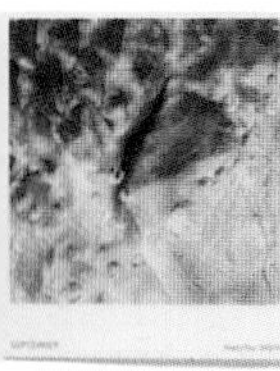

475

476

squaregain

477

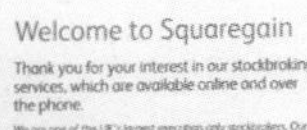

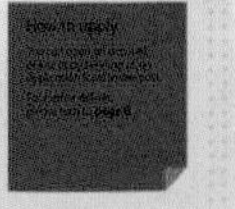

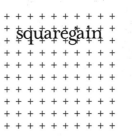

478 *Lunar Phase Calendar by Ric Bell is a process-driven piece of design charting the phases of the moon. The gradient pattern only became apparent halfway through the project.*

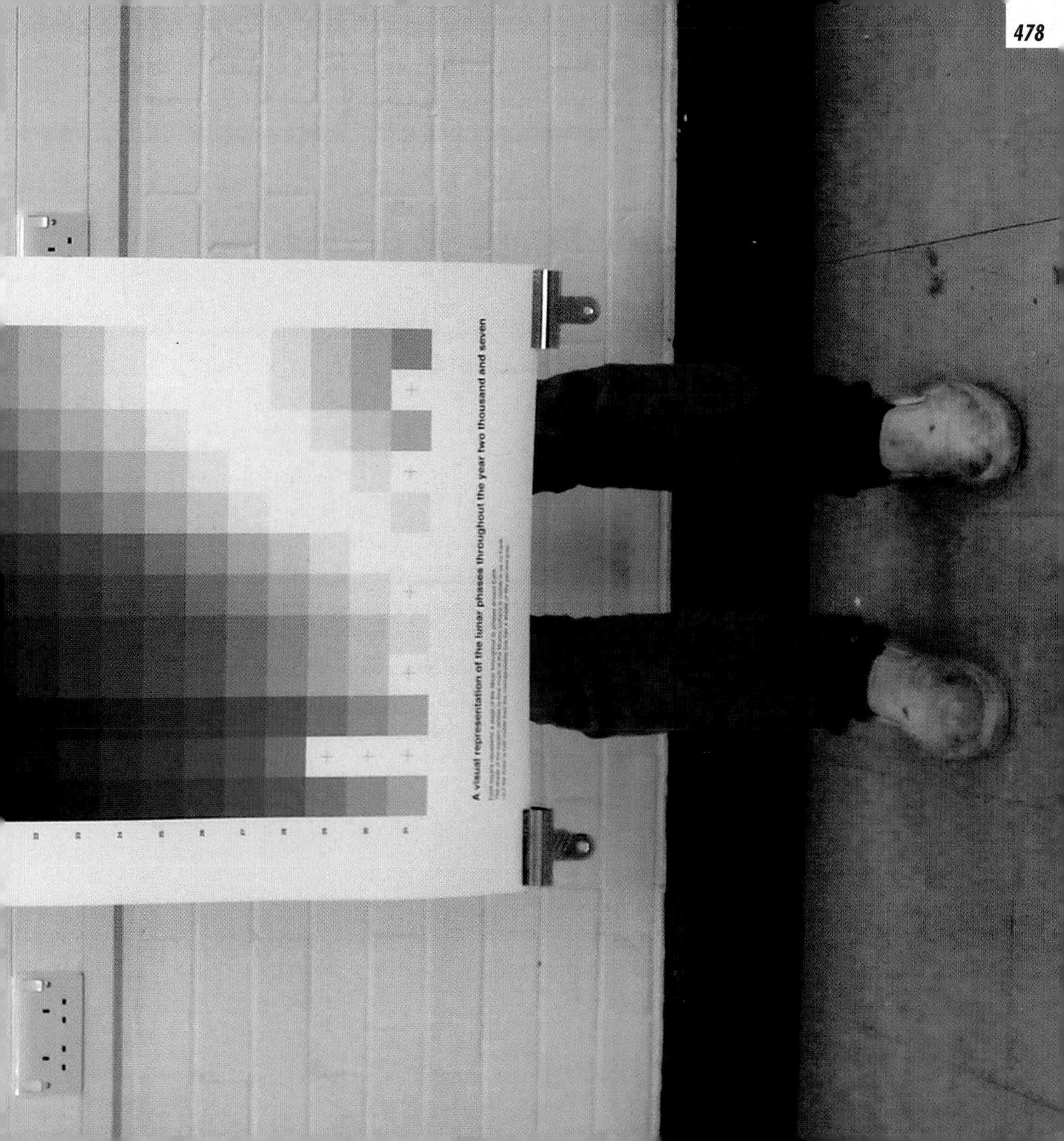
A visual representation of the lunar phases throughout the year two thousand and seven

→ Graph paper comes in various formats to enable the plotting of different types of data on graphs and charts. French exercise books are usually made up of graph paper because it offers multifunctionality—used for writing, drawing, or plotting data. Recently, artists and designers have found a renewed fascination with graph paper. It offers a canvas for consumer customizable artwork, like the CD cover for Beck's *The Information* by Big Active, or can sit in stark contrast to freehand drawing.

"The use of graph paper is akin to comfort eating. There is a ready-made background, a space that seems to add weight to any drawing no matter how incomplete or technically deficient. It is evocative of a time when doodling in the maths book was more fun than doing the maths; when drawing on graph paper was frowned upon by the art teacher as being vulgar. Graph paper is for rebels."

Bob Milner
Milk, Two Sugars

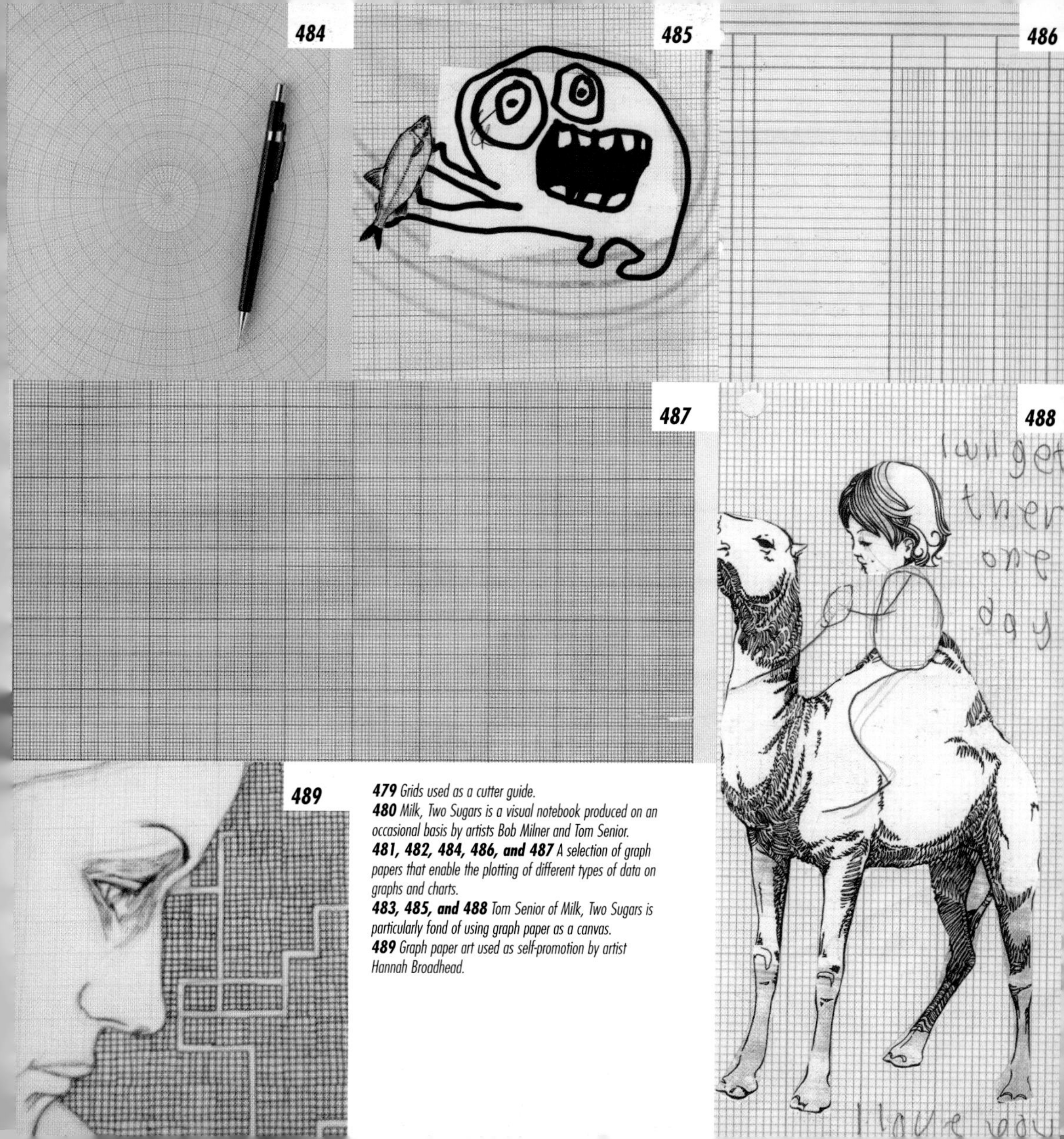

479 *Grids used as a cutter guide.*
480 *Milk, Two Sugars is a visual notebook produced on an occasional basis by artists Bob Milner and Tom Senior.*
481, 482, 484, 486, and 487 *A selection of graph papers that enable the plotting of different types of data on graphs and charts.*
483, 485, and 488 *Tom Senior of Milk, Two Sugars is particularly fond of using graph paper as a canvas.*
489 *Graph paper art used as self-promotion by artist Hannah Broadhead.*

BECK

BECK

BECK

BECK

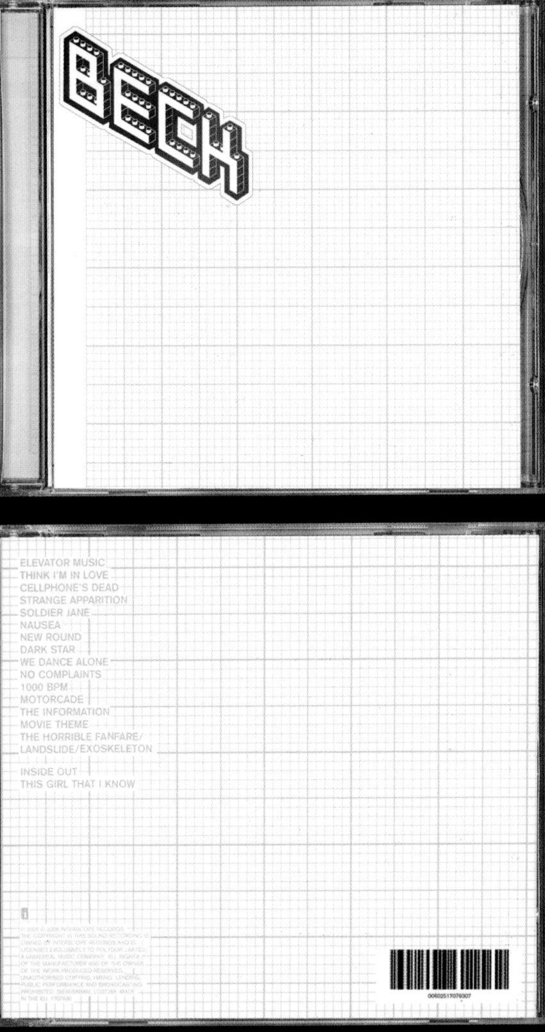

BECK
ELEVATOR MUSIC
THINK I'M IN LOVE
CELLPHONE'S DEAD
STRANGE APPARITION
SOLDIER JANE
NAUSEA
NEW ROUND
DARK STAR
WE DANCE ALONE
NO COMPLAINTS
1000 BPM
MOTORCADE
THE INFORMATION
MOVIE THEME
THE HORRIBLE FANFARE/
LANDSLIDE/EXOSKELETON
INSIDE OUT
THIS GIRL THAT I KNOW

"The album is designed to be sold featuring blank packaging. This is implied by using a plain graph paper grid as the cover and insides of the CD booklet and back inlay of the package. Each CD contains one of four different sticker sheets, each featuring original images by 20 different artists commissioned and curated to form almost 250 different stickers in total. The idea is that the listener is then free to customize their CD or create their own album cover and booklet using the kit of source material contained within, participating in the album experience in a way that is highly reflective of Beck's idiosyncratic style. The listener is then further encouraged to scan and upload their individual designs to share with other fans on-line. The packaging was conceived to clearly differentiate the physical album artifact from the digital download version of the release."

Gerard Saint, Creative Director
Big Active

490 *Beck's "The Information" album.*
Art Direction: Mat Maitland and Gerard Saint at Big Active with Beck.
Design: Mat Maitland at Big Active.
Sticker Images: Jody Barton, Juliette Cezzar, Estelle & Simon, David Foldvari, Genevieve Gauckler, Michael Gillette, Jasper Goodall, Mercedes Helnwein, Han Lee, Mat Maitland, Ari Michelson, Parra, Melanie Pullen, Gay Ribisi, Aleksey Shirokov, Will Sweeney, Kam Tang, Adam Tullie, Kensei Yabuno, and Vania Zouravliov.
Record Label: Interscope/2006.

Form and Function

Mosaics and Tiles
Trellis, Nets, and Mesh
Weaves
Patchwork and Quilts
Frames and Compartments
Windows and Glass Blocks
Cubes
Street Grids and Public Squares

Form and Function

Squares that are intrinsic to the form and function of materials and objects are largely formed through tessellation, grids, and weaves. Modern design uses mesh construction to achieve the optimum balance of lightness and strength. The square is a regular polygon. This and its many lines of symmetry make it tile regularly across a surface—exemplified by mosaic covered walls, neatly sewn patchwork squares, and windows in regular rows and columns.

The square helps us to order and organize. In three dimensions, the cube offers basic multifunctionality and a means of measuring volume. Frames help compartmentalize objects and grids formalize the urban environment, aiding navigation and maximizing the usage of space. Nowhere is the square more evidently a symbol of the human civilizing instinct than in the town square: a public space created for political exposition and social interaction.

491 *New Balance 576 in Harris Tweed, courtesy of Hikmet Sugoer at Solebox.*
492 *Side Chair with full covers by Bertoia, from Knoll International.*
493 *Graphic pattern in mosaic tiles.*
494 *Knitted patchwork squares demonstrate tessellation.*
495 *Detail of Lace Fence by Demakersvan. Photography by Bas Helbers.*
496 *Lacy fishnet tights.*
497 *Fabric with a large open weave.*
498 *Newspaper stands have large mesh fronts to hold daily headline sheets.*
499 *Decorative Parisian security screen.*
500 *Standard mesh fence evokes a hard urban edge.*
501 *Tinted windows and panels create a graphic pattern on this building's exterior.*
502 *Plastic crates derive strength and lightness from their mesh construction.*
503 *Detail of Bertoia side chair.*
504 *A sunny mosaic.*

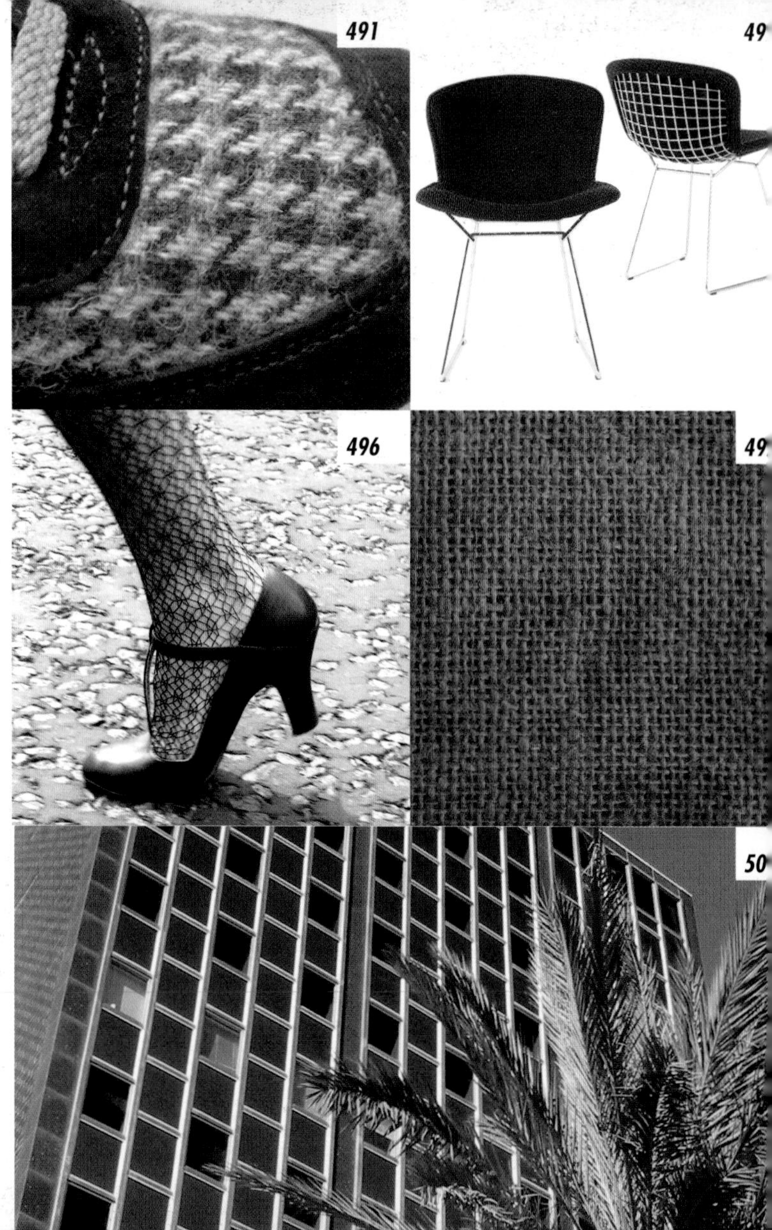

493 494 495

498 499 500

502 503 504

Mosaics and Tiles

Mosaics and tiles exploit the square's ability to tessellate. The square is one of only three shapes that offers regular tessellations—where equal size polygons with sides of the same length fill a plane with no gaps or overlaps—the other two being triangles and hexagons. Mathematics aside, mosaics have endured as a decorative covering for floors and walls since around 4BC. Earlier techniques had used pebbles of varying colors to create patterned flooring designs. The Greeks refined this approach, manufacturing small pieces of square tile (the word "tessellation" is derived from the Greek word "tessera," meaning "four") to make up more precise designs featuring scenes of people, animals, gods, and geometric patterns such as the interwoven rope border called "guilloche." Greek artists were responsible for many of the mosaics preserved at Pompeii and Herculaneum, and the expansion of the Roman Empire spread the art form around the world. →

505, 506, 508, and 510 *Mosaic tiles can range in use from figurative applications to abstract. Here they are used in random colors and patterns to create an exciting visual explosion of color and texture.*
507 *Rough edges give these monochromatic mosaic tiles an aged effect.*
509 *Even single color mosaics can make a big statement as seen here in the Hotel on Rivington.*

511 and 514 *Watery colors are used in the mosaics covering the pool at the Commune of the Children, Commune by the Great Wall.*
512 *A mosaic fish gives an undersea theme to a New York subway station.*
513 *Faith Fate artwork as seen on another part of the New York subway.*

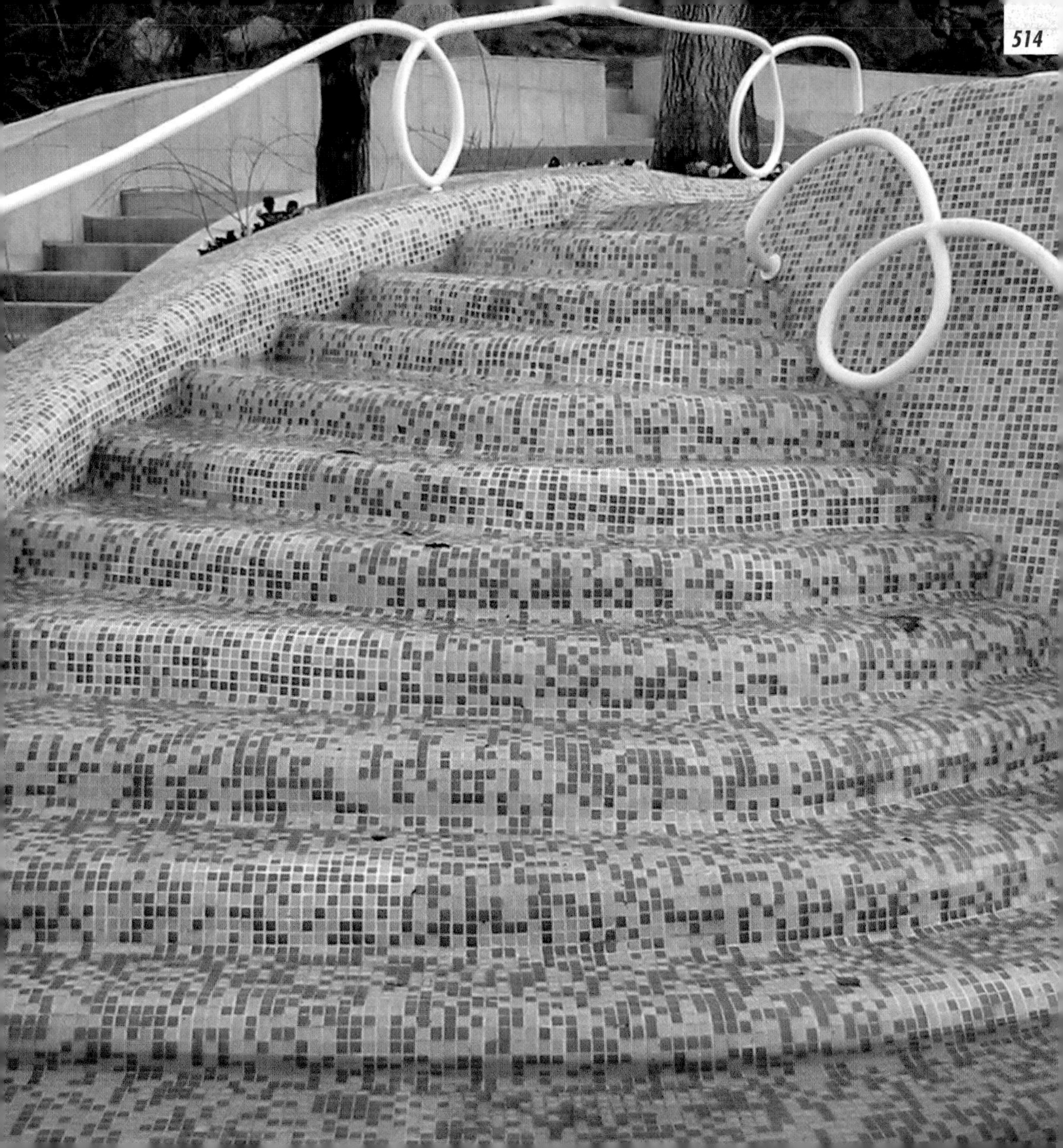

514

515–525 *Colorful, cheerful, and durable, mosaics are a popular medium for public and community art. These bollards and wall mosaics were all captured by photographer Alan Campbell.*

516
517
518
519
520
523
524
525

→ Modern mosaic applications encompass abstract, figurative, and graphic designs in domestic and public settings. The small scale of the tiles makes them perfect for creating subtle gradation of color across a large surface, or random effects using either multicolored or tonally similar tiles—greens and blues the popular choice for watery environments. In small areas, mosaics in single block colors serve to make the space seem bigger.

Apt for creating durable decoration, mosaic is frequently used in public art, sometimes made by members of the community, celebrating themes of love, peace, and happiness with a naive charm. And just as pixels act like digital mosaics, so the technique lends itself to communicate information—letters and words being easily spelled out in contrasting colored tiles, as evinced in these elegant examples from the New York subway. →

526–536 *Mosaics used to give directions or identify the various stations on the New York subway.*

532
NG
534
535
CLINTO
533
AVE
ET.
536
ST.

***537** Untitled, a broken ceramic tile mosaic portrait by Ken Knowlton.*

***538–543** These mosaics in the classical style pay homage to the mosaics that adorned Roman residences in Pompeii and Herculaneum.*

538
541
540
542
543

→ Examples of ceramic tiles have been found in the pyramids and ancient ruins of Greek cities, and they have been used to adorn walls and floors ever since. Throughout history, tiles have been decorated using a variety of techniques including stamping, handpainting, carving, modeling, luster painting, and sgraffito. Plain tiles, on the other hand, can be arranged in geometric patterns, like the classic checkered black and white synonymous with hygiene and cleanliness. Transfer printing is responsible for much of what is produced commercially now, but artists are rediscovering the ceramic tile as a medium for one-offs and limited editions. Often, a design or scene will cover a block of individual tiles, only coming together when assembled in situ. Intricate designs, once in repeat, help to mask the square form of the individual tiles.

Tiling can also have graphic applications. Old style dropped capitals and monograms were the inspiration behind US designer Michael Browers' Geistig typeface. Each letter is framed within an individual square and is intertwined with stylized flowing foliage, evoking the relief patterns of Art Nouveau tiles.

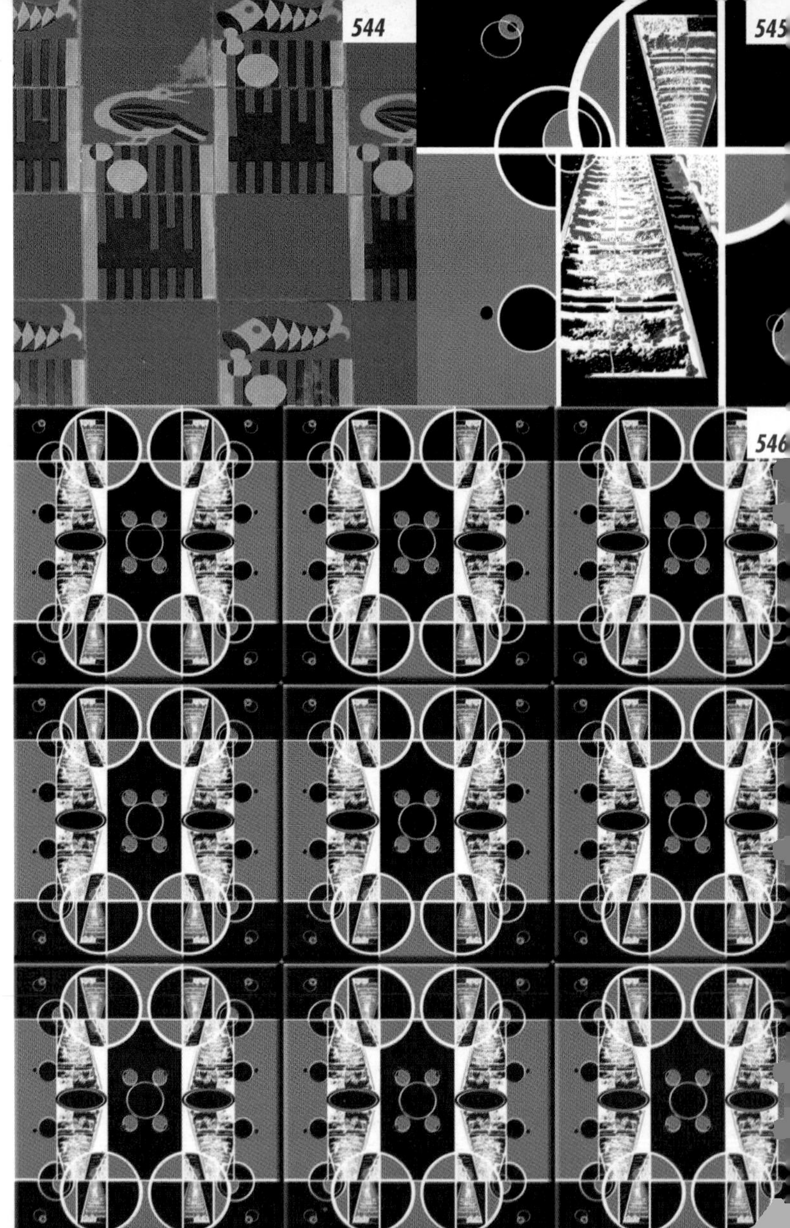

544 *The strongly graphic tiles in Ernest Hemingway's bathroom at his house in Key West.*
545 and 546 *Contemporary tiles by Annette Taylor-Anderson at ATADesigns.*
547 *Pristine and hygienic bathroom tiles photographed by Gianmaria Zanotti.*
548 *Geistig typeface by Michael Browers.*
549 and 550 *Vintage tiles with Art Nouveau designs.*

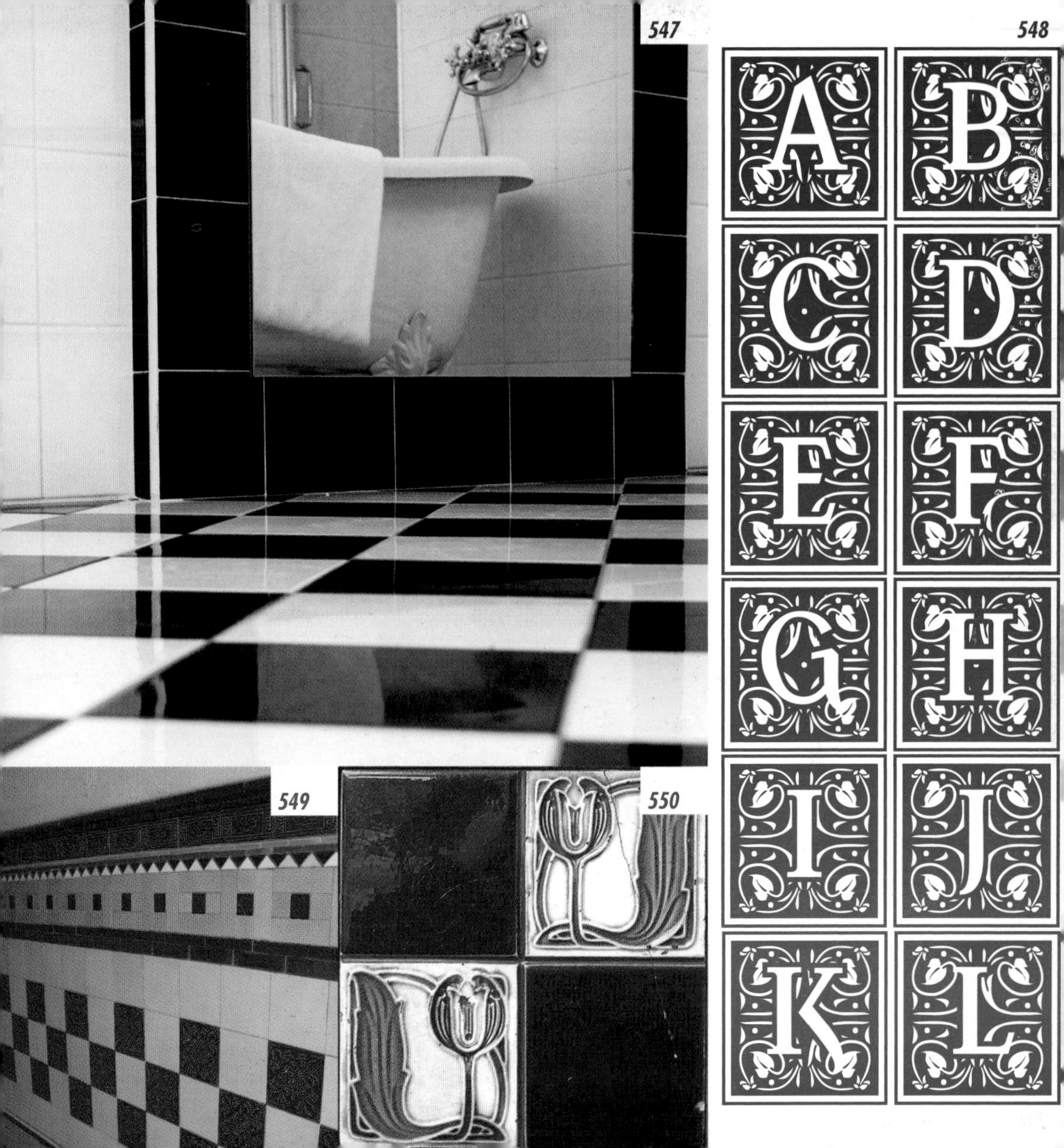
547
548
549
550

Trellis, Nets, and Mesh

Used for support, capture, protection, and division, these functional fabrications have virtually the same construction, differentiated by material: trellis is usually made from wood, netting from string or rope, and mesh is largely metal.

The purpose of trellis is to support climbing plants. Made from interwoven slats of wood or bamboo, trellis has the advantage of being light enough to mount on a fence or wall while offering a framework for the plant to grow up. Trellis is not really intended for display—the ultimate goal being that the climbing plant flourishes and covers it entirely—yet while its purpose is purely functional, its aesthetic has merit in its own right. Used to construct a pergola or arbor, trellis has a lightness and elegance that can convey an English country garden or faded colonial grandeur. →

551–556 *Trellis offers support to climbing plants and provides privacy while allowing light into an outdoor space.*
557 *Contemporary bamboo trellis used as a courtyard screen.*

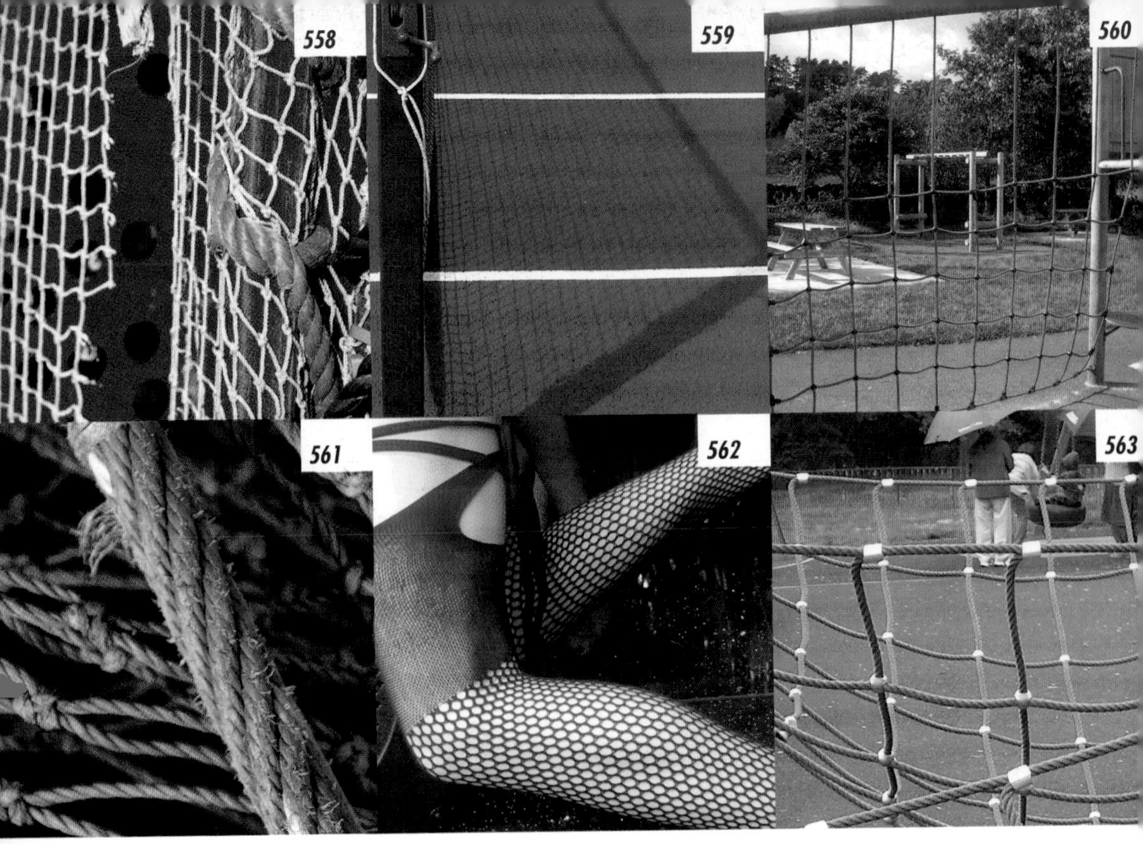

→ Net can describe any fabric where the warp and weft yarns are knotted at their intersection. This creates a fabric that derives its functionality from its openness. Nets are designed to capture only the things you want; their open weave allows the free passage of air and water. So fishing nets are woven to a specific gauge to catch the desirable sized fish and let the tiddlers through. Associations with capture and entrapment are perhaps the reason why net stockings—or fishnets—have subtly fetishistic overtones.

Nets are commonly used in sports applications, particularly in tennis, soccer, and basketball. In the language of sports, the net symbolizes scoring. "Back of the net" is a term appropriated from soccer commentary to describe a small victory like the winning of an argument.

Wire mesh has an industrial look and a protective quality. Encased within glass, a fine metal mesh adds strength and also creates a visual signal of security. Designer Alex Brown has created elaborately patterned versions of safety glass; central to the success of the work is that it breaks an accepted visual code, reinterpreting the strengthening mesh as ornament. →

558, 561, and 562 *From fishing nets to fishnets.*
559 *Shadows cast by a tennis net.*
560 and 563 *Climbing nets in a playground, seen by Jannie Armstrong.*
564 and 566 *Basketball net and an abstract version rendered on a retail fascia in stone relief, complete with metal basketball.*
565 *"The back of the net"—nets inside a playground soccer goal.*

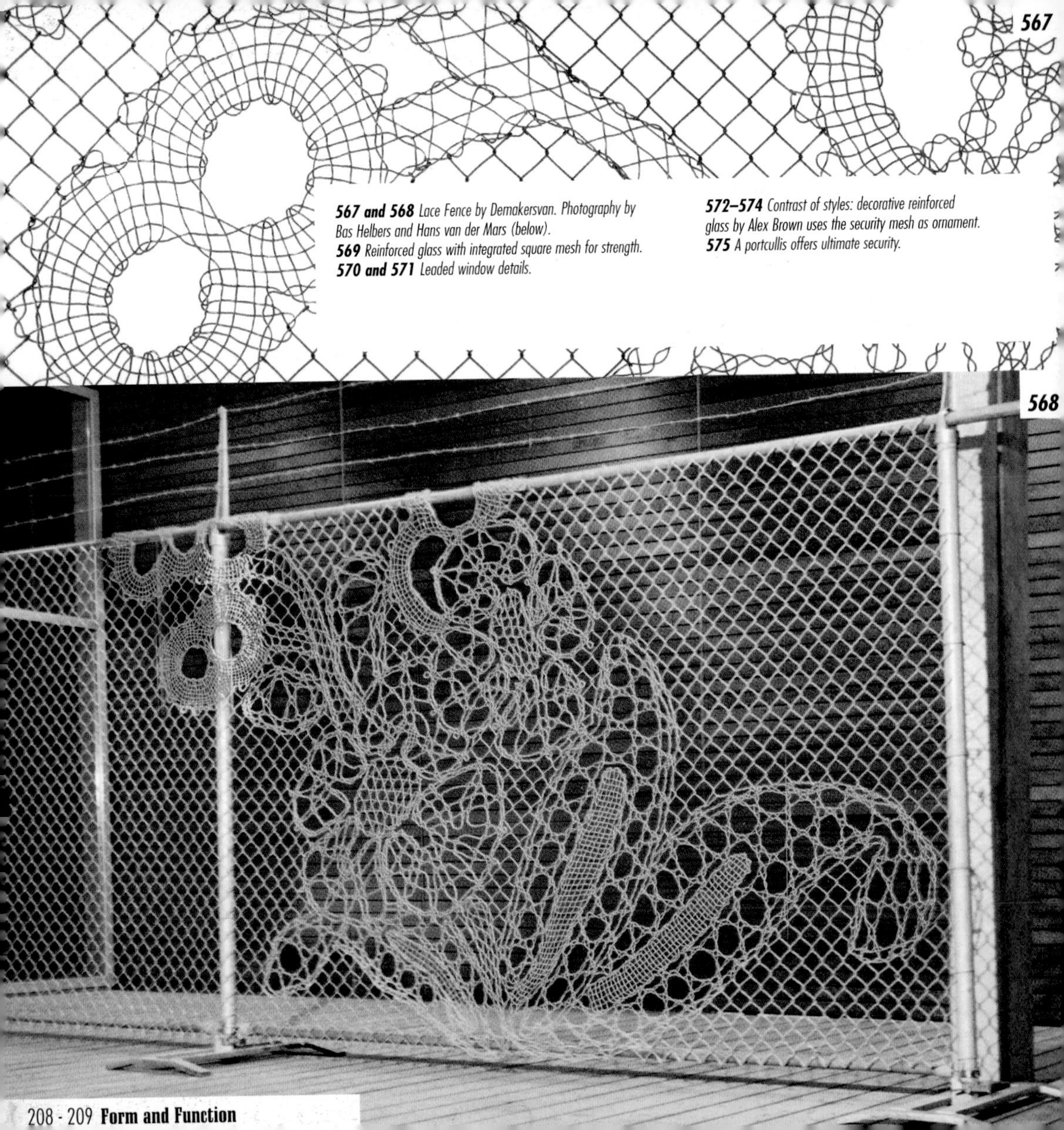

567

568

567 and 568 *Lace Fence by Demakersvan. Photography by Bas Helbers and Hans van der Mars (below).*
569 *Reinforced glass with integrated square mesh for strength.*
570 and 571 *Leaded window details.*
572–574 *Contrast of styles: decorative reinforced glass by Alex Brown uses the security mesh as ornament.*
575 *A portcullis offers ultimate security.*

569
570
571
572
573
574
575

→ The use of metal in domestic design owes much to the modernist fascination with industrial materials and manufacturing processes. The Bertoia chair has become a design classic. Its mesh construction lends it technical precision, yet its sculpted form has a lightness that transcends interior design trends. Val Bertoia says of his father's work: "The Bertoia Chair of the 1950s was designed by a sculptor, not a furniture designer. The chairs Harry designed were definitely sculptures that contained the human (physical) body comfortably above the floor. The chair, then, is a 3D line sculpture."

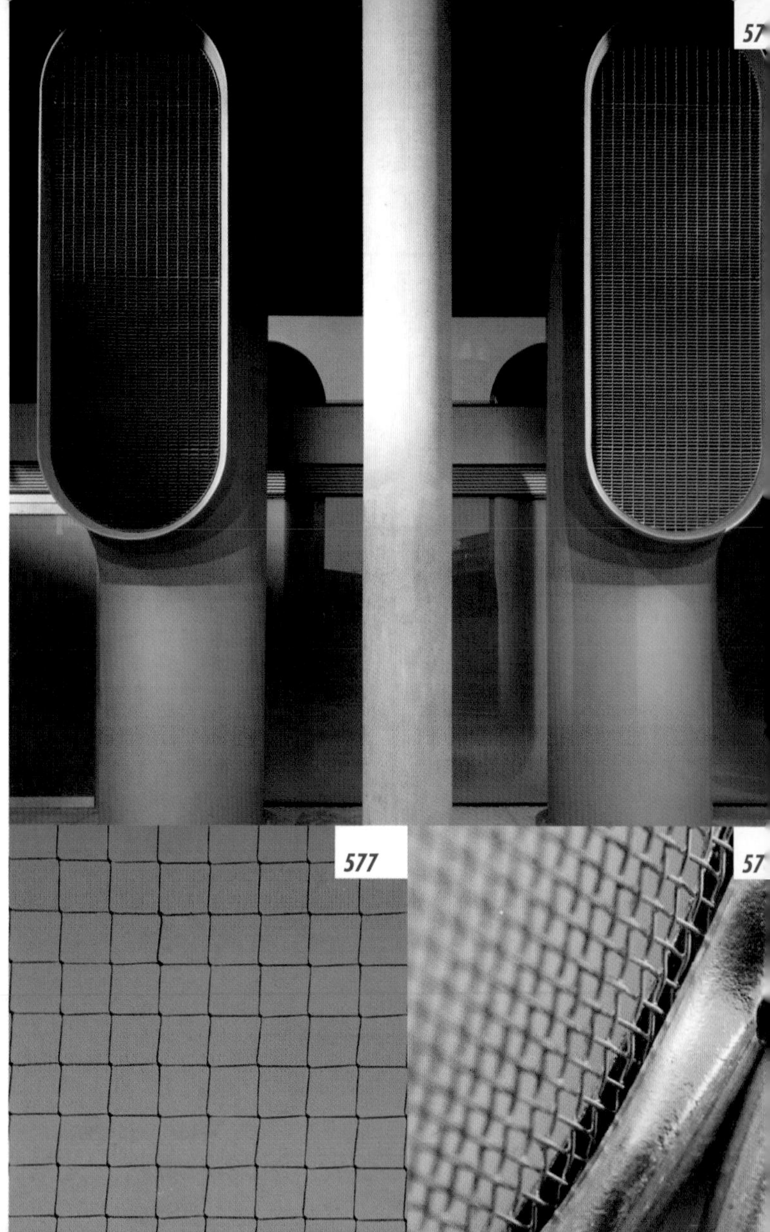

576 *Funnels use mesh to keep out unwanted things while allowing the free flow of air. Photographed by Robin Hayes.*
577 *A mesh fence.*
578 *Guess the object—it's a sieve.*
579 *Harry Bertoia's Diamond Chair from Knoll International.*

580 *Bertoia asymmetric chaise from Knoll International.*
581 *Bertoia colored side chairs from Knoll International.*

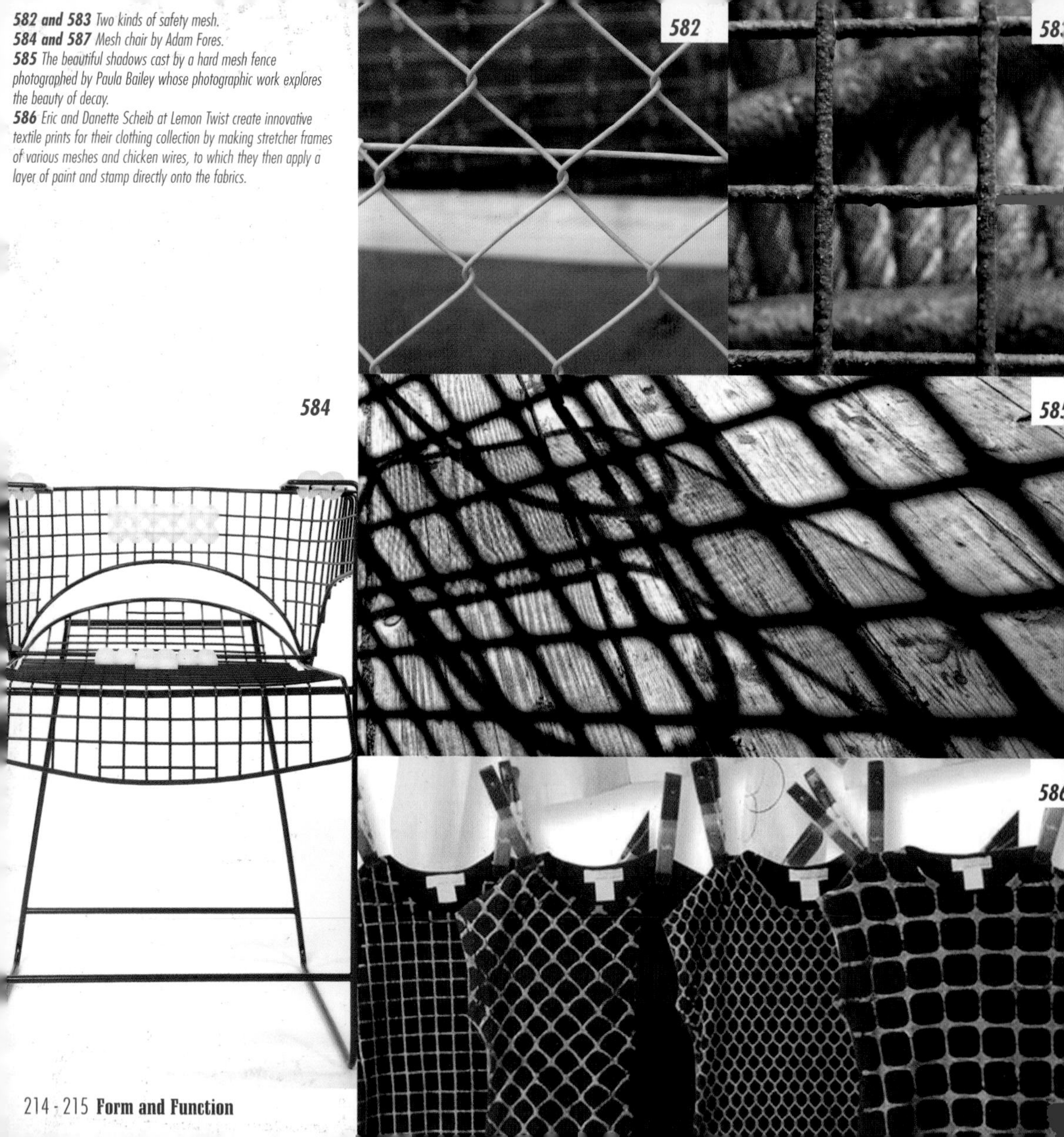

582 and 583 *Two kinds of safety mesh.*
584 and 587 *Mesh chair by Adam Fores.*
585 *The beautiful shadows cast by a hard mesh fence photographed by Paula Bailey whose photographic work explores the beauty of decay.*
586 *Eric and Danette Scheib at Lemon Twist create innovative textile prints for their clothing collection by making stretcher frames of various meshes and chicken wires, to which they then apply a layer of paint and stamp directly onto the fabrics.*

582

583

584

585

586

Weaves

A fabric's thread count is measured as the number of horizontal and vertical threads in one square inch. While most textiles derive their quality through fine yarns and a high thread count, some get their character from a deliberately open weave. Hessian, for instance, has an earthy roughness that feels honest and natural. Tweed is a handwoven twill made from best quality wool with a richly rustic appeal. US artist Cat Chow produces sculptural garments from handwoven tape measures that offer a checkerboard effect. The basic principle of interlacing strips to create a solid sheet of material can also be applied to wool, wicker, and wood. Traditional basket weaving employs techniques such as plaiting, coiling, and twining in materials that include grasses, rushes, reed, cane, and willow. Basketware was popular until the 1970s when its homespun charm fell out of favor; now it is enjoying a renaissance in the collections of US designer Jonathan Adler, applied as a graphic print to a range of home accessories.

588 *Traditional pie decorated with a lattice pastry top.*
589 *An industrial weave seen here by photographer Paula Bailey.*
590 *New Balance 576 in Harris Tweed, courtesy of Hikmet Sugoer at Solebox.*
591 *The iconic Harris Tweed stamp, featuring their trademark orb and scepter.*
592 *Woven printed duvet set in brown by Jonathan Adler.*

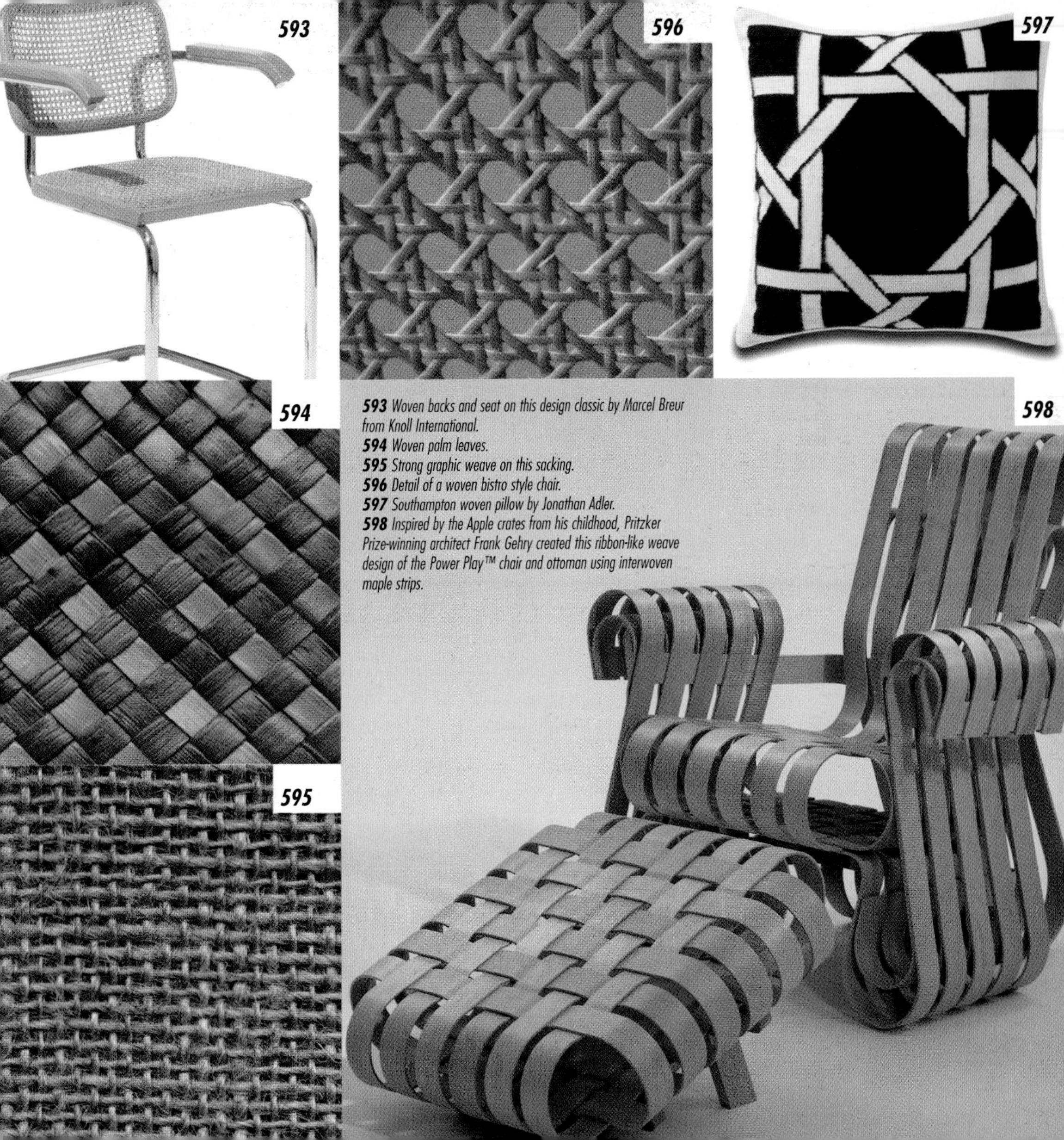

593 Woven backs and seat on this design classic by Marcel Breur from Knoll International.
594 Woven palm leaves.
595 Strong graphic weave on this sacking.
596 Detail of a woven bistro style chair.
597 Southampton woven pillow by Jonathan Adler.
598 Inspired by the Apple crates from his childhood, Pritzker Prize-winning architect Frank Gehry created this ribbon-like weave design of the Power Play™ chair and ottoman using interwoven maple strips.

COMBINATIONS OF LINES IN TWENTY FOUR COLOURS, FOUR DIRECTIONS AND THREE WEIGHTS USING LETRASET TRIA SHONEN-MANGA PENS 2006 TO LEWITT

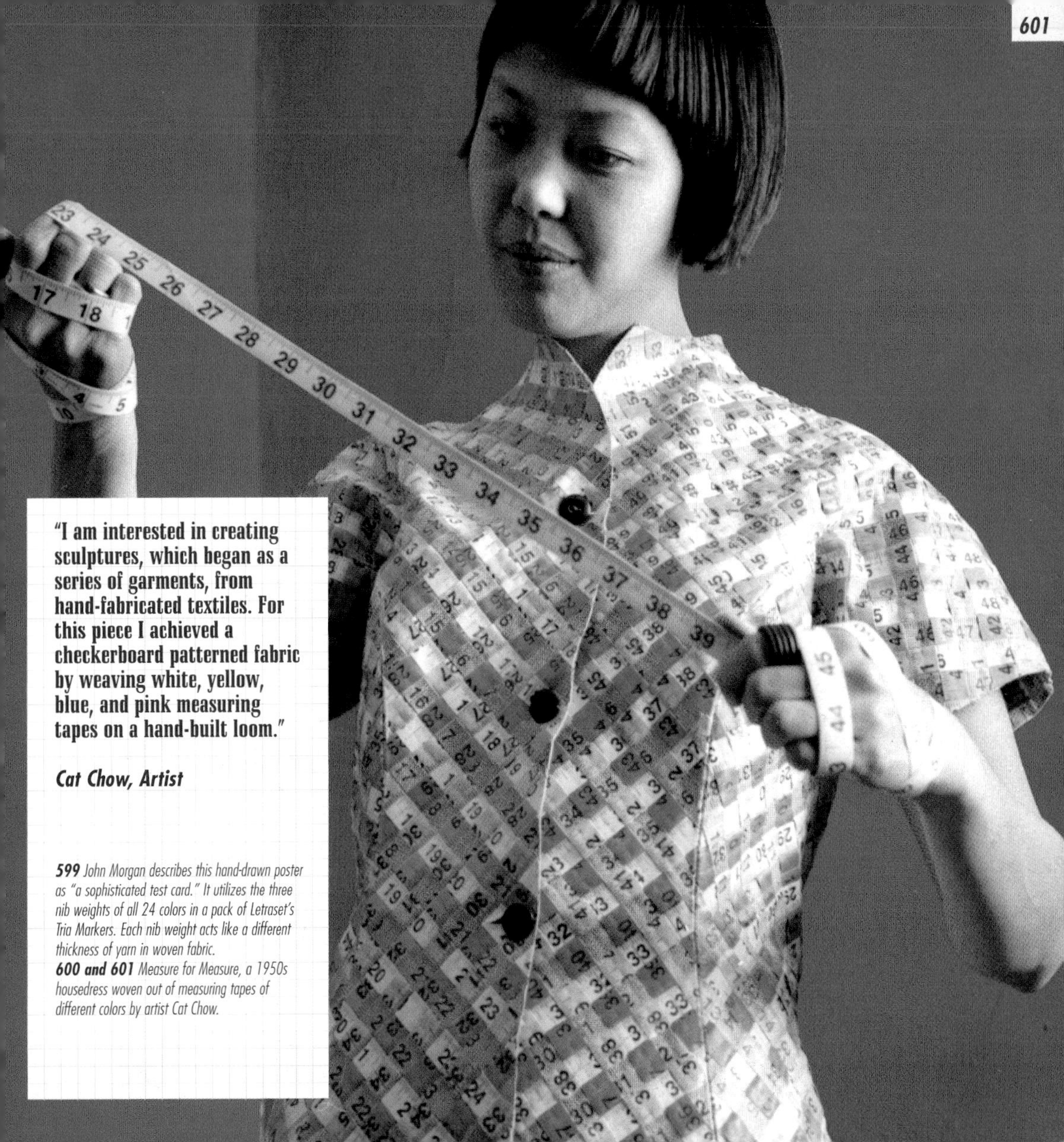

"I am interested in creating sculptures, which began as a series of garments, from hand-fabricated textiles. For this piece I achieved a checkerboard patterned fabric by weaving white, yellow, blue, and pink measuring tapes on a hand-built loom."

Cat Chow, Artist

599 *John Morgan describes this hand-drawn poster as "a sophisticated test card." It utilizes the three nib weights of all 24 colors in a pack of Letraset's Tria Markers. Each nib weight acts like a different thickness of yarn in woven fabric.*
600 and 601 *Measure for Measure, a 1950s housedress woven out of measuring tapes of different colors by artist Cat Chow.*

Patchwork and Quilts

On 12 May 2007, UK campaigners marched to Westminster with a petition for WaterAid's End Water Poverty campaign. The petition was like none other—a 250 meter (c. 820ft) river knitted by WaterAid campaigners from across the world in support of the billions worldwide who don't have safe water to drink, or access to toilets. The knitted river represents a novel way to bring the campaign to life and taps into the tradition of communal quilting. Its 100,000 individual blue squares were assembled by people brought together by a common cause, just as American Abolitionists united in the fight to end slavery would make quilts incorporating antislavery poems and messages.

Agricultural landscapes are often described as a "patchwork of fields" because the different crops and grasses of adjoining fields juxtapose to create an effect like a traditional quilt. Patchwork and quilting is tessellation in fabric. Like other forms of tiling, any shape can be used, but squares make the process easier. More regular to work with, squares create less wastage for a craft that is essentially a form of recycling. →

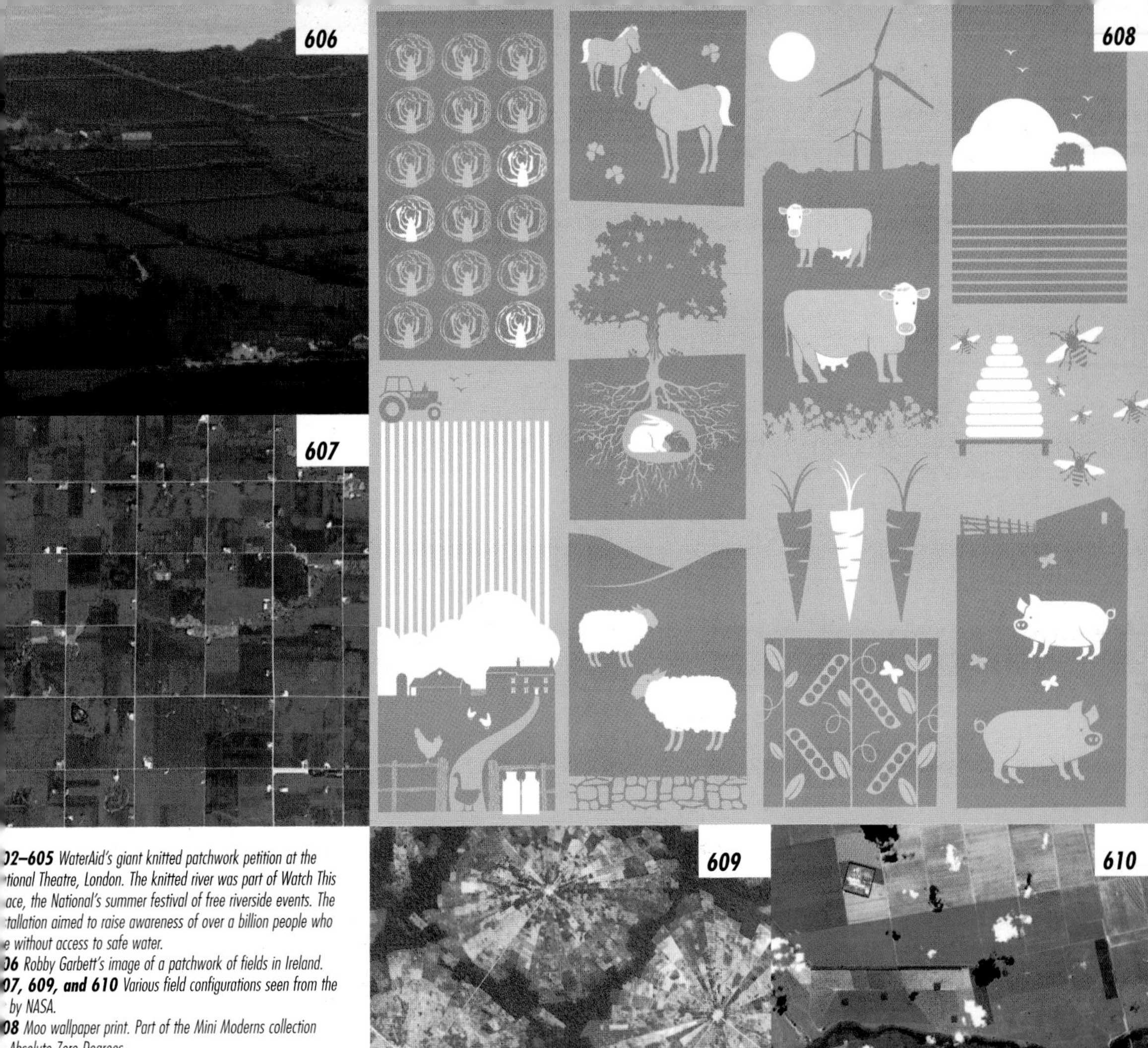

)2–605 WaterAid's giant knitted patchwork petition at the
'tional Theatre, London. The knitted river was part of Watch This
ace, the National's summer festival of free riverside events. The
tallation aimed to raise awareness of over a billion people who
e without access to safe water.
)6 Robby Garbett's image of a patchwork of fields in Ireland.
)7, 609, and 610 Various field configurations seen from the
' by NASA.
)8 Moo wallpaper print. Part of the Mini Moderns collection
Absolute Zero Degrees.

611

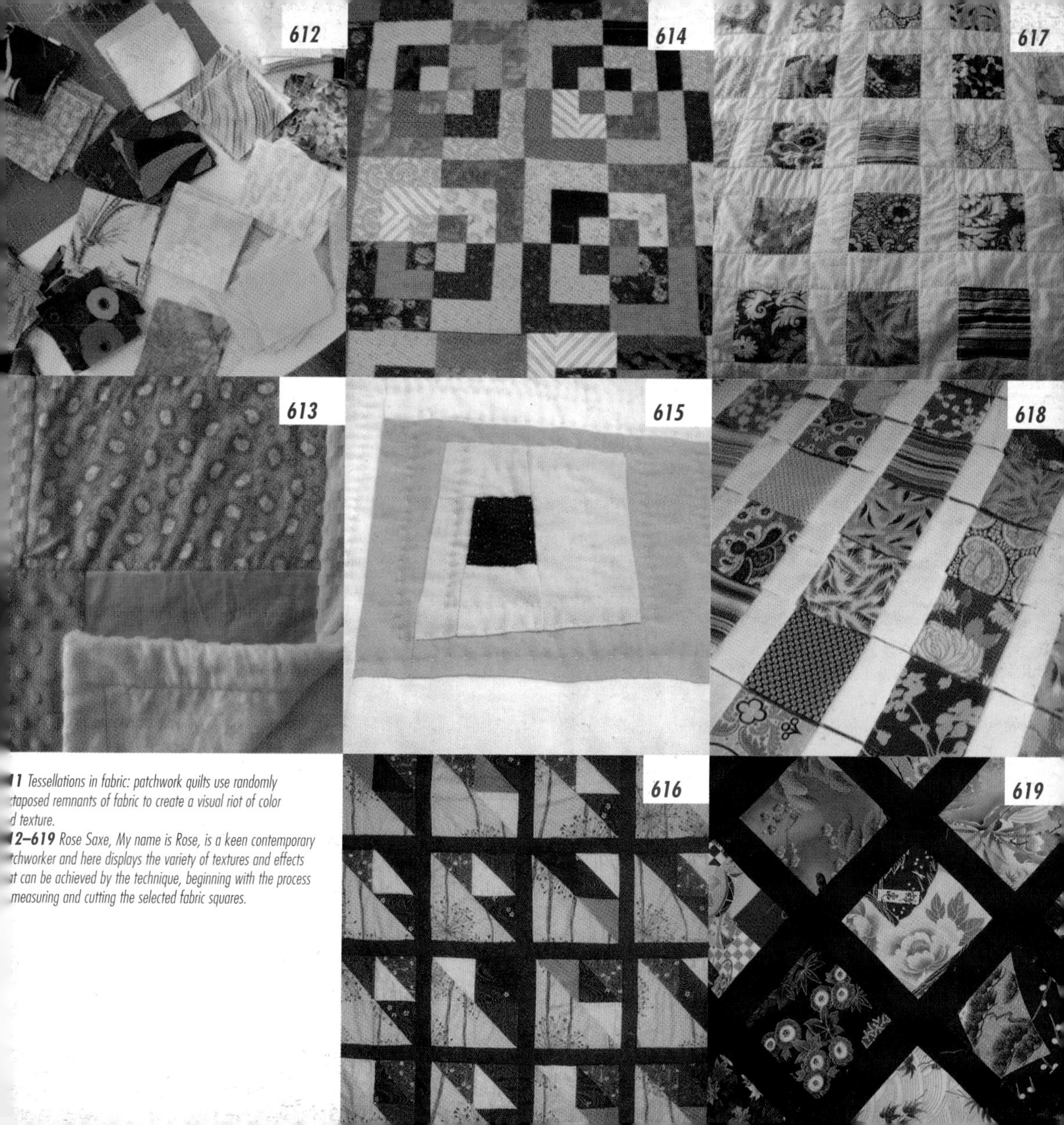

11 Tessellations in fabric: patchwork quilts use randomly *taposed remnants of fabric to create a visual riot of color* *d texture.*

12–619 Rose Saxe, My name is Rose, is a keen contemporary *tchworker and here displays the variety of textures and effects* *at can be achieved by the technique, beginning with the process* *measuring and cutting the selected fabric squares.*

→ When applied to materials other than textiles, quilting takes on a diverse range of appearances and effects. Buttoned and paneled squares of leather give a sleek, yet luxurious look to furniture by mid-20th century legends Mies Van Der Rohe and Florence Knoll. Technical fabrics can benefit from the quilted treatment too, with tiny stamped dots used to seal the pockets in place of traditional stitching.

Quilting techniques can lend a soft appearance to hard materials. American street food stalls are often made from a kind of quilted pressed steel that makes the metallic surface surprisingly tactile, while individual squares of wood yield to give a quilted appearance and function, turning Stephen Reed's table into a seating bench.

620

621

622

620 The Florence Knoll bench, designed in 1954, from Knoll International.
621 and 622 Square paneled leather upholstery features on both the Florence Knoll chair and the Barcelona chair by Ludwig Mies van der Rohe, both available from Knoll International.
623 Stamped quilted fabric.
624 The slates on this Belgian house give a quilted look to the structure.
625 This New York fast-food counter—turned into a plant display—used its quilting to retain heat and insulate the hot plate.
626 Stephen Reed created this Soft Spot table with a quilted, flexible wood cushion, perfect for guests who perch on the end of your coffee table. The wood tiles are connected by elastic cords held in tension, creating a flat tabletop that bows to provide cushioned seating.

Frames and Compartments

The suitability of squares and rectangles for framing and compartmentalizing comes down to the ordering function of the square—it literally boxes something in. Many common phrases evoke the restrictive, constraining properties of the square: "you've been framed," "don't box yourself in,"and "try to think outside the box." But compartments have positive applications and connotations too. Storage systems and desk tidies work on a similar principle—employing squares and rectangles to order disparate objects and make them easily locatable. When merchandising, displaying groups of items within compartments helps to create coherent stories based on color, shape, or function.

Framing bestows merit or value on an image, helping to focus attention on the subject matter, whether it's a gilt-framed old master or a window positioned to frame a beautiful view. A white border can offer "breathing space" that gives pace to a busy visual composition. The distinctive frame of a Polaroid print is often used graphically to suggest capturing a moment in time.

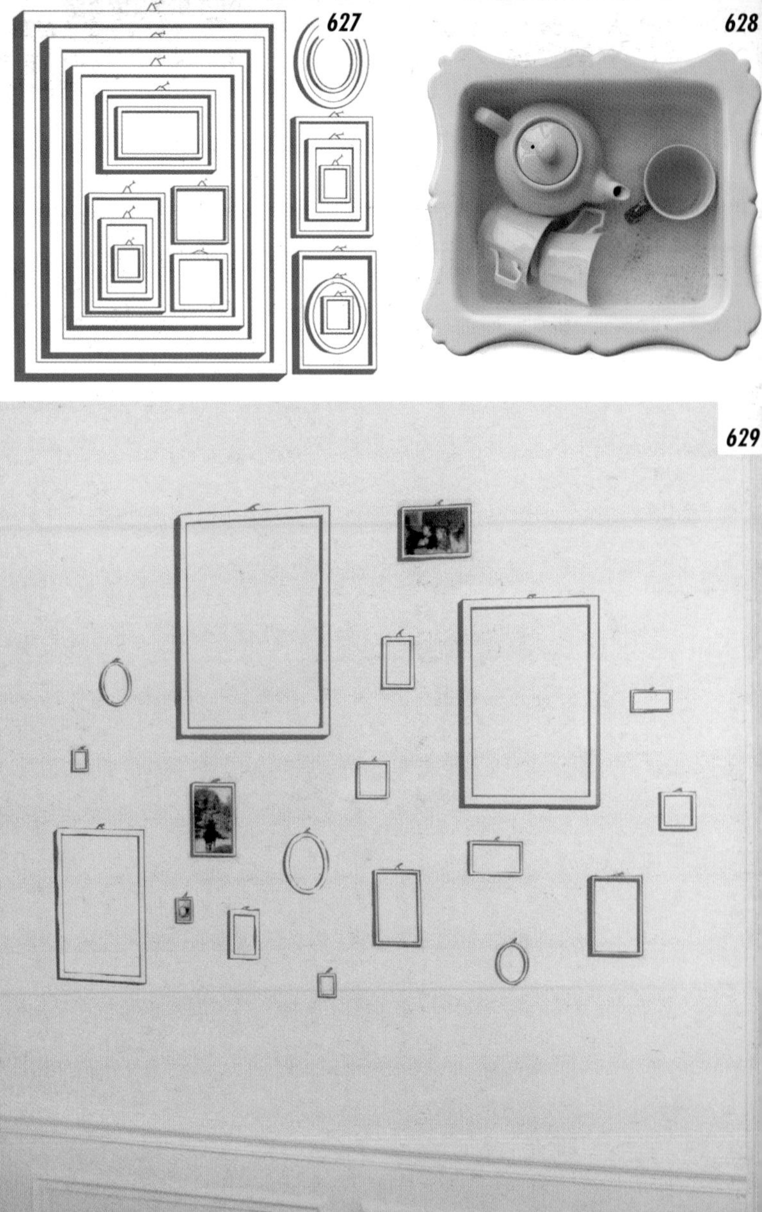
627

628

629

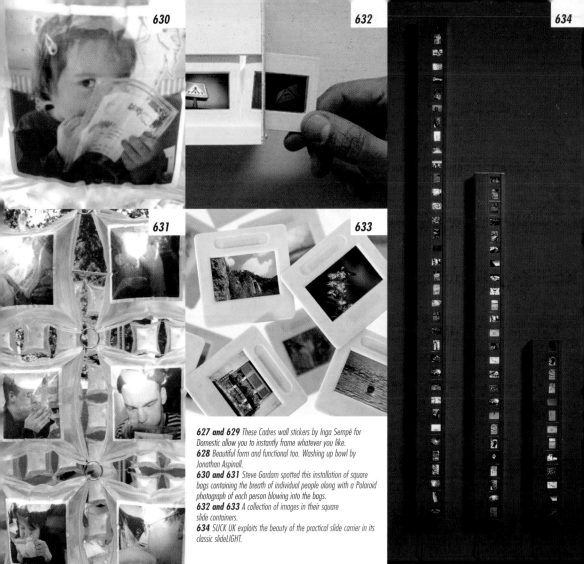

630

631

632

633

634

627 and 629 *These Cadres wall stickers by Inga Sempé for Domestic allow you to instantly frame whatever you like.*
628 *Beautiful form and functional too. Washing up bowl by Jonathan Aspinall.*
630 and 631 *Steve Gardam spotted this installation of square bags containing the breath of individual people along with a Polaroid photograph of each person blowing into the bags.*
632 and 633 *A collection of images in their square slide containers.*
634 *SUCK UK exploits the beauty of the practical slide carrier in its classic slideLIGHT.*

635
Mercedes-Benz
636
637
MON
TUE
WED
THU
638
639

643

635 *Compartments of extreme scale. The architecture of this Mercedes-Benz showroom in Munich creates a framework within which to showcase the cars. Captured by Robin Hayes.*
636 *Golden Time Cupboard by Lola Lely.*
637 *A pill tray helps to regulate dosage.*
638 and 639 *Attractive and practical wine storage solutions.*
640 *A desk tidy.*
641 *Lifestyle stores group coordinating items to create a coherent story that the consumer can buy into.*
642 and 643 *Modular shelving by designer Massimo Meta allows the user to create functional shelves and usable negative space depending on the orientation and stacking of the units. Additional metal sheet boxes stabilize the structure and offer extra storage.*

Windows and Glass Blocks

Advanced building technologies and materials afford 21st-century architecture a pared down aesthetic with minimal exterior ornamentation. The construction technique used on most large-scale commercial buildings means that exterior walls are free of any load-bearing function, allowing them to exist simply as a curtain of glass and steel.

Thus, the most common pattern that can be seen in the modern built environment is the grid: a framework of steel encasing glass panels spanning a building's facade, maximizing natural light inside the building, and reflecting the modernist principle of "form follows function." →

644 *Alsop Architects' Palestra, London, photographed by Robin Hayes.*
645–651 *A collection of modern facades demonstrating the curtain of glass achievable by modern building techniques.*

645
646
650
647
648
651
649

→ Before technology allowed glass to be suspended within such a simple framework, the glass block was a commonly used construction material as it offered sturdy support, yet maximized natural light. Machine production made glass blocks popular in the 1930s. Sometimes textured or frosted, they are often incorporated as a dramatic feature stairwell of an art deco apartment block, or found in commercial applications such as factories or stadiums.

Mid-20th century buildings would often include panels of relief decorated concrete or simple blocks of color to break up the glass exterior. Geometric configurations of colored glass panels can also offer a facade an element of graphic pattern, creating visual interest without compromising the building's design integrity.

652 *Grids of glass and relief concrete panels feature on this mid-20th century building—perhaps a college. Its signage, depicting the word "Graphical," gives it maximum designer appeal.*
653 *Windows used as a strong graphic device on the HQ building for Seven Network in Melbourne's docklands area.*
654 *Graphic glass window blocks seen in Sheffield.*
655–659 *Glass blocks give a modernist edge to a building.*

654
657
658
655
656
659

Cubes

As the square is to the power of two, so the cube represents the power of three. Squares indicate 2D area, cubes 3D volume. Cubes have a solid appearance and can fulfill several functions. A simple wooden block can be used as a table or stool; blocks of concrete are sturdy enough to act as tidal defense.

The cube is unique among the Platonic solids for having faces with an even number of sides and being able to tile space regularly. When rotated to view three faces of equal area, the functional cube loses its "boxiness" and the straight sides become dynamic diagonals. This isometric representation offers designers a simple way of representing 3D objects on the 2D page. Ric Bell's Triso is a conceptual typeface based on isometric grids and cubes. The letterforms are created out of the edges of a single cube on an isometric grid. The result is a modular typeface that makes up a geometric pattern when used in sentence format.

660

660 *Ric Bell's Three Cubed is a typographic interpretation of a space 3m high, 3m wide, and 3m long.*
661 *Sea cubes, photographed in France by Robin Hayes.*
662 *Robert L. Segal captured this vivid green block on the outskirts of Chicago.*
663 *The Bloq Solid Stool/Table by Bloq makes a feature of the cutoff corner—a reference to the statement "chip off the old block," also demonstrated on the company's branding.*

"We use clean lines and solid shapes to produce precisely detailed, minimalist, and elegant forms that have a host of uses, from functional to social. When creating a new product or range, I look at the tasks involved before finding a fresh and clever design solution. I take a corner off every product to create a triangle on the corner—a physical manifestation of the saying 'a chip off the old block' (or Bloq) which my dad used in reference to me."

Paul Johnson
Bloq

664

664 Ric Bell's Triso typeface—the sentence reads: "the quick brown fox jumps over the lazy dog," demonstrating every letter in this isometric-inspired font.
665 Learning tools that teach volume through cubes.
666 and 667 Cubic houses seen in Rotterdam.

668 and 669 The Cardboard Network by Kate Pemberton comprises a series of units linked together via electrical cables that also power the work. A selection of artists were invited to "remix" a unit, including Pamina Stewart, Jacob Masters, Alex Johnson, and Tom Ranahan.

Street Grids and Public Squares

An aerial shot of any modern city demonstrates how the street grid represents the triumph of human civilization over the earth's organic form. The system of laying out towns and cities according to a grid pattern dates back as far as 2600 BC, with settlements in India, Pakistan, and Egypt built using blocks laid along north/south and east/west axes. The UK new town of Milton Keynes, built in 1967, employed a famously rigid grid of roads set out 1km apart. Critics use this as evidence of a built environment lacking soul. The benefits and drawbacks of the grid are clearly held in fine balance: logic versus over-regimentation.

Every visitor to Manhattan feels the benefits of a regular street grid, at least above 14th Street. From 1811, this area of New York was developed with avenues running north/south and streets running east/west, providing the most efficient means of developing the land. Uptown, any visitor can navigate by means of the grid; downtown, such logic goes out the window. Some would say this reflects the differing attitudes of the inhabitants of these two distinct halves of the city. →

***670** The street grids of downtown San Francisco—seen from above by NASA.*
***671** Universal Everything created this city scape for the Universal Everything exhibition at Maxalot Gallery, Barcelona in November 2005.*

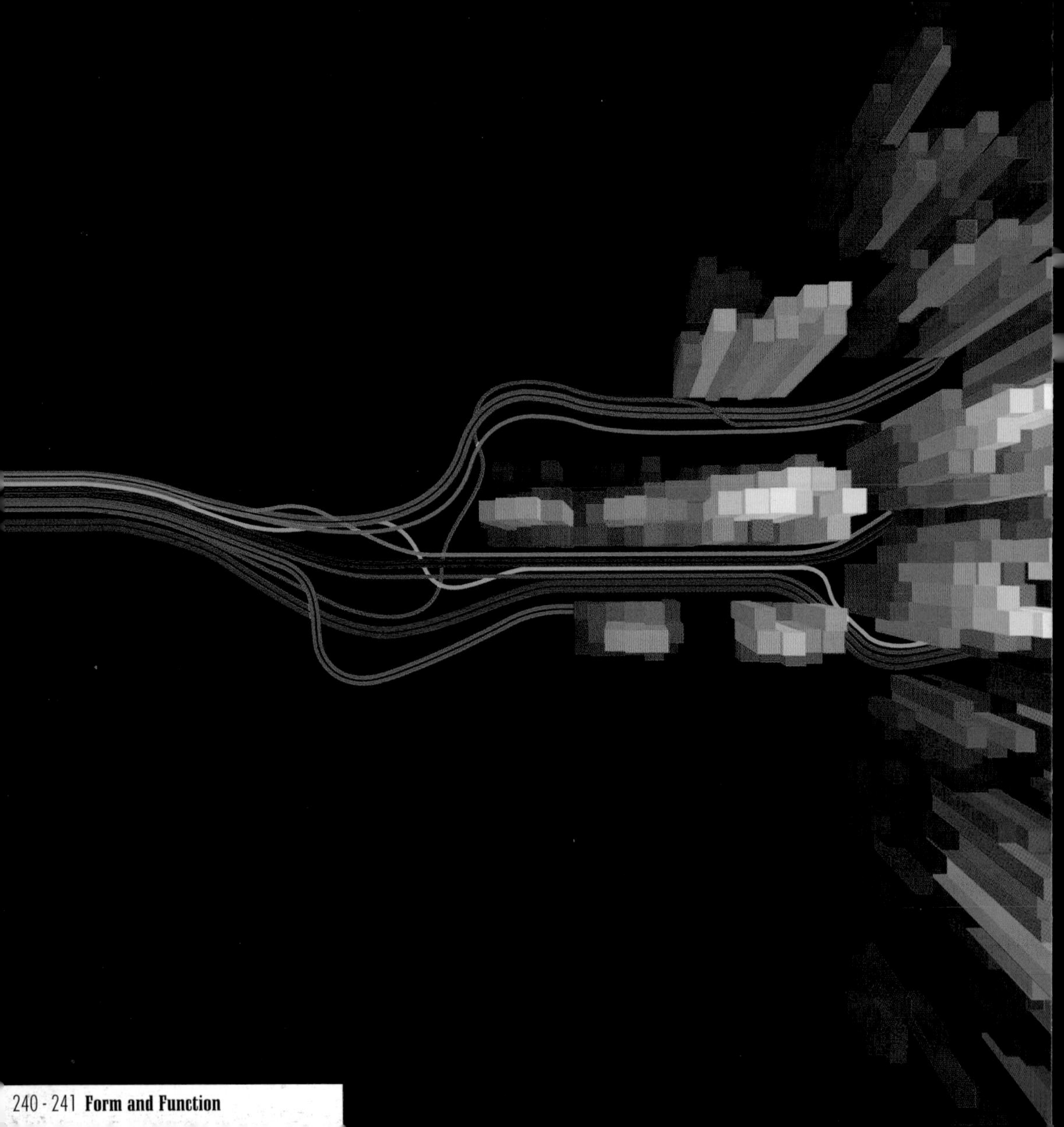

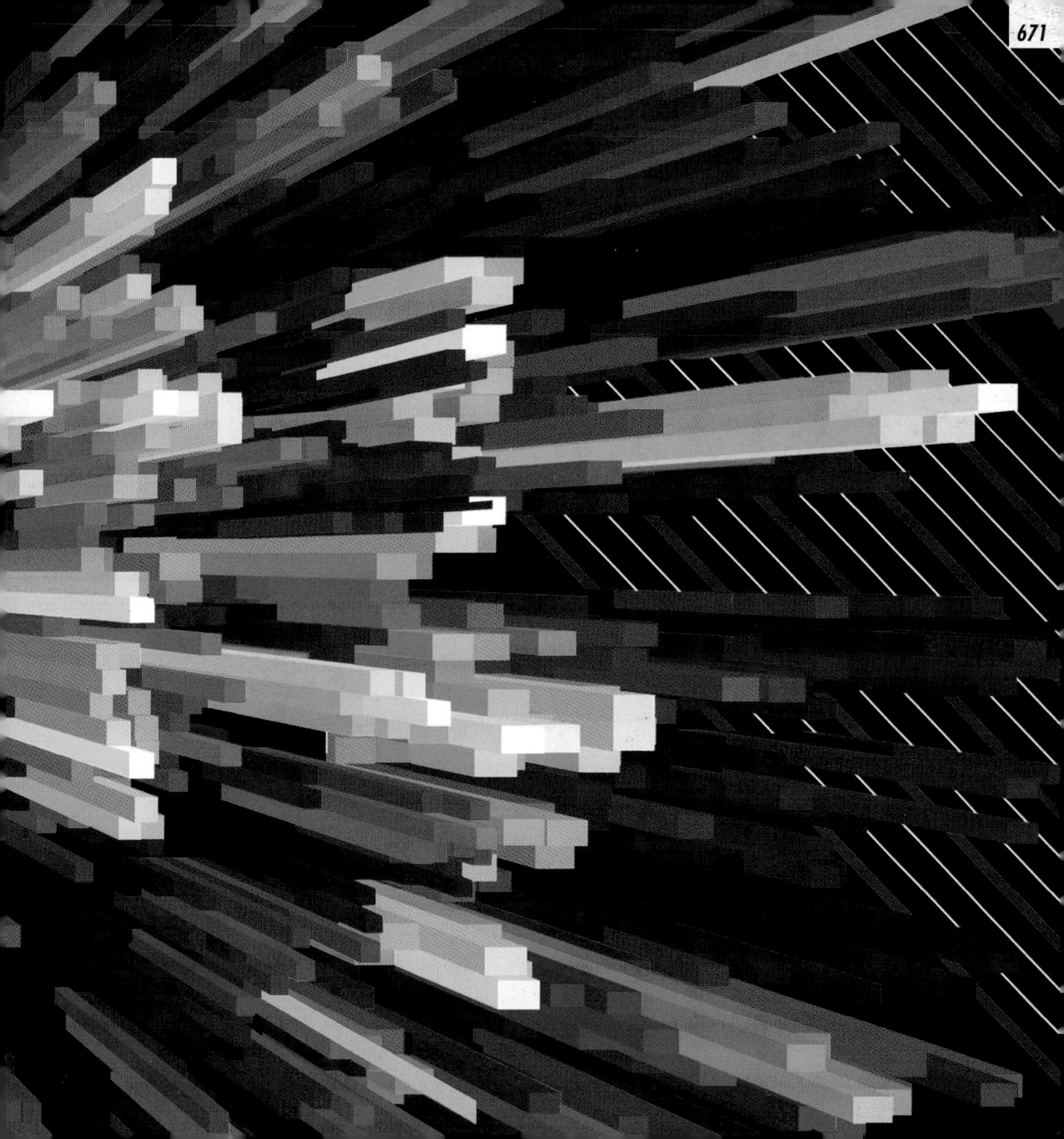

→ The grid has created a language for New Yorkers—"drop me at 23rd and 5th"—and a visual identity too. Featuring a grid within the Big Apple, Lance Wyman's identity for the NYC Block Associations could represent no other city.

The forum was the commercial and judicial heart of every Roman city. Today, plazas, piazzas, and town squares continue to feature in the modern built environment—symbols of civic pride and community spirit, offering public recreational space in our cities and towns.

67

672 *NYC Block Associations identity by Lance Wyman.*
673 *NASA's aerial view of Barcelona.*
674 *A street plan of Key West.*
675 *Manhattan street plan.*
676 and 679 *Two views of Chicago: one taken from the air by Tony Webster, the other, taken by Robert L. Segal, is a sidewalk diagram which celebrates Chicago's street grid system.*
677 *A promotional poster seen on the NY subway that uses the street grid of Manhattan as a graphic device.*
678 *The unmistakable footprint of the New York Twin Towers is used on this commemorative Tribute WTC 9/11 keychain designed by Lance Wyman and Peter Arnell.*

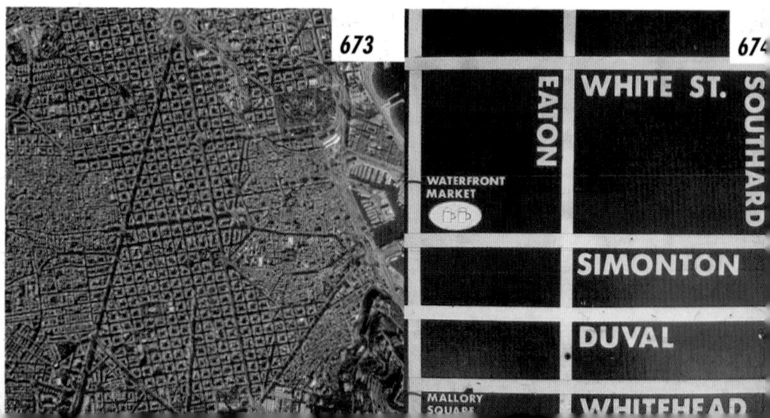

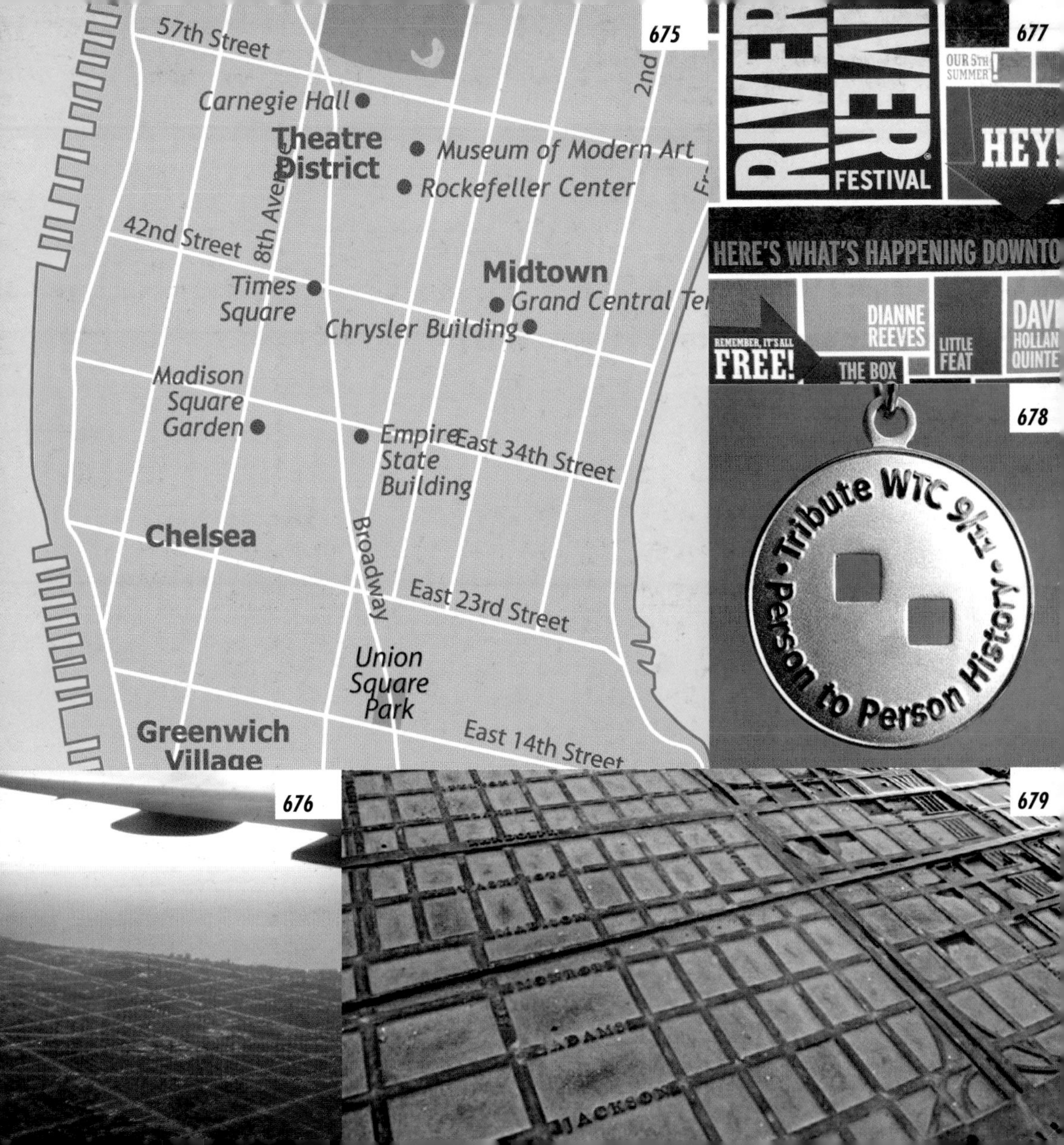
675
57th Street
Carnegie Hall
Theatre District
Museum of Modern Art
Rockefeller Center
2nd
8th Avenue
42nd Street
Midtown
Times Square
Grand Central Ter
Chrysler Building
Madison Square Garden
Empire State Building
East 34th Street
Chelsea
Broadway
East 23rd Street
Union Square Park
Greenwich Village
East 14th Street
676
677
RIVER TO RIVER FESTIVAL
OUR 5TH SUMMER!
HEY!
HERE'S WHAT'S HAPPENING DOWNTO
REMEMBER, IT'S ALL FREE!
DIANNE REEVES
LITTLE FEAT
DAVE HOLLAN QUINTE
THE BOX
678
Tribute WTC 9/11
Person to Person History
679
MADISON
MONROE
ADAMS
JACKSON

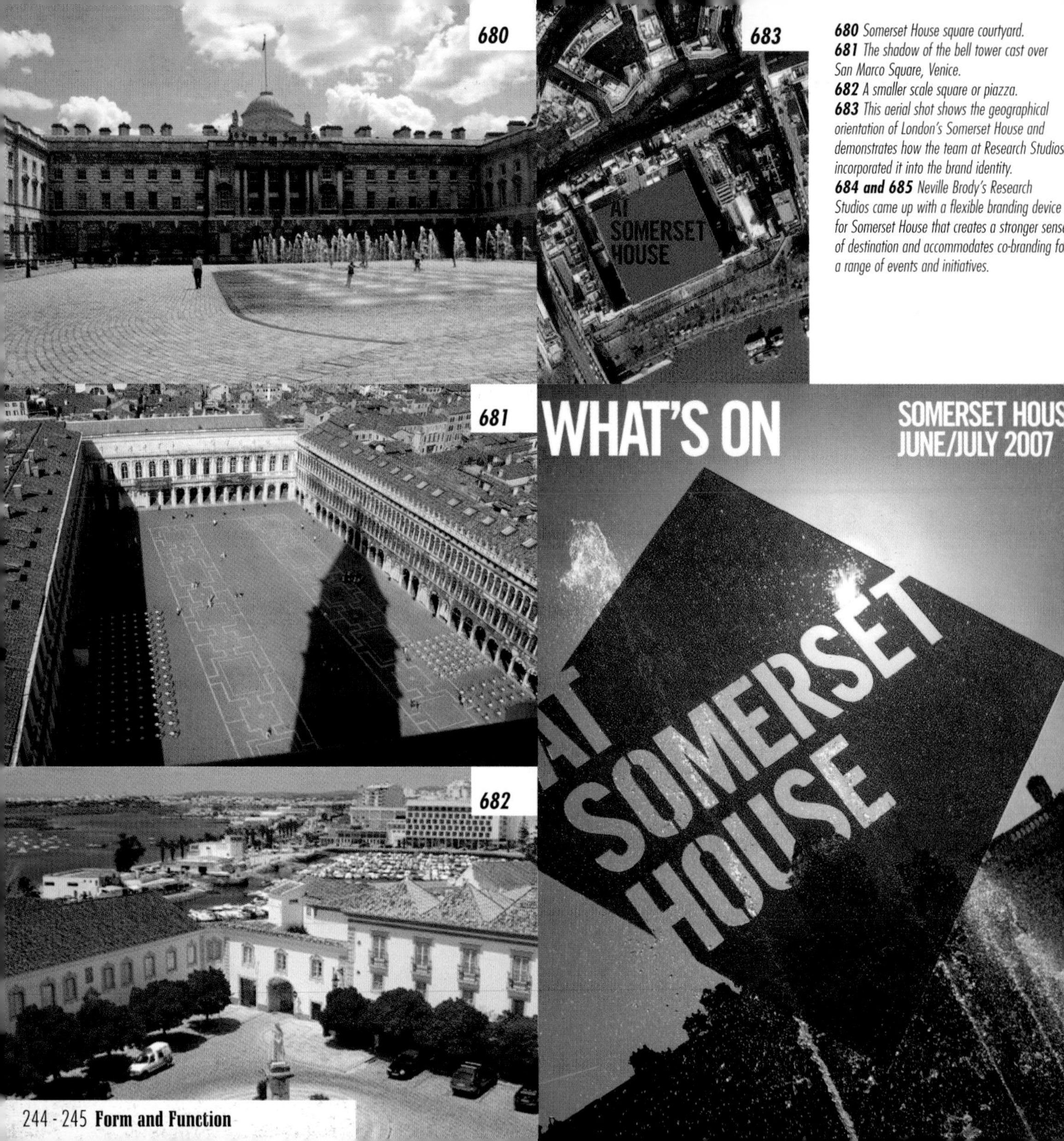

680 *Somerset House square courtyard.*
681 *The shadow of the bell tower cast over San Marco Square, Venice.*
682 *A smaller scale square or piazza.*
683 *This aerial shot shows the geographical orientation of London's Somerset House and demonstrates how the team at Research Studios incorporated it into the brand identity.*
684 and 685 *Neville Brody's Research Studios came up with a flexible branding device for Somerset House that creates a stronger sense of destination and accommodates co-branding for a range of events and initiatives.*

684

"Somerset House is a number of things; it is a building, a public space, a venue for public events, and a home to galleries and restaurants. The verbal identity aimed to solve this through the use of the phrase 'At Somerset House,' allowing the building to be branded in conjunction with other parties."

Neville Brody, Research Studios

"Using the topographic view of the building, the idea of a tilted square became the iconic visual element for the brand. It resembles a portal and the building itself set at a 24-degree angle from the north-south axis."

Nick Hard, Research Studios

685

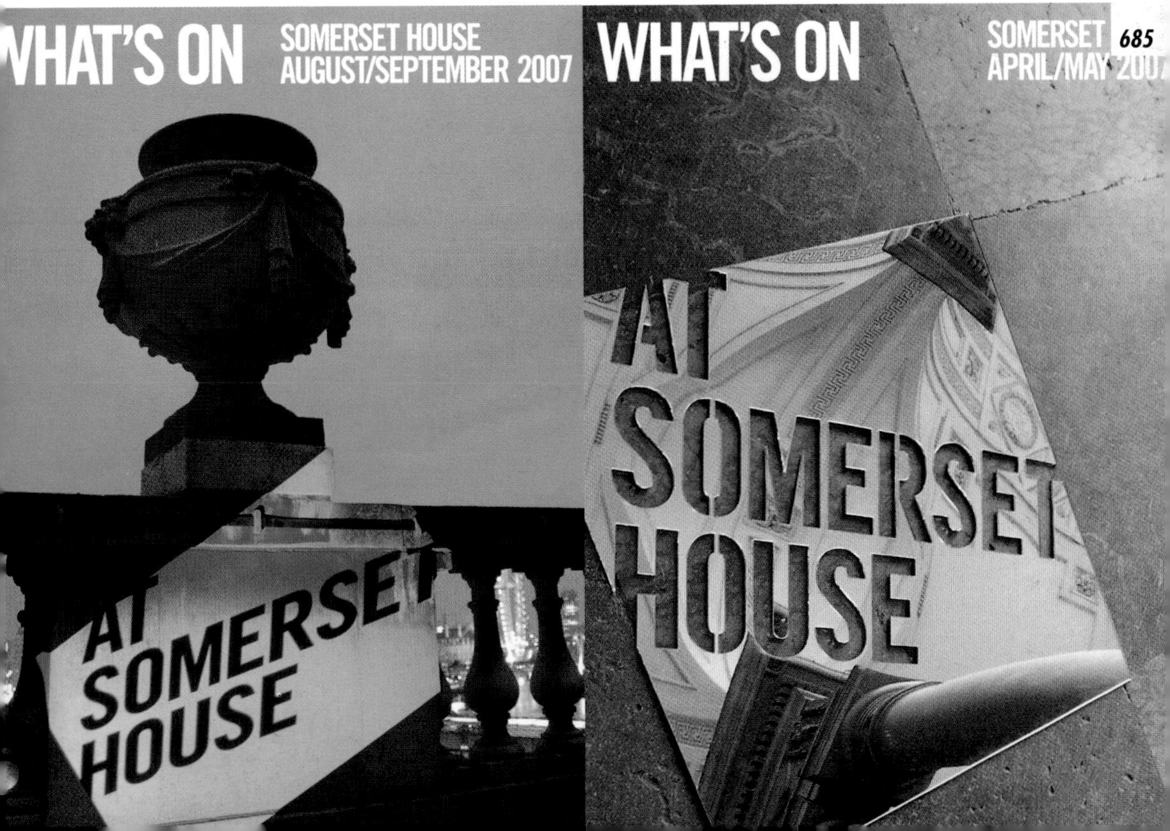

WHAT'S ON SOMERSET HOUSE AUGUST/SEPTEMBER 2007

AT SOMERSET HOUSE

WHAT'S ON SOMERSET APRIL/MAY 200

AT SOMERSET HOUSE

686

687

688

686–688 *Interior of Museo de Arte Contemporaneo, Monterrey.*
689 *Branding for Museo de Arte Contemporaneo by Lance Wyman Ltd. The "O" of the acronym "MARCO" (which means "frame" in Spanish) was squared to reflect the central patio of the museum's iconic building, designed by architect Ricardo Legorreta.*

marco

Appendix

Index
Contributors
Photography Credits
Acknowledgments

Index

A

2 Tone 98, 105
Absolute Zero Degrees 82–83, 148, 221
Adler, Jonathan 99, 100, 216–17
Alba 78–79
Albers, Josef 6–7, 98
Alsop Architects 230
architecture 22, 66, 67, 74, 87, 98–99, 108–11, 114–25, 190, 228, 230–33, 237
Argyle check 10–11, 16–17
art deco 230
Art Meets Matter 148–49, 152
Art Nouveau 202–3
Arts and Crafts movement 66–67, 108–11
ATADesigns 202
Atelier LaDurance 22–23
automotive design 66, 106–7

B

Bailey, Paula 214
Banksy 54–55
basket weaving 216–17
Bauhaus 118–21
beds 145, 146
Bell, Ric 90, 178, 182–83, 234, 236–37
Berlin Cameron Partners 26–27
Bertoia chairs 210–13
bespoke tartans 40–41, 42
Beyond the Valley 70
Bierut, Michael 81
Big Active 186–87
Blake, Scott 138
Bloomberg 76–77
Bloq 84–85, 96, 129, 142–44, 235
bondage trousers 34, 42–45
book covers 11, 25
brand identity 34, 48–49
Breuer, Marcel 118–19, 217
Broadhead, Hannah 174–75, 185
Brody, Neville 245
Browers, Michael 202
Brown, Alex 207, 209
building blocks 66, 94–97
Bullus, Anna 173, 174
Burberry Check 10–13

C

camouflage 166–69, 171
Campbell, Alan 50–53, 110–11, 196–97
chairs 85, 100–101, 119, 172–73, 190–91, 211–15, 217, 224–25
Chanter, Sarah 154–55
checkerboards 72, 74, 104–5, 111, 202–3, 216, 218–19
checkered flags 66, 106–7
checks 6, 8–54
chess 72, 74
The Chicken Kid 129, 172
Chow, Cat 216, 218–19
Clay, Emily 18–19
coats of arms 46–47, 62
Commedia dell'Arte 34–35, 56–57
compartments 70, 96, 142–43, 226–29
Cordon, Eva 91
cover art 11, 25, 78, 100, 186–87
cross-stitch 140–41, 144
crosswords 66, 68–73
cubes 234–37
Cubism 112
Curious 180–81

D

date plaques 34, 50–53
dazzle camouflage 166–69, 171
De Stijl 112–21
Demakersvan 191, 208
diamonds 128–33
Dior house 29
Dipper, Hannah 122
Doane Paper 72–73
draughts 72
DSquared 28, 31
Dunant, Henry 58

E

eBoy 154–55
El Chivo 91
embroidery 140–41, 144

F

Fischer, Bobby 72
fishnets 190, 206
flags 34–35, 46, 58–63, 66
flat-packed products 102–3
floor coverings 20, 82, 144, 171, 175
FLOR 20, 82–83, 171
frames 190, 226–27
Froshaug, Anthony 176

G

games 66–93
Garns, Howard 68
Gehry, Frank 217
gingham 10–11, 22–27
Glasgow School of Art 66–67, 108–11
glass blocks 232–33
Goldfinger, Ernö 120–23
graph paper 72–73, 128–29, 184–87
graphs 128, 176–87
Grid-it! Notepads 178–79
grids 6, 46–47, 66–67, 128, 166–67, 176–87, 190, 230–34, 236–43
Gropius, Walter 120

H

Hard, Nick 245
harlequins 34–35, 56–57
Harris Tweed 190, 216
hazard symbols 129, 130, 132–33
Hemingway Design 142–43, 144
heraldry 34, 46–49, 62
Hermann grid illusion 166–67
hessian 216
Hoover, Chris 66, 112–13
hopscotch 88, 92–93
houndstooth 10–11, 18–21

I

Identica 181
Illera, Jakob 150
Impagination Inc. 84
Inseq Design 128–29, 150–51
intarsia 16
Isaksson, Sandra 96
isometric grids 234, 236–37

J

jigsaw puzzles 82–83
Johnson, Paul 235

K

Kasparov, Garry 72
keyboards 129, 164–65
kilts 22, 35, 37, 40
Knoll International 190, 211–13, 217, 224–25
Knowlton, Ken 69, 129, 147, 164–65, 200
Kreuger, Amanda 66

L

landscapes 220–21
lattices 216
Le Corbusier 67, 118–19, 120
leaded windows 209
learning tools 66, 94–97, 237
Lego 94–95
Lely, Lola 228
Lemon Twist 215
Lianos, Nuggy 125
little bird 115, 129, 172
Ljubicic, Boris 34, 58, 62–63, 74–75, 146
Lo Shu Square 68
Lopez Estudillo, Rosario 45
Loungecore 100
Lyle and Scott 16–17

M

Mackintosh, Charles Rennie 66–67, 108–11
McLaren, Malcolm 42
Magic Squares 68
meshes 191, 204, 207, 210–15
Meta, Massimo 229
Milk, Two Sugars 184–85
milliondollarhomepage.com 134
Milner, Bob 184–85
Minipops 128, 136–37
Mio 20, 101–3, 144
Modernism 6, 66, 108–25, 233
modism 66
modular design 84–85, 96, 229
Mondrian, Piet 66, 112–19
Morgan, John 166–69, 171, 218
mosaics 128, 148–49, 190–201
msk7 70

N

national flags 34–35, 58–63
Necker Cube 172–73, 174
netting 191, 204, 206–7
noughts and crosses 66, 88–89
Novarese, Aldo 98

O

Op Art 6
open weaves 190, 216–19
optical effects 166–75
ORCO 98–99

P

Pallent, Alex 143, 171
panels 224–25
patchwork 190–91, 220–25
Pemberton, Kate 140–41, 144, 158–59, 237
Penny, Stuart 134
Pentagram 78, 80–81
People Will Always Need Plates 122–23
Periodic Table 6, 128, 160–63
piazzas 242, 244–45
Pinch, Russell 78–79
pixels 6, 18, 128–29, 134–59, 198
plaid 10, 28–37
plazas 242, 244–45
police uniforms 34–35, 54–55
Ponti, Gio 108
Pop Art 18
portcullis 209
Pringle 16
punk tartans 34, 42–45
puzzles 66, 68–93

Q

Quad 124–25
quilts 191, 220, 222–23

R

Railfreight 34, 48–49
Red Cross flag 58
Reed, Stephen 76–77, 224–25
reinforced glass 207, 209
Remias, Jennifer 173
Research Studios 244–45
retro design 98–105
Reynolds, Leo 68
Rietveld Schröder House 118–19
road signs 128–33
Robinson, Craig 136
Rockmount Ranch Wear 28
Rothwell, Tom 160, 162
Roundel 48–49, 95, 96
Router, Ben 89
Rubik's Cube® 66, 86–87

S

Saint, Gerard 187
Saint Laurent, Yves 112–13
Saks Fifth Avenue 78, 80–81
Salge, Michael 78, 164–65
Saxe, Rose 223
Scabetti 100
Schleifer, Fritz 120–21
Schock, Aaron 96
Scott, Sir Walter 40
Scrabble 72, 75–77
screen blocks 98–99
screens 21
Sholes, Christopher 164
Sillitoe's Tartan 34–35, 54–55
ska revival 66, 98, 105
Skott, Courtney 21, 144–45
sliding tile puzzles 78
snakes and ladders 66–67, 74
soft furnishing 76–77, 100–101, 158–59, 216
Somerset House 224–25
Space Invaders 128, 148–49, 152–55
Stavro, Astrid 178–79
Stevens, Claire 174
stools 172–73
storage systems 70, 79, 83–85, 96, 142–43
StormHand 138, 171
street grids 238–43
SUCK UK 227
Sudoku 68

T

tables 89, 225
tartans 22, 34–45
Tati 22, 24–25
Tattersall check 10–11, 14–15
tessellation 190, 192, 220, 222–23
Tew, Alex 134
tic-tac-toe 66, 88–89
tiles 129, 175, 190, 198–99, 202–3
Tomlinson, Rory 164
town squares 242, 244–45
Tozzi, Gianni 134
Trellick Tower 122–23
trellis 204–5
Tschaen, Ninon 19
Tschichold, Jan 176
Turner Duckworth 166
tweeds 14–15, 190, 216
typography 90, 98, 176–79, 202–3, 234

U

Universal Everything 238, 240–41

V

van der Rohe, Mies 66, 224
van Doesburg, Theo 112

W

Wade, Beau 152, 154–55
warning signs 128–33
warp/weft 26, 36, 206
Wassily Chair 118–19
weaves 190, 216–19
Weil, Jack A. 28
Western plaid *see plaid*
Westwood, Vivienne 42, 56–57
White, Luke 83, 84
Wilmott, Alistair 76–77
Wilton, Brian 36, 39
windows 88, 109–11, 119–20, 122–25, 152–53, 190, 228, 230–32
Wright, Frank Lloyd 108
Wyman, Lance 242, 247
Wynne, Arthur 68

Y

Yang Rutherford 135

Z

Zuse toaster 128–29, 150–51

Contributors

Featured Designers and Suppliers

Absolute Zero°
www.absolutezerodegrees.com

Adam Fores
foresy@hotmail.co.uk

Alex Brown
www.spiderandfly.co.uk

Anna Bullus
ab@annabullusdesign.com

Art Meets Matter
www.artmeetsmatter.com

Astrid Stavro
www.astridstavro.com

ATADesigns
www.atadesigns.com

Atelier LaDurance
www.atelierladurance.com

Ben Router
benrouterdesign@googlemail.com

Berlin Cameron Partners/ Berlin Cameron United
www.bc-p.com

Beyond the Valley
www.beyondthevalley.com

Big Active
www.bigactive.com

Bloq
www.bloq.co.uk

Boris Ljubicic
www.studio-international.com

Burberry
www.burberry.com

Cat Chow
www.cat-chow.com

Chris Hoover
www.crvhoover.com

Claire Stevens
www.clairesjstevens.co.uk

Commune By The Great Wall
www.communebythegreatwall.com

Cordings
www.cordings.com

Courtney Skott
www.courtneyskott.com

Curious
www.curiousdesign.com

DSquared
www.dsquared2.com

Demakersvan
www.demakersvan.com

DIY Kyoto
www.diykyoto.com

Doane Paper
www.doanepaper.com

eBoy
hello.eboy.com

Emily Clay
em_clay@hotmail.com

Eva Cardon
www.ephameron.com

FLOR
www.flor.com

Frank
www.frankhome.co.uk

Gianni Tozzi and Stuart Penny
www.giannitozzi.com

Goodwood Revival
www.goodwood.co.uk/revival/

Harris Tweed Authority
www.harristweed.com

Hannah Broadhead
iccle_scamp@yahoo.co.uk

Hemingway Design
www.hemingwaydesign.com

Identica
www.identica.com

Impagination Inc.
www.impaginationinc.com

Inga Sempé
www.ingasempe.com

Inseq Design
www.inseq.net

ISAK
www.isak.co.uk

John Morgan Studio
www.morganstudio.co.uk

Jonathan Adler
www.jonathanadler.com

Jonathan Aspinall
www.jonaspinalldesign.co.uk

Kate Pemberton
www.katepemberton.com

Ken Knowlton
www.knowltonmosaics.com

Knoll International
www.knollint.com

Lance Wyman
www.lancewyman.com

Lemon Twist
www.lemontwist.net

Lola Lely
lolalely@AOL.com

Luke White
luke.white@students.plymouth.ac.uk

Massimo Meta
mazmeta@hotmail.com

Martin Bull
www.shellshockphotos.co.uk

Maxalot
www.maxalot.com

Michael Browers
www.michaelbrowers.com

Michael Salge
info@salge-design.de

Milk, Two Sugars
www.milktwosugars.org

Minipops
www.flipflopflyin.com/minipops

Mini Moderns
www.minimoderns.com

Mio
www.mioculture.com

Nicholas Felton
www.mgfn.net

Nora Brown
www.norabrowndesign.com

Pentagram
www.pentagram.com

People Will Always Need Plates
www.peoplewillalwaysneedplates.co.uk

Pinch
www.pinchdesign.com

Quad
www.quadprojects.com

Research Studios
www.researchstudios.com

Ric Bell
www.ricbellnthat.co.uk

Roundel
www.roundel.com

Robin Hayes Photography
www.robinhayes.co.uk

Scabetti
www.scabetti.co.uk

Schnitzel Records
www.schnitzel.co.uk

Scott Blake
www.barcodeart.com

Scottish Tartans Authority
www.tartansauthority.com

Seven Towns Ltd
www.rubiks.com

Stephen Reed Industrial Design
www.stephenreed.net

StormHand
www.stormhand.com

SUCK UK
www.suck.uk.com

Tom Rothwell
rotherty@yahoo.com

Turner Duckworth
www.turnerduckworth.com

Vibrandt
www.vibrandt.com

WaterAid
www.wateraid.org.uk

Yang Rutherford
www.yangrutherford.com

Photography Credits

By image number

Classic Checks
002 *Aundrea King*
003, 011, and 013 *Patrick Quinnelly*
006 and 008 *Source: iStockphoto*
009 *Keith Stephenson*
010 *Source: iStockphoto*
012 *Abra Carroll Nardo*
015 *Mario Testino*
© Copyright Burberry/Testino
018–020, 022, and 023
Source: iStockphoto
021 *Keith Stephenson*
024 and 030 *Karin Ost*
025 *Michael Yagoda*
027 *Ninon Tschaen*
026 and 029 *Keith Stephenson*
028 *Source: iStockphoto*
035 *Sarah Holmes*
036 *Dan Iggers*
038 *Raphael Mazor*
041 and 042 *Patrick Quinnelly*
043 *Christian Spanring*
044 *Mark Hampshire*
046, 048, and 049 *Abra Carroll Nardo*
047 *Christy Bindas*
050–053 *Source: iStockphoto*
054 *Source: www.firstview.com*

Membership and Identity
055 *Source: iStockphoto*
056 *Mark Henderson*
060 *Source: iStockphoto*
061 *Bob Milner*
062 *Stephen Forbes*
063, 065, and 082 *Alan Campbell*
067 *Source: iStockphoto*
086 *Keith Stephenson*
087 *David Leip*
090 *Robert Innes*
093 *Mark Henderson*
094 *Jennifer Gonzalez*
096 *Mark Henderson*
099 *Daniel Morris*
100 *Rosario Lopez Estudillo*
103 *Keith Stephenson*
104 *Martin Ivison*
105 *Source: iStockphoto*
106 *Keith Stephenson*
107–110 *Source: iStockphoto*
116–129 *Alan Campbell*
130 *Source: iStockphoto: Chris Schmidt*
131 *Source: iStockphoto*
132 *Alex Pallent*
133 *Martin Bull*
134 and 135 *Source: iStockphoto*
136 *Stephen Forbes*
138 *Source: iStockphoto*
139 *Malene Thyssen*
141 *Diana Lee*
142 *Mark Hampshire*
159 *Source: iStockphoto*

Themes and Moods
167 *Chris Hoover*
168 *Jennifer Remias*
169 *Amanda Krueger*
170 *Patrick Quinnelly*
171 *Robby Garbett*
172 *Alan Campbell*
173 *Alex Pallent*
175 *Taylor Ozimac*
176 *Robert L Segal*
177 *Abra Carroll Nardo*
179 *Leo Reynolds*
180 *Alan Campbell*
182 *Jannie Armstrong*
184 *Katya Rostock*
187 and 188 *Keith Stephenson*
189 *Alex Pallent*
192 *Keith Stephenson*
193 *Peter Bihr*
194 and 196 *Alex Pallent*
197 *Robby Garbett*
198 *Leo Reynolds*
199 *Abra Carroll Nardo*
200 *Patrick Quinnelly*
206 *Keith Stephenson*
221 *Kevin Minnis*
225–227 *Alex Pallent*
228 *Anton Bogomolov*
229 *Kees de Vos*
232 *Keith Stephenson*
233 *Joren Frielink*
234 *Glenn Arango*
235 *Marina Loram*
236 *Jan Tik*
238 *David Dunsmore*
240 *Liliana Cholerton-Bozier*
241 *Aaron Schock*
243 *Erika Padilla-Morales*
245 *Tama Leaver*
246 *Fernando G.M. (ArchEnemy)*
248 *Sally Blackmore*
250 *Source: iStockphoto*
251 and 254 *Jennifer Remias*
252, 253, 257, 258, and 261
Keith Stephenson
265 *Source: iStockphoto*
267–273 and 275–279
Mark Hampshire
280 *Source: iStockphoto*
282 and 284 *Keith Stephenson*
283 *Source: iStockphoto*
285 *Steve Gardam*
286 *Kevin McDonnell*
287, 290, 291, 296, 297,
298, and 302 *Melina Hunter*
288 *Angie Bacskocky*
289, 293, 295, and 299–301
Alan Campbell
292 *Brian Ledgard*
294 *Cherry Welsh*
303 and 305 *Chris Hoover*
304 *Polyphoto*
306 *V&A Images/*
Victoria and Albert Museum
307 *Bruce Grant*
309 *Neil Crocodile*
310 *Austin Cross*
311 *Olivier Bareau*
312 *Aaron Kapor*
313 and 317 *Gail Dedrick*
314 *Mascia Serafini*
315 and 318 *Jennifer Remias*
316 *Marek Bakajsa*
319 323, and 324
Luis Reyes Galindo(GF)
320–322 *Robby Garbett*
326, 331, and 332 *Hans Munk*
327 *Peter Segerstrom*
328–330 and 333–339 *John Levett*
341–345 *Keith Stephenson*
346–348 *Charlotte Wood*

Acknowledgments

As ever, we owe a huge debt of gratitude to our supportive team at RotoVision—Jane Roe, Tony Seddon, and April Sankey. We are particularly grateful for the elastic deadline we've been allowed this time around. From our team, we thank Spike for his patience and late nights.

We are constantly encouraged by the generosity of our contributors. Our thanks, in no particular order, go to: Brian Wilton at the Scottish Tartans Authority, Turner Duckworth, Hikmet Sugoer at Solebox, Lara Sinclair and Justin Cooke at Burberry, Rosie Dixon at Cordings, Ken Knowlton, Michael Bierut and Susannah McDonald at Pentagram, Gina Forst at Flor, Fara Carty at Vibrandt, David Hedley Jones at Seven Towns, Janet Bradley at Goodwood, Paul Johnson at Bloq, Lavinia Galieti at Knoll Europe, Gez at Big Active, Kate Pemberton, Boris Ljubicic, Martin Bull, Craig Robinson, Allison Julius at Jonathan Adler, Jaime Salm at Mio, Courtney Skott, Cat Chow, Ric Bell, Abra Carroll Nardo, John Morgan, Bob and Tom of Milk, Two Sugars, Lotje at Maxalot, Nick Hard and Neville Brody at Research Studios, Jane Quinn, Lance Wyman, NASA, Lyndsay at firstVIEW, Stephanie Fawcett at V&A Images, Emily Clay, Boy Bastiaens, Inga Sempé, Jimmy Yang, Malene Thyssen, Nuggy at Quad, The Chicken Kid and little bird.

We say it every time, so why break a habit? We are indebted to the infinitely creative and collaborative community of photographers on Flickr.com. Particular thanks to Alan Campbell, Neil Crocodile, Jennifer Remias, Melina Hunter, Alex Pallent. and Robby Garbett. Finally, thanks to Robin Hayes for generously contributing photography from his professional portfolio.

Signals and Information
351 *Source: iStockphoto*
353, 354, and 357 *Keith Stephenson*
360 *Alex Pallent*
362 *Source: iStockphoto*
363 *Source: iStockphoto: Daniel Thomson*
364 and 369 *Keith Stephenson*
370, 373, and 374 *Source: iStockphoto*
371 and 372 *Neil Crocodile*
377 and 378 *Source: iStockphoto*
380–383 and 389 *Keith Stephenson*
402 *Alex Pallent*
408 and 409 *Keith Stephenson*
411, 412, and 414 *Adam Lewensohn*
415 *Sarah King*
416 *Ryan Popoff*
419 *Jonathan Stilts*
421 *Ryan Popoff*
422 *Martijn Eerens*
423 *Beau Wade*
424 *Brenda Janish*
429 *Keith Stephenson*
430 *Mike Mertz*
432 *Jonathan Tony Lau*
433 *Mark Hampshire*
434 *Brian Kennedy*
436 and 438 *Source: iStockphoto*
439 *Keith Stephenson*
444 *Hans Munk*
449 *Alex Pallent*
458 *Jennifer Remias*
465 *Keith Stephenson*
467 and 468 *Elisa Renouard*
469 *Mauricio Salinas*
471–473 *Source: iStockphoto*
479 *Jeannine Walker*
481, 482, 484, 486, and 487 *Source: iStockphoto*

Form and Function
491 *Hikmet Sugoer*
493, 496, and 504 *Alan Campbell*
494 and 498–501 *Keith Stephenson*
495 *Bas Helbers*
497 *Source: iStockphoto*
502 *Alex Pallent*
505–514 *Keith Stephenson*
515–525 *Alan Campbell*
526–536 *Keith Stephenson*
538–543 *Alan Campbell*
544 *Keith Stephenson*
547 *Gianmaria Zanotti*
549 and 550 *Alan Campbell*
551–557 *Keith Stephenson*
558 and 561 *Robby Garbett*
559, 560, 563, and 565 *Jannie Armstrong*
562, 564, and 566 *Keith Stephenson*
567 *Bas Helbers*
568 *Hans van der Mars*
569 *Robby Garbett*
570 *Keith Stephenson*
571 and 575 *Alex Pallent*
576 *Robin Hayes*
577 and 578 *Source: iStockphoto*
582 and 583 *Robby Garbett*
585 *Paula Bailey*
588 *Source: iStockphoto*
589 *Paula Bailey*
590 *Hikmet Sugoer*
594 and 595 *Source: iStockphoto*
596 *Jannie Armstrong*
602–605 *Keith Stephenson*
606 *Robby Garbett*
607, 609, and 610 *NASA*
611 *Source: iStockphoto*
612–619 *Rose Saxe*
623 *Source: iStockphoto*
624 and 625 *Keith Stephenson*
630 and 631 *Steve Gardam*
633 *Source: iStockphoto*
635 *Robin Hayes*
637–640 *Source: iStockphoto*
644 and 651 *Robin Hayes*
645 *Keith Stephenson*
646 *Karen Miles*
647 *Abra Carroll Nardo*
648–650 *Robert L Segal*
652 *Alan Campbell*
653 *Alex Pallent*
654 *David Elliott www.flickr.com/photos/cdell*
655 and 657–659 *Keith Stephenson*
656 *Alan Campbell*
661 *Robin Hayes*
662 *Robert L Segal*
665 *Keith Stephenson*
666 and 667 *Steve Gardam*
670 and 673 *NASA*
674 and 677 *Keith Stephenson*
676 *Tony Webster*
679 *Robert L Segal*
680 and 682 *Source: iStockphoto*
681 *Tama Leaver*
686–688 *Ulises Muñiz*